The Kaiju Connection

ALSO BY JASON BARR
AND FROM MCFARLAND

Gender and Werewolf Cinema (2020)

Video Gaming in Science Fiction:
A Critical Study (2018)

Giant Creatures in Our World: Essays on Kaiju
and American Popular Culture (2017)

The Kaiju Film: A Critical Study
of Cinema's Biggest Monsters (2016)

The Kaiju Connection
Giant Monsters and Ourselves

Jason Barr

McFarland & Company, Inc., Publishers
Jefferson, North Carolina

LIBRARY OF CONGRESS CATALOGUING-IN-PUBLICATION DATA

Names: Barr, Jason, 1976– author.
Title: The kaiju connection : giant monsters and ourselves / Jason Barr.
Description: Jefferson, North Carolina : McFarland & Company, Inc.,
Publishers, 2023. | Includes bibliographical references and index.
Identifiers: LCCN 2023038172 | ISBN 9781476693514 (paperback : acid free paper) ∞
ISBN 9781476651507 (ebook)
Subjects: LCSH: Monster films—Japan—History and criticism. |
Monsters in motion pictures. | LCGFT: Film criticism.
Classification: LCC PN1995.9.M6 B36 2023 | DDC 791.43/6750952—dc23/eng/20230814
LC record available at https://lccn.loc.gov/2023038172

BRITISH LIBRARY CATALOGUING DATA ARE AVAILABLE

ISBN (print) 978-1-4766-9351-4
ISBN (ebook) 978-1-4766-5150-7

© 2023 Jason Barr. All rights reserved

*No part of this book may be reproduced or transmitted in any form
or by any means, electronic or mechanical, including photocopying
or recording, or by any information storage and retrieval system,
without permission in writing from the publisher.*

Front cover images © 2023 Digital Images Studio/Shutterstock

Printed in the United States of America

*McFarland & Company, Inc., Publishers
Box 611, Jefferson, North Carolina 28640
www.mcfarlandpub.com*

This one is for my wife, Tracey,
who is stronger than Godzilla.

Acknowledgments

Every book has an author, but there's almost always an invisible army who supports that author in everything they do. Top of the list for me will always be my wife Tracey, who was smart enough to see something different in me than what a lot of people thought they had seen, and changed my life's trajectory so that I could do cool stuff like write critical texts on kaiju.

Of course, my children, Vincent and Lily, watched and re-watched these films with me, and their patience and their company will always give me fond memories, a sort of Heisei to Reiwa-era reboot of my own Showa-era childhood of watching kaiju movies with my own parents.

Which naturally leads me to my parents, who of course provided for me as a child, but were always ready to watch a science fiction film with me, no matter how bad it turned out to be. I will always remember watching late-night episodes of *The Outer Limits* or the final chunks of a Godzilla marathon until we could barely stay awake.

The wonderful staff at McFarland were also quite patient and gracious as they worked with me on this latest batch of thoughts.

Thanks to all for their patience as I worked on this project.

Table of Contents

Acknowledgments	vi
Introduction	1
1. Categorizing the Kaiju	13
2. Toys and Dinosaurs and Nostalgia	26
3. An Appreciation of *Godzilla Raids Again*	34
4. Science and Faith: The Solo Kaiju Adventures	40
5. "The Third Fire": *Agon, the Atomic Dragon*	56
6. The Wor(l)ds Get Stuck in My Throat: Aliens from Sea and Space	62
7. Reigo, Raiga, Ohga: The (Sometimes Loving) Basement of Kaiju Film	76
8. An Ode to Baragon and Barugon	89
9. It Turns Out Gamera *Is* Really Neat: The Heisei Trilogy	99
10. The Legendary Dr. Serizawa	109
11. Kong, Again and Again: The Son[s] of Kong	121
12. Toward the Past and the Future at the Same Time: *Colossal* and *Godzilla vs. Kong*	143
13. Men as Kaiju: *Big Man Japan* and *Kaiju Mono*	160
14. When Even Humans Are (Almost) Kaiju: *The Amazing Colossal Man* and *Attack of the 50 Foot Woman*	173
Conclusion	189
Filmography	195
Bibliography	197
Index	201

Introduction

Many kaiju fans can tell you about their first kaiju film, and how they got immediately hooked on the genre. It's almost a way of gaining membership in the club; across numerous message boards online and at many more in-person conventions, the question is always the first thing that is asked of strangers: *What was your first kaiju film?* The answer itself doesn't really matter. If you say *War of the Gargantuas* or *The X from Outer Space*, that's not really the point of the question. No, the point is that you're sharing the *experience* of your first kaiju film: where you were, who you were with (if anyone), and how old you were. What is the "you" in the kaiju film, where do you place your identity? For most of us, that first moment was coming across a Godzilla or Gamera film while we scrolled through the television late at night, the bright colors and bizarre action waking us from our drifting half-sleep. And, if you ask fans, they will happily tell you their first film and where they were and how they responded to it, as if they were dunking a madeline in atomic breath and watching the smoke curl into the ash-laden memories of what came before.

For me, in our tiny one-television household, the Saturday morning cartoons would eventually give way to a show out of Washington, D.C., that would have an afternoon matinee. Now, this was usually boring cop dramas or heavily cut action films with a decided lack of blood and cursing, but every once in a while, they would choose a science fiction film, and so, that's where I would see parts of movies such as *Space Monster X-7* or *The Thing from Another World* or *Them!* or *It Came from Outer Space*.

But once, I turned on the television and saw blood spurting out of the mouth of a large, mutated ankylosaurus as a large tyrannosaurus-like creature bent down and broke the spiked beast's jaw. Now *this* was something interesting! And so I watched the rest of the film, struggling with the dubbing, wrestling with the relative lack of monsters after that point for what felt like an eternity. But then there they were again, just at the end of the film: a robot, a giant fishlike dinosaur and our heroes, the large

Introduction

dinosaur and the big puppy. And they were all fighting one another. Pure mana for a seven-year-old boy.

From there, the movies would occasionally pop up from week to week. Crime movie? Flip the channel. Romance? Flip the channel. Godzilla? Turn it up, and sit down about four inches from the screen, close enough that you could see the individual horizontal lines run across the screen.

Of course, it wasn't just Godzilla; over time, Gamera started to appear, as well as Mothra, Rodan, King Ghidorah, Sanda, Gaira, and some of the lesser-known kaiju that just didn't seem to fit anywhere, such as Ganimes or Guilala.

Almost forty years later, kaiju films, especially Showa-era Godzilla films, remain a comforting presence, queued up during times of stress or sickness.*

I suspect a lot of fans of the genre have kaiju "built in" to their bad days, a whiff of nostalgic comfort that reminds us of simpler times where two guys in rubber suits could run into each other while knocking down cardboard and plaster buildings.

* * *

It was around a decade ago that I started to write *The Kaiju Film: A Critical History of Cinema's Biggest Monsters*, a book that took a strange voyage from one press to another and metamorphosed from an in-depth study of Godzilla to a broader and wide-ranging work on the kaiju genre as a whole. As I finished the book in 2016, I wrote about the potential for kaiju film to become more mainstream over the intervening years, especially with projects such as *Shin Godzilla* and *Godzilla vs. Kong* scheduled for release.

Has that resurgence happened? Has there been a push for greater mainstream viability?

Probably not. For every *Godzilla vs. Kong* blockbuster, there's a few other kaiju films that simply escape (or, in some cases, repulse) mainstream attention. There's a lot of cultural forces at play in the world of pop culture and cinema, and there's a lot of blame to go around. Goodness, even *Godzilla: King of the Monsters* was a bit of a box office disappointment, if only because it was pressed against the release of several other massive films such as *Avengers: Endgame*. About that: kaiju films tend to get washed in the same sort of polish as the current blockbuster trend of superhero films and large corporate-driven franchise spectacles. Although *Godzilla vs. Kong* fared amazingly well during the Covid shutdowns— relying primarily on streaming through HBOMax rather than in-theater

---

*Gamera, too, although I found those films were much more entertaining if I watched them via *Mystery Science Theater 3000*.

Introduction

3

distribution—that's essentially the only "big" blockbuster-sized kaiju film since *Godzilla: King of the Monsters* two years prior, which was, again, not well received by fans or critics.

Of course, with the slow rise in accessibility for quality, or at least decent, CGI, and the ready availability of professional grade cameras and audio, kaiju films have become a little bit easier for amateurs and low-budget studios to produce. This has led to some unfortunate films that are just not good: *Monster Seafood Wars, War of the God Monsters, Notzilla,* and the woeful *Zillafoot.* Even the *Reigo* and *Raiga* films, which at least, on the surface, give kaiju films the old college try, and are born from a distinct desire to pay homage to kaiju film, tend to be painful to watch. Each of these films have the unfortunate effect of heightening the biases and assumptions of mainstream movie critics: for every successful kaiju film, not just in terms of popularity and box office, but rather in terms of historical and cultural context, it feels like there's three or four more that embrace the cheese of some of the worst kaiju films of the 1970s or 1980s, or are otherwise quick cash-ins. The poor fellow who rents *Atlantic Rim* hoping for quality kaiju action is bound to experience suddenly lowered expectations for the genre as a whole.

It goes without saying, of course, that one of the biggest bugaboos about kaiju film is the widely varying quality of the main franchises themselves. Both *Godzilla* and *Gamera, The Giant Monster* spawned numerous sequels, and many of those sequels are problematic in terms of quality. Godzilla and Gamera still labor under the wild hokiness of the 1960s and the 1970s, and there's little doubt that people who see Gamera doing backflips or Godzilla flying backwards have consigned kaiju film as a whole to the "silly" category.

As such, kaiju film remains woefully underappreciated and under-studied. That's hopefully where this book comes in. If this is not a book that's an academic text in the strictest sense, perhaps it is more of an apologia for the continued study of the kaiju film.

If you read *The Kaiju Film*, you'll notice that, in this volume, I will revise and revamp some of my thoughts and opinions in this work, specifically in regard to *King Kong* as well as the kaiju genre in general—what "qualifies" and what doesn't. This is the result of interacting with quite a few people along the way as I worked on a variety of projects, re-watched films, or read new critical works. So, like every good academic, I'm going to spend time arguing with myself and coming to new conclusions. But ultimately, this work follows a different path from *The Kaiju Film.* In this volume, my primary exploration will be about how we, as viewers, interact with, judge, and ultimately understand kaiju, and, as a result, how these shifting boundaries affect or reveal our own perceptions about humanity itself, and what makes someone—or some*thing*—"human." And, more interestingly, what makes some humans "monsters."

For people who purchased or borrowed (or pirated) *The Kaiju Film* and later spoke to me or wrote to me, one of the questions that was almost always omnipresent was about the academic stylings of the work; as these things go, I was often too academic or not academic enough. Discussions on various aspects of kaiju were too in-depth or were too surface-level, and let's not even discuss my lack of discussion for movies like *Son of Kong* (which I mostly ignore in this volume, too, so there). But, my goal for the work was to prompt an academic discussion rather than to be the alpha and omega text about the kaiju film genre, and I think, or hope, that this happened. I followed up that effort by coediting with Camille Mustachio a book of essays called *Giant Creatures in Our World* and other works soon appeared as well, including the great book *Japan's Green Monsters*, written by Sean Rhoads and Brooke McCorkle.

You'll no doubt wonder if *The Kaiju Connection* is going to be in the same sort of academic-ese as *The Kaiju Film* and I will respond: nah. Essentially, my rubric for this book is going to be much more loose and informal, and it will be mostly critical and personal musings on a wide array of kaiju films and similar topics, with some emphasis on simply interrogating and exploring the sometimes ragged edges of the form.

So, for those who are wondering which direction I will go, the answers are simple:

Q: What will you write about? A: Whatever I want.

Q: What movies will you choose to discuss? A: Whichever ones strike my fancy at the moment.

As you can imagine, this will lead to a more scattered feel than *The Kaiju Film*, and to me, at this stage, it is a more productive approach. It will allow me, for example, to mention *Shin Ultraman* mostly in passing because it relies on such a deep knowledge of the original *Ultraman* series that I tend to view it as a prolonged television episode rather than a film, and thus, because it straddles that border, I'm reluctant to explore it beyond a few notes and mentions here and there.

You'll also note some assorted very short essays and musings scattered throughout the book; these are just that: scattered musings. Ideas that are there and maybe don't need as much exposition as others, but, taken as a part of a whole, can provide a different insight into what we've seen as kaiju fans and scholars. Not every essay can be a full study of the lineage of *King Kong*; but almost every essay (I hope) can add a new perspective to the conversation, no matter how short.

Introduction 5

There will still be some research, of course, and there will be plenty of cultural contexts … it will just be presented in a different, looser way, and, hopefully, will be a bit more approachable in tone. For all of my soon-to-be digressions, however, I will ask for patience and forgiveness in advance.

This also means I'm subjecting myself to some real stinkers out there. While films like *The X From Outer Space* aren't *too* bad, others, like *Yeti: Giant of the 20th Century* and *Konga*, were truly tests of patience, with several attempts being made to successfully complete one viewing. Of course, tastes can be different, and if you have *Yeti* posters on your wall and were happy when Code Red DVD released the upgraded version of the film, I humbly apologize in advance for upsetting you. Yet, even though these don't quite fit the "Japanese only"–style lineage discussion, the bad films can tell us about kaiju and their place in the world by showing us how things can go wrong, and they can also help us understand our own perceptions of kaiju. We can learn a lot about what makes *King Kong* so successful in part *because* of these often bad films, because they can show us what worked so well by making mistakes. And we can understand what makes Godzilla so popular by examining and gauging our own reactions—and our expectations—to other borderline kaiju films.

* * *

There have been quite a few kaiju films released since *The Kaiju Film*, and more that I didn't discuss from prior eras, or simply didn't have the space or resources at the time. To better facilitate the inclusion of works such as *Kaiju Mono*, *Big Man Japan*, *Mighty Peking Man* and *Agon* alongside their vastly different kaiju film counterparts such as *Godzilla vs. Kong*, I have decided to structure this work as a series of essays built around a set of themes, focusing on subsets of the genre. And I will even revisit some films from *The Kaiju Film* that I felt may have received short shrift because of time or research constraints, or just because they were so new that precious little was known about them. Thus, alongside some of the more off-the-beaten-path discussions, there will be highlights and discussions of *Colossal*, *Shin Godzilla*, and even the often overlooked *Godzilla Raids Again*, which, even though it is indeed a sequel, mostly stands beside the 1954 *Godzilla* as creating a new spin on the genre: here is Anguirus, and the resulting blow-by-blow battle between the new Godzilla and this hedgehog/ankylosaurus hybrid immediately resulted in the "versus" format that dominates so many kaiju films today.*

---

*Indeed, outside of the original *Gamera*, every Gamera film has relied on kaiju duking it out for whatever reason, and precious few *Godzilla* films feature only Godzilla: the original, of course, and then thirty years would pass before Godzilla would solo his own film with *The Return of Godzilla* in 1984. The next one (setting aside the much-maligned 1998 American *Godzilla*) would be *Shin Godzilla* in 2016, a length of 32 years.

6   Introduction

* * *

Most introductions to academic texts, especially collected volumes of essays, always give away the plot by summarizing each individual essay. I suppose I should do so here, too, because I have a picture in my mind of someone reading this introduction and thinking "will he just get to the point already"? I'll keep this overview brief, though, in the hopes that you dive in more deeply to the rest of the book.

My first task is to reexamine what "kaiju" truly means. Well, we know what "kaiju" means, but my focus is more on what makes something a kaiju. It's a topic I visited in *The Kaiju Film* and again as part of a round-table discussion in *Giant Creatures in Our World*. It's a topic that has zero easy answers, but I will give it a try here, with a specific emphasis on delineating kaiju and what could be considered kaiju-adjacent films.

Then, it is time to broaden things out a little more, as I explore how nostalgia, dinosaurs, and science fiction all combine to undergird the kaiju film, and kaiju fandom.

From there, I move toward an appreciation of a flawed and often overlooked *Godzilla Raids Again*, which provides what I feel is a depiction of a country slowly staggering to its feet after several years of war and after unprecedented atomic bombings.

Moving on, I explore the "solo" kaiju films, and how science and religion tend to be the focus when there's only one kaiju in the film.

Agon, The Atomic Dragon was a short television series recut into a film, and I examine how it "fits" with the solo kaiju themes but also draw heavily on horror elements in order to refresh the message of *Godzilla* (1954), and was so successful at it that the film is often dismissed as a rip-off.

An exploration of aliens is due, and how aliens battling kaiju tend to invert the traditional science fiction narrative of alien invasions and the Othering that occurs within them. In many Godzilla films, for example, the aliens are often versions of himself.

The next chapter explores the fan-made and fan-focused films of *Reigo, Raiga,* and *Ohga* and how these films, in spite of their often deep flaws, reveal the borders of acceptability for the kaiju genre.

Then, an ode to Baragon and Barugon, and a discussion about what makes some kaiju "stick" in our minds and what makes others quite forgettable.

I then explore the Gamera Heisei trilogy, featuring a story arc spread across three films and directed by Shusuke Kaneko. Within these films is a broader message of what makes a kaiju heroic … or not.

And then, a little bit of controversy, as I explore the slow Americanization of the legendary version of Godzilla through the marginalization and then outright absence of the character of Dr. Daisuke Serizawa.

Introduction 7

There's a whole bunch of different Kongs out there, and there's even knock-off Kongs, and each of them have something to tell us about the borders of the kaiju genre—even if you argue that Kong isn't a kaiju—and the way we expect kaiju to interact with humans, and even how we sometimes expect kaiju to *be* human.

I compare two very different films, *Colossal* and *Godzilla vs. Kong*, and I will admit my bias early so that you can skip to the end if you like, but these two kaiju films show two very different futures for the kaiju genre and where the genre as a whole can go next.

The final two chapters build on exploring the borders between humanity and kaiju. First comes discussions of two films in which Japanese men become kaiju-sized and battle kaiju: *Big Man Japan* and *Kaiju Mono*, and how masculinity functions in these films.

After that is our most remote discussion, the furthest from what we could claim to be "real" kaiju film, as we take a look at *The Amazing Colossal Man, War of the Colossal Beast*, and *Attack of the 50 Foot Woman*. I argue, however, that by examining these films, we can more easily ascertain what makes a person a monster, and how their sudden growth into giants pushes them toward monstrosity, leading them to sit outside of the borders of kaiju-adjacent films.

Finally, near the end of *The Kaiju Film*, I made several predictions about where the genre was headed, but I admit I think I missed a newer trend that's really just beginning, starting in 2016 or 2017. As such, I feel it's only fair that I take a few moments to update my failed predictions. I will have more soon-to-be failed predictions at the end of this volume.

* * *

Before I begin and launch us together into this book of random thoughts, ideas, and observations, I should, at the risk of repeating myself, mention briefly some of the "rules" of this volume; namely, what a "kaiju film" truly is. The etymology and origins of the word—shortened from daikaiju*—is well-known and clear in translation; however, the application of the word and all of the fraught subtexts and themes is decidedly less clear. As I discussed in *The Kaiju Film*, there's a whole lot of movies out there that don't necessarily fit the reductive "it has to have something to do with Japan" notion, but are sometimes more of a kaiju film than those films that do nod toward Japan. Films like *Cloverfield* and even

---

*In fact, it's often something that's changed in translation. I'm reluctant to call it an error, but it's more of a way for translators to smooth out the transition from Japanese to English. In Japan, it's *Daikaiju Mono*; in the West, it's *Kaiju Mono*. That extra syllable carries a lot of importance and weight in how to literally translate the concept, but not enough importance that most of the idea carries over to the West as simply "kaiju."

8 **Introduction**

the old *Rudolph the Red-Nosed Reindeer* feature mentions or have direct origins from Japan, which is more than can be said for works like *King Kong* or *Beast from 20,000 Fathoms*, yet *Kong* and *Beast* are often classically considered kaiju works, if only because of the notion of "big creature wrecks city" plotting that propels the climaxes of the films. Yet, *Cloverfield* is sometimes derided as not being a kaiju film because the kaiju is barely seen and the only tangible connection to Japan is a mention at the beginning of the film that a going-away party is happening because a character is going away to Japan to work.

And, let's just set aside any consideration of the Bumble in *Rudolph* as a kaiju, right? It's only huge and terrorizes people ... and was animated by a group of talented Japanese puppeteers, designers, and animators.

But, then again, does this mean the Indominus Rex in *Jurassic World* is a kaiju? It's a big creature wrecking stuff, and no, it isn't Japanese, but it *does* carry the additional anxiety of science run amok, in this case, genetic manipulation. After all, numerous Godzilla and Gamera films focus on how science stretches the boundaries of ethics, creating all sorts of issues, from the Absolute Zero weapon to Biollante herself. And so, the Rex carries those same symbols and codings, which point to at least an intent to acknowledge its potential heritage as a kaiju.

Things get more complex from there, because films such as *Attack of the 50 Foot Woman* and *The Amazing Colossal Man* aren't traditionally considered kaiju films, or even kaiju-type films, as the giant beings aren't creatures or monsters, but just humans grown freakishly large, with an emphasis on freakishly. Within these films come some of the earliest strains of body horror in cinema, a continuing theme of displacement and pain because of one's body, a discussion reminiscent, say, of *Shin Godzilla*, featuring a Godzilla with scar tissue and endless agony from its own malformed existence. But neither *Attack of the 50 Foot Woman* nor *The Amazing Colossal Man* have any relationship with Japan.

Of course, strictly keeping the idea of Japanese origins in place would mean that big creatures such as King Kong are sometimes kaiju (*King Kong Escapes*) and sometimes not (1933, *Son of Kong*), and even sometimes within the same set of circumstances. After all, *Kong: Skull Island* doesn't have strictly Japanese heritage or associations, but then, the sequel, with the same creature, is in *Godzilla vs. Kong*. So does this mean that Kong is a sort of honorary kaiju, depending on which creature he is facing, and at what time in the genre's history? Or, more confounding, is the 2014 Legendary Godzilla story cycle, playing out across at least four films now, features a Godzilla that isn't a kaiju? After all, as we shall see, Legendary has worked overtime to reinvent Godzilla as a distinctly American version.

And so, then we get to the Japanese film *Kaiju Mono*, where a fair

Introduction 9

debate can be had that it isn't really a kaiju film because of a decided lack of kaiju, save for one, and the main characters are giant-sized humans … *even though the word "*kaiju*" appears in the title!*

Set all of this aside, for the debate will go on and on; in fact, in one Facebook forum after the book was released, I stood by and watched the debate rage over the use of Gorgo on the cover of my *The Kaiju Film. Gorgo?* the argument went, *How can Gorgo be on the cover of a book when it isn't even a kaiju?* And so it continued, with more reasonable people (I call them this because they affirmed my views) rightfully pointing out the difficulty of licensing Godzilla or Gamera images and that Gorgo was at least available via stock photography. And besides, these heroes argued on my behalf: Gorgo was big and it crushed cities, and isn't that kaiju enough?

Of course, the other, rather small, group of individuals continued their naysaying for a brief spell before finally throwing their hands in the air, promising never to purchase the book and wondering what has gone wrong in the world today.

So, this is the debate, and I won't go too much further into it outside of the first chapter; others can pick up the torch and carry it on into the darkest corners of social media, but I will use the more reductive logic of "big creature" and leave it at that, with a little more explanation to come. This allows me some comfort in drawing broader inferences at times when I need to, such as discussing the Italian/Canadian *Yeti: Giant of the 20th Century* and films such as *Colossal.* I sometimes worry that containing kaiju film to "just Japanese origin or influence" is a boundary at once too firm and too soft, and this sort of wishy-washiness can lead to immense amounts of confusion in what makes a kaiju film. I think in order to explore the sometimes rigid boundaries of what we can easily appreciate as de facto kaiju franchises—Godzilla, Gamera, Ultraman, and so on—it helps to take a look at the resulting homages, parodies, and outright rip-offs.

* * *

One relatively newfound trend, or at least a retro trend, is the use of kaiju to explore pressing social issues. Of course, we're quite aware of how the original *Godzilla* symbolized the continuing concerns of nuclear tests around the Japanese mainland. And, in fits and spurts, kaiju films have occasionally brushed up against other issues, from the collective growing popular amnesia of World War II (*Giant Monsters All-Out Attack*), the ethical boundaries of genetic manipulation (*Godzilla vs. Biollante*) and pollution (*Pacific Rim* and *What to Do with Dead Kaiju?*). At times, however, it feels that these social lessons are incidental, or added in to spur the human-based plot, which naturally shrinks in size the moment you add large monsters destroying cities, and, as such, kaiju films have generally placed a much lower emphasis on the realities of the world we live in.

Perhaps that's a bonus. How often do I hear, among fans of both science fiction and horror, that the purpose of movies is to let people escape the "real world"? In those fantastic renderings of supernatural murderers, space battles, and, yes, even kaiju, there's a tacit agreement between viewer and producers: we'll watch and we'll discuss, so long as you don't push any "real" narratives into our faces for the next few hours. This is why, as I argued in *The Kaiju Film*, the genre tends to take an academic backseat to, yes, even science fiction and horror, which over the years, have been more naked in their ambitions (especially science fiction during the Cold War and onward), and why critical acceptance of these films is sorely lacking. Indeed, I at times found during the writing of *The Kaiju Film* several moments—well, more than several—where I needed to stretch my writing to incorporate the bridges I needed in order to explore any depth in some kaiju films that were simply lacking in almost any purpose other than "big monsters fighting." Yes, that will include some of the obvious, such as *Gamera: Super Monster* and *Son of Godzilla*, among a few others.

Enter the film *Colossal*, which I will argue is really one of the first films, along with, perhaps, *Shin Godzilla*, to successfully move the kaiju film not only away from "big monsters fighting," but to ironically move from the macro level: worldly concerns such as war, pollution, disease, and the like, to the micro level. In the case of *Colossal*, the kaiju don't necessarily represent or interact with any issue much larger than addiction and domestic violence, which one could no doubt suggest is indeed endemic in much of the world, but are, well, very *personal*. *Colossal*, in other words, doesn't focus on statistics and sweeping symbolization of the issues of addiction or domestic violence; instead, it focuses on two very broken individuals who can summon kaiju on their behalf. And the film gets much darker from there.

There have been, in the past several years, growing discussion about the roles that underrepresented people play in film genres, and the horror genre, in particular, has been a hotbed of discussion, spurred forward primarily by the efforts of Jordan Peele, director and writer of *Get Out* and *Us*, among others. Peele successfully reintegrated a mainstream Black experience into American horror films that moved the prevailing narrative beyond the "blaxploitation" films of the 1960s and 1970s, instead providing genuinely terrifying and uncomfortable films that featured a predominantly Black cast, but also a Black viewpoint.

And, of course, to turn the clock back even further, horror has struggled at times with the integration and inclusion of LGBTQ individuals. Of course, there's a long history of gay—both closeted and open—directors

Introduction   11

and writers in the horror genre, and the struggles of marginalization can be felt in the narratives we see on the screen. James Whale's *Frankenstein,* for example, or *Nightmare on Elm Street 2: Freddy's Revenge* can be easily read as commentaries on the marginalization of non-heterosexual and non–LGBTQ individuals.

Okay. One review of *The Kaiju Film* was that it was "too PC," so I won't go much further other than to make a fair prediction that the kaiju film can, and will, begin to incorporate and explore themes of marginalized and underrepresented populations, and it can be done successfully, if *Colossal* is an example. Or the genre can explore the incompetence of government bureaucracy and the everyday drone of red tape, if *Shin Godzilla* or *What to Do with Dead Kaiju?* is an example, or, perhaps some combination thereof. *Shin Godzilla,* too, rather nakedly aligned itself, perhaps more than any other film outside of *Godzilla* (1954) with current events and a sort of real-worldliness that made the film, at times, less of a kaiju or monster film and more of a retelling of parts of a dismal reality.

Just a quick pitch: imagine a kaiju film that opens in the typical manner: a massive beast comes ashore, starts destroying a city, and then, eventually, falls asleep, much as in *The Return of Godzilla,* or is simply frozen, as in *Shin Godzilla.* But, what if the kaiju were to fall asleep in a poorer section of the city? And what if the government just simply decided to say "good enough" and leave the slumbering kaiju there, leaving families to deal with the snoring and possibly soon-to-be awakened creature?

Hard to imagine? Maybe, but keep in mind that *Shin Godzilla* practically begged the viewer to consider this conundrum: an already inept government, in a miracle of miracles, manages to temporarily freeze a rapidly mutating kaiju ... and we're left with the image of Shin Godzilla standing in the middle of a ruined city while a pair of government bureaucrats wonder what's next. They've stopped the threat temporarily, and there's no plan beyond that. That ending begs for a sequel, of course, with Shin Godzilla reawakening, but what about the in-between? How do the citizens live with a massive frozen kaiju in their midst and a government that seems to shrug about it? Or how do they deal with the sudden displacement spurred on by a giant creature run amok?

Anyway.

You haven't purchased, borrowed, or pirated (though I much prefer the first two options to the latter, but reality intrudes) this book to hear me pontificate and speculate on my own individual pitches for kaiju film.* What I hope to provide here is a fresh set of eyes on changes to the kaiju genre, or to provide a sort of resurrection of lesser-known or less popular

---

*Although I have a few more…Hollywood, give me a call.

kaiju films and how they have impacted the genre in negative or positive ways.

Oh, and one more note: although these appear to be separate chapters, all self-contained, I view them more as a consistent staircase of sorts, with ideas building and reappearing as we progress from one essay to the next. I hope that the structure of this volume leads clearly through one essay to the next so that we can better understand exactly how this whole kaiju craze kicked off and why it continues, almost unabated, seventy (or more, depending on who you ask) years later. Ultimately, throughout this work, I reach out for potential answers to the questions of *what are kaiju?* and *what do kaiju teach us about our own perceptions about ourselves?* Whether or not I succeed in this, even incrementally (or incidentally), will be left up to you. I hope that the looser structure and the avoidance of a lot of academic-ese will help clarify some of the ideas presented in *The Kaiju Film*, and, as you'll note, in the intervening years, I've found some reason, through new research and new films, to challenge my own old assumptions and ideas as well.

But, first, a few of the usual notes, the ones that are required when a Western author and a Western press discuss Japanese films. First, I refer to most kaiju as "he" with few exceptions. As Norman England notes, Mothra being female is a "Western contrivance" (xvii), but, like him, I kept it here.

Japanese names are Westernized to personal names first and family names second.

I have attempted to stick with the most popular English translation of the film titles. In some cases, especially with films like *Reigo*, there are numerous translations that overlap or otherwise confound; I chose one that differentiates it from the others and went with that. I also shortened the film titles to a more usable function after their first mention, so films such as *Godzilla, Mothra*, and *King Ghidorah: Giant Monsters All-Out Attack* became *Giant Monsters All-Out Attack*, or, if I felt particularly lazy, *All-Out Attack*.

There are some films that repeat the title. In these instances, if the text doesn't make it absolutely clear, I have placed the year of release immediately after. In other words: *King Kong* (1933) or *King Kong* (1976) or *King Kong* (2005); *Godzilla* (1954) or *Godzilla* (1998) or *Godzilla* (2014). And so on.

As you have no doubt figured out, this volume focuses exclusively on films or the film properties, so *Ultraman* or *Kamen Rider* fans: I apologize in advance. I know that there are films for these television franchises (and several others), but there's such a long history alongside the series and the various iterations that it would be impossible to contain them all in one volume, much less a chapter or two. I know, I know: I cheated a little bit by discussing *Agon*, but that was only four episodes long, and besides, it was later edited into a movie, so I didn't entirely break my own rules.

Let's begin.

1

Categorizing the Kaiju

Okay, so, if you took some time with the Introduction to this book, you'll have read about just a small number of the issues surrounding the word "kaiju" and how this has come to represent a distinct genre in cinema, although no one seems to be able to build boundaries based on this genre that make any sort of sense, or at least hold up to prolonged interrogation. I also discussed this in my prior book, *The Kaiju Film*, but to no avail, as the discussion itself burned on in my absence. It was even the focus of a group write-up/discussion in the introduction to the edited collection *Giant Creatures in Our World*, and, even with a group of great academics, we were unable to come to any sort of consensus on what constitutes a kaiju, and, therefore, what makes a kaiju film.

Does this mean I'm changing my mind on what makes a kaiju film? Which includes the very low bar of a state of anxiety that mirrors the concerns about science and destruction we find in so many Godzilla films, for example? Maybe? Not quite? But I do think it may be time to modify, and hopefully, clarify the discussion a bit. Perhaps it is important here to call back to much of the inspiration for our earliest big monsters on film: dinosaurs. As W.J.T. Marshall notes, "[t]he word 'dinosaur,' unlike mammal, may not denote a natural group of animals with a coherent group of derived characteristics; it may instead be an artificial, arbitrary construct..." (23). It only follows, then, that the nebulous borders for what makes a "dinosaur" perhaps transfer over to the potentially nebulous borders of what makes something a "kaiju."

So, here's a working proposal, perhaps, and we can take it or leave it, but the lineage of Japanese relationships to kaiju film is just too large to overstate, and it's also too large to ignore.

Of course, the concept of monsters appearing at the edges of our consciousness isn't uniquely Japanese, but the adoption or conversion of that rich folkloric history seems to be much richer in modern Japan. Let's face it, if you've ever read *Kwaidan* (or even seen the movie, which adapts a group of four tales from the book), then you know that Japanese folklore

13

hovers in the realm of the fully uncanny. This uncanniness has trickled down through pop culture in Japan and then exported abroad, moving creations as diverse as Godzilla and Gamera and Pokémon to an international stage, resulting in a hodgepodge of cultural adaptations and adoptions, As Miri Nakamura puts it:

> Monsters have haunted the Japanese literary imagination since the earliest recorded writing. Eight-headed snakes, giant spiders, water spirits, mountain goblins—frightening, supernatural creatures of all sorts infest premodern Japanese literature. Spectacular bodies to behold, colorful demons, and human-animal hybrids adorned the pages of religious anecdotes and vernacular tales. But monsters are not just creations of the past; modern Japanese literature is haunted by myriad monsters, not remnants of an earlier time but new creatures imagined through advances in technology and medical sciences [1].

This means that films that feature kaiju-style creatures but don't carry any relationship with Japan couldn't, on paper, be considered kaiju films. They would just be films with big monsters in them. Films such as *Colossal*, *Rampage* and *Trollhunter,* for example, wouldn't be considered "true" kaiju films, in spite of the big monsters that appear on the screen. As for *Colossal* and *Rampage*, well, those are distinctly different films: one a dramatic comedy about toxic relationships and the other a relatively brainless action go-getter. Still, in the case of *Trollhunter*, there's no doubt that Scandinavian legends, of course, feature their own creepy monsters, but there's a sort of robust transference that occurs in Japanese folklore that readily adapts itself to a new time period and a new era. While trolls can indeed appear in modern circumstances, as in *Trollhunter*, they still remain the same trolls that tales were told about several centuries earlier: in fact, their sort of "out of time" quality is what gives them a new meaning in the modern context. The trolls, in other words, remain the same, but the world around them changed.

Yet, with Japanese folklore, as one can see in J-horror films including *Ringu*, *One Missed Call*, *Pulse*, and *Noroi: The Curse*, the uncanny and the weird simply adapt themselves to the new world they find themselves in and continue to march forward—in fact, in many cases, actually incorporating technology into their scare tactics—spreading almost ceaseless terror among a modernized populace that can no longer find comfort in the very modern trappings that were supposed to advance them beyond "superstitious" beliefs in the first place.

Justin Mullis is indeed correct when he points to Western monsters as being more inclined "to chase us down, attack us, violate us, eat us, kill us, or make us into one of their own," with the only possible strategy to victory is to accomplish the "God-given dominance over nature by killing the monster" (9). And, as we take a brief glance at horror and sci-fi

1. Categorizing the Kaiju

films ranging from *Frankenstein* to *Dracula* to *Friday the 13th* to *Cloverfield*, the monster's unrelenting destruction of the main characters is true, and there's always the obvious solution: kill them before they kill you. We see this play out all the time in the slasher genre: Jason Voorhees, Michael Myers, and Freddy Krueger, among others, even when they are cast as unstoppable undead demons, *can* ultimately be destroyed or otherwise sent away until the next film. As noted, films like *Cloverfield* follow this formula: the kaiju nicknamed "Clover" is there to wreak havoc and ramp up the body count: nothing more, nothing less, and the only way to stop it is to bomb the living daylights out of it (but, along the way, spend a lot of time fleeing in terror).

But these Western monsters, unlike Sadako in *Ringu* and unlike Kagutaba in *Noroi*, *can* be defeated, albeit temporarily, and they retain much of their primitiveness in their roles: Jason will mercilessly walk (setting aside the ill-fated reboot of *Friday the 13th*, where he's much more agile) toward his victims, stalking them, and then usually crushing them or hacking them to death. Simply put, Western monsters, as a concept, necessarily include Western kaiju, for the most part (Kong, as a "hero" of sorts, seems to be the exception here), and their baseline characterization as an unstoppable but ultimately defeatable force, contradicts how Japanese monsters seem to flourish: nothing will stop them. There's little defeat to be seen at the end of Godzilla films where he functions as the antagonist: he simply strolls, falls, or is tossed into the sea, and is always a present and existent threat. Chon Noriega writes,

> Most Godzilla films end with the monster(s) swimming out to sea. [...] Rather than celebrate the monster's retreat, the films reveal the narrative "resolution" to be incomplete [...] The end also indicates a prescience of the monster's (re) return, or worse [75].

In the world of Godzilla, kaiju are treated almost as mass weather events, with constant monitoring, warnings, and evacuations, a plot device which finds its origins in *Godzilla Raids Again*.* The kaiju show up, damage things, and then go away again.

To return to *Trollhunter*: in that film, the trolls are indeed taken from old folkloric traditions, but it's modernity that *saves* the populace: long electrical wires are strung up by the government to prevent trespassing trolls; Hans gathers blood samples from them to take to a laboratory; massive strobe lights and trucks are deployed to battle or frighten trolls. Yet, in films such as *One Missed Call*, cell phones aren't the new weapon

---

*This is so apparent in Japanese kaiju films that *The Simpsons* poked fun at it in "Thirty Minutes Over Tokyo," where a pilot nonchalantly announces a flight delay due to the presence of, among others, Mothra and Godzilla.

16   **The Kaiju Connection**

that keeps spirits at bay: they instead provide a new avenue for attack and destruction, leaving people to distrust modernity itself. In *Pulse*, ghosts transmit themselves via the internet. The evil spirit Sadako comes through the television in *Ringu*. A professor tries in vain to figure out why a demon is awakening, recording his research as a documentary that eventually becomes evidence of the demon's presence (and destructiveness) in *Noroi*. In each of these films, contrary to many international works that draw from folklore, the modern is not the savior of the people; it's the enabler of the folkloric creatures that were supposed to be kept at bay and roundly dismissed as superstitions.*

Turning back to the kaiju themselves, there's one other thing to mention: so many of them are regarded as gods in their narratives: Godzilla is introduced as a deity, as is King Kong, as well as Mothra, and even at certain points, even King Ghidorah and lesser kaiju such as King Caesar and Megalon. It makes sense, of course: what else could these gigantic creatures of awe-inspiring power be? But this is also the very same duality that tends to define the monstrous in many kaiju films, and it's an aspect of the genre that we rarely see repeated outside of Japan (again, with Kong being the exception). For many of these Japanese-based kaiju, this duality, where the kaiju is "both demonized and deified, reveal[s] a deep sense of ambivalence about the relation between the monstrous and the divine, and intensifying the sense of paradox" (Beal 298), creates an uncomfortable friction that both alienates and embraces the kaiju at the same time.

Returning to *Trollhunter* as the comparative example, we can see that the trolls in the film do not—nor, for example, does Santa in the Finnish film *Rare Exports*—exhibit the discomfort of being both a destructive force to be feared and also worshiped, or at least held in awe. This tension between these opposite poles fuels *Godzilla* (1954), and it's a facet of Japanese kaiju film that continues to dominate even through the kid-friendly Showa era, as Godzilla, mostly shorn of godlike status and now a bona fide hero, has to battle other deities on behalf of an endangered Japan.

Even Gamera is initially introduced as a creature to be worshiped in the Showa era, and his Heisei appearance directly confronts, especially in *Revenge of Iris*, his godlike and heroic status, juxtaposed with the massive amount of destruction he brings while trying to save humanity. Godzilla and Gamera become what W.J.T. Marshall describes as "transitional object[s],"

---

*To show the adaptability of Japanese folklore, one needs only to turn to the Kuchisake-onna, who wanders around with a mask covering the lower half of her face and carries a pair of scissors. If you fail to answer questions she asks satisfactorily, you end up dead or disfigured. As you can imagine, the lower half of one's face covering possibly evil actions became a renewed, yet slightly altered, trope during the Covid pandemic–a few centuries after the first appearance of the Kuchisake-onna in folklore.

1. Categorizing the Kaiju

creations that exist to be "adapted and remolded" based on the prevailing mores of the time (197, 198). This strain of duality is less pronounced in Kong films, and in films such as *Colossal* and *Cloverfield*, it's completely absent.

I suppose a good way of looking at this would be for me to call forth an example from my very 1980s childhood that helps explain the authenticity (and also provides an undertow of nostalgia). I collected Transformers. These were authentic Transformers: Autobots and Decepticons, Dinobots, and so on. But, along the way, I also started to collect the rather cheap knock-offs known as Go-Bots. Go-Bots, of course, were somewhat less expensive than Transformers, but also more cheaply made. And the less that's said about the Transforming Robots I could find at the local dollar store, the better.

But all of these were, indeed, built under the conceit of the Cool Robots That Transform Into Something Else Cool. Go-Bots turned into motorcycles, airplanes, and so on. Transformers turned into jets, guns, and cassette tapes, among other things. And you could fold in half the dollar store robots to turn them from a Robot into … well, some sort of squarish car or something. So, the very basic idea here is that all of them shared a very large category, and they all held the values of that very large category in common.

But we all know, and we certainly knew then, that the "real thing" were the Transformers. They were the first and the best, and the originators (in theory) of the concept of Cool Robots That Transform Into Something Else Cool. So, what's to be made of Go-Bots and the dollar store Transforming Robots? Essentially, as one category (or, to put it less politely, rip-off) took inspiration from the other, they became their own entities, the classic Xerox-style copy of a copy of a copy that loses definition each time, but still retains the very basic individual properties that would allow the layman to pick up the toy and say: "This looks like one of those Transformers, my son would probably like this equally as much as the real thing."

This is where we could delve into deeper concerns about capitalism and pop culture, and how a studio can take a successful film and spawn endless copies until the original itself seems to fade in importance, often getting lumped in with the poorer and less memorable copies. Has the original *Godzilla* (1954) lost its impact, not due to dated special effects and acting, but because new viewers, as we have seen, carry the weight of every single iteration of Godzilla long before they see the original? And does this constant mining of the property lessen the film's importance as every new version is released?

Is this all rambling? Perhaps, but there's a definitive purpose to this analogy, because there can be considered three different categories of the kaiju film: The Real Thing, The Reasonable Facsimile, and The Cheap

Knock-Offs. There's another category, too, which encompasses related ideas but which strays too far from the original subject to be necessarily included in the discussion, except for when that discussion allows us to explore and understand the boundaries of categorization. This category is essentially the G.I. Joe's to the Transformers: still toys marketed to a segment of the population, even with some crossover potential between the two separate "universes," the same very black-and-white militaristic views of good versus evil, but different enough that we can hold up a G.I. Joe and wonder what they bring to the discussion that Transformers do not, and vice versa.

More about this category a bit later, but these films would be so reduced as to be generally recognized primarily as science fiction films, but have some very basic overlaps with kaiju film, at least enough that we can more fully understand kaiju films by understanding what these science fiction films are *not*. In the end, though, these borders remain ragged, as we will see.

I suppose the best way to visualize what is about to follow is to picture a straight line with the following four categories, all in a row, on that line. But, as you proceed from the "authentic" kaiju films, the distance between each category grows, so that you have more and more space between the final three categories, and much more distance from the "authentic" kaiju films.

The "authentic" Kaiju Films

"For some reason, kaiju only appear in Japan." This idea, spoken by a government official in *Shin Ultraman,* reveals a certain understated desire for authenticity concerning the concept of the "kaiju." There have been numerous convincing arguments over the years that point to a kaiju film as necessarily having some sort of Japanese origin to it (or otherwise "borrow" Japanese characters). These films are the "purest" example of kaiju film, and they include some of the most well-known heavy hitters in the kaiju canon: Godzilla, Gamera, and Mothra, among others. But this also includes far lesser known kaiju films such as *The X From Outer Space* and *Space Amoeba*. Alongside the mighty Godzilla stands Gezora, Ganimes, and Guilala. Even the American adaptations of Godzilla would be considered kaiju films because they share that same essential DNA as their Japanese counterparts: in this case, the established kaiju themselves.*

---

*This brings to mind a constant debate over *Godzilla* (1998), in which the Godzilla of that film bares so little resemblance to the original Godzilla that it seems to qualify in name only. The design of the 1998 Godzilla places it closer to films like *Jurassic Park*, and I hold some sympathy to the idea that *Godzilla* (1998) would have been a more well-received film if it just didn't call itself "Godzilla" and instead just embraced the "big dinosaur" motifs and left the few trappings of Japanese kaiju film completely behind.

1. Categorizing the Kaiju 19

What makes something a "kaiju" stands at the center of this discussion, of course, and so it makes a difference if we delineate between the terms "kaiju" and "daikaiju." For our purposes, ironically, "daikaiju," which translates to something along the lines of "great strange beast" is more appropriate than "kaiju," which means, simply, "strange beast." If we use the term "kaiju" literally, then other creatures such as the mushroom people in *Matango* and Gokemidoro from *Goke, Body Snatcher from Hell* would essentially be on the same level and consideration as Gamera.

Thus, it's important to establish, I suppose, that the term "kaiju" has been popularized to the point that it is generally meant, in the West, to be the term that points toward a combination of size and monster-ness as a prerequisite.

There are, of course, issues with this definition, and, as I argued in *The Kaiju Film*, this means that some films may sort of trickle into being more genuine as kaiju films than fans would like to think. Films such as *Pacific Rim* don't really have much of a Japanese origin, but the film itself makes no bones about referring to its own giant creatures as kaiju.

Another issue with this categorization can be best illustrated by the film *Kaiju Mono,* which uses humans as giant-sized characters (more on that below), but also features a kaiju character that is so worn and, well, cheap, that it belabors the point as a low-budget film, or a tribute to the cash-strapped kaiju films and television shows featuring suits that were clearly slapdash or in poor repair. The true question, then, in the case of *Kaiju Mono* and *Big Man Japan* is whether or not parodies and satire can be considered an authentic use of the form. For now, I'll say that they do, as they still, in this case, check off the other boxes: kaiju, with Japanese origins, and they also explore some of the same anxieties and concerns that dominate many kaiju films.

Another set of oddballs to consider, as I mentioned in *The Kaiju Film*: this definition: a large creature with Japanese DNA means that The Bumble from *Rudolph, the Red-Nosed Reindeer* may fit into the kaiju genre, or at least there's a tangible argument to be made. After all, Rankin/Bass relied on Japanese animators to "put together" the models for the holiday special. And what about *Gappa, the Triphibian Monster?* It's a Japanese production from Nikkatsu studios, but it's so painfully taken from both *King Kong* and *Gorgo*—an American film, and an American and United Kingdom co-production—that it hardly has any originality at all.

To make the issue more problematic is what counts as authenticity. Films such as *Colossal* and *Cloverfield* pay homage to Japan in very understated ways. At the start of *Cloverfield*, Rob is attending a going away party in his honor, as he's transferring to a position in Japan. And, during *Colossal*, we see that Gloria's laptop has a skin of Katsushiki Hokusai's "The

Great Wave off Kanagawa" woodblock print. Are these homages enough to give the film a sort of Japanese "credibility"?

Here's another sticky wicket: Steven Rawle, in his book *Transnational Kaiju: Exploitation, Globalisation, and Cult Monster Movies*, points out, quite rightfully, that kaiju film is a direct result of transnational politics, and has rarely been strictly "national" in outlook or in execution. I'm reluctant to go too far down this path, because the idea of transnational cinema as a theory has long been problematic and vague to the point of being like, well, the term kaiju.

The "knockoff" Kaiju Films

These would be films that have no tangible connection to Japanese culture or history, but do feature similar large monsters dominating the plot and the action. These films would be fairly obvious, because they lack Japanese origins, but still feature giant monsters. *Cloverfield* and *Colossal* would be two of the most salient examples of these films. You could also include other international efforts such as *Gorgo, Trollhunter,* and *Pulgasari.** As such, these films are often international and are homages to the kaiju film, but miss on the vital Japanese origination points. The different culture and differing cultural experiences that background numerous Godzilla and Gamera films, for instance, are severely lacking in films such as *Cloverfield* and *Gorgo*, and instead, provide a unique, but ultimately hollow, spin on the film. Of course, some films such as *Trollhunter* are successful in their own way by melding their own cultural values and perspectives with the concept of giant creatures; however, more likely, this category will remain dominated by what could fairly be considered quick cash-ins on the prevailing popularity of the "real" kaiju films, such as *Zillafoot*.

Yet, as noted above, even *Trollhunter* doesn't manage to capture the distrust or adaptability of the folkloric tradition: the time period changes, but the trolls remain intrinsically the same, a plot device which assists the narrative as Hans battles to keep the trolls under wraps away from the rest of the country (and world). Another example is the film *Rare Exports*, a Finnish Christmas film that depicts Santa in his initial guise of cruelty, essentially commanding an army of elves that stuff children in sacks and beat them if they're naughty. Santa, who is frozen in a block of ice throughout the film, is shown as nearly kaiju-sized, but he and his elves are

---

*The bizarre creation of *Pulgasari* has been the topic of much conversation this past decade, especially Paul Fischer's book *A Kim Jong-Il Production*. If a film is made by a well-respected South Korean director and a Japanese suit actor, but under duress, does it qualify? Who knows?

1. Categorizing the Kaiju 21

ultimately defeated by the modern world and technology: Santa is blown up with hundreds of sticks of dynamite, and the elves are rounded up in an electrified reindeer pen and trained to be the "real" Santas, complete with red outfits lined with white trim, for each country in the world. Modernity wins the day in these films.

You'll notice I just wrote a paragraph that unfortunately categorized what I would consider to be superior and more interesting films like *Colossal* and *Trollhunter* with the cheap and significantly lower quality films like *Zillafoot* and almost anything from Asylum, including *Monster Island*, *Atlantic Rim*, and *Mega Piranha*.* There's clearly a difference in motivation and philosophy among these films, with some being "inauthentic" in not wearing obvious Japanese origins or ideas and the others are "inauthentic" in a purely philosophical movie-making sense, often rushed through production and given clever names to confuse people stopping by a Redbox or scrolling through their preferred streaming platform.

Perhaps it's that films like *Atlantic Rim* barely qualify themselves as actual films, given their low production values, general soullessness, and lack of any semblance of technical or artistic skill. If that's the case, then it's easy to avoid including them in this category not because they aren't kaiju films, and not because they aren't "knockoff" kaiju films, but because they barely qualify as films at all.

The "big, familiar creature" Films

King Kong and all of the Kong and Kong-like films out there would fit into this category. Shorn of Japanese origins, but also ostensibly avoiding the "monstrous" nature of their look by having "real" animals be larger than usual. These creatures—often dinosaurs, dinosaur-like creatures, or apes—are inherently "real" to people, and thus don't fulfill the rubric of the "monster" aspect of the film. One question for these films is whether or not dinosaurs—or vaguely recognizable dinosaurs—such as the Indominus Rex in *Jurassic World* would be a more familiar creature, or if it would be genetically manipulated or spliced enough to reach toward the bizarre … just enough to make it feel more like a kaiju than a dinosaur.

Of course, there are more nakedly straightforward examples here, too, many of them legendary and created in the 1950s sci-fi "make them bigger" films: *Them!*, *The Deadly Mantis,* even, perhaps, *The Beast from 20,000 Fathoms.* There's, simply put, a Freudian *uncanniness* aspect to these

---

*At the time of this writing, Asylum was hopping aboard the promotional wave surrounding the horror/comedy film *Cocaine Bear* by releasing a poster for their own soon-to-be-released film, *Attack of the Meth Gator* (Perine).

creatures, for they look similar to what we as humans can recognize: ants, praying mantises, pictures of dinosaurs we see in books or when we visit museums, but just not quite the "real" article. Their size heightens all of their garish freakishness, and emphasizes their displacement in our reality.

In fact, we can see the reverse play out with much the same results. In movies like *Fantastic Voyage, The Incredible Shrinking Man*, and even *Honey, I Shrunk the Kids!*, the uncanniness of the mis-sized human body (this will be important for the next category) as well as the surrounding animals and creatures quite remarkably exposes and explodes the strangeness of the world that we choose, through most of our lives, to ignore.* In many ways, we as humans are rarely confronted with the bizarre nature of an ant—all fuzzy and pointy with gigantic eyes—until they become bigger than we are, and we simply can't escape that reality.

Returning to Kong, there's a sense of the uncanny with him as well, even though he is frequently the most "human" of the familiar creatures we see mega-sized. Ants, mantises, blood cells, cats, and flies, even when enlarged, remain intrinsically animalistic or otherwise foreign to our sensibilities. Kong is familiar, even, at times, almost human in his mannerisms, much like the apes that he represents. However, his size and his displacement from his home in many movies (a cycle that occurs in numerous Kong knock-offs, too) turns him more uncanny: a familiar sight in an unfamiliar world, and vice versa. Very few films outside of *Kong: Skull Island* and *Son of Kong* keep the giant ape in his own home territory for the entirety of the film; in fact, most of the "homages" to Kong, from *Mighty Joe Young* to *Konga* to *Yeti* to *Mighty Peking Man* all present the formula of taking the vaguely familiar and pushing them outside into a foreign place in order to heighten their absurdity and their bizarre-ness.

And so, the uncanny. Recognizable, but also just enough removed that they no longer remind the viewer of the kind or innocuous creatures they once were. There is indeed something "strange" in these creatures that provokes a sense of discontent or discomfort, especially when their unseemly and moralistic origins are considered. After all, almost all of the creatures in this category, save for King Kong and maybe Mighty Joe Young, came about as a result of scientific experimentation with the "forbidden" or unethical worlds of radioactivity or genetic manipulation, or even transgressions of cultural or societal ideals.

---

*We see some examples of the shrinking person phenomenon as early as 1929, with David Keller's "The Jelly-Fish," in which an unpopular professor—"We hope some evil might befall him," the narrator gloomily intones—attempts to educate his pupils on an expedition by shrinking himself down and lecturing from a microscope slide. That is, before a small jellyfish-like protozoan eats him in front of the horrified, but probably also relieved, students (583).

Human Kaiju

This is a misnomer, of course, because, if we set aside the idea of kaiju being strictly Japanese in origin, to be a kaiju means to be monstrous (and monstrously large) to the point of the uncannily identifiable. But films such as *Attack of the 50 Foot Woman*, *The Amazing Colossal Man*, and *War of the Colossal Beast* delve into, primarily, body horror,* because the growth of that particular individual immediately ostracizes them from society and makes them into outcasts. Their problems grow alongside their bodies, and we're left with a massive-sized set of issues that are exacerbated by their newfound size. Inevitably, their growth leads not only to their ostracization from society, but also numerous deaths (including their own) and untold destruction. Their giant stature is ultimately isolating, even maddening, and tends to force them to embrace their more animalistic natures. Glenn Manning and Nancy Archer are everyday people driven to madness by their newfound stigmatization. In becoming giant humans, they lose all sense of humanity.

Of course, their size makes them different from other body horror works such as *The Fly* or *The Wasp Woman*, as well as any number of werewolf films. In other words, *Attack of the 50 Foot Woman* isn't a "kaijin" film, a term which Brad Weismann defines as "humanoid supervillain" (102), but contains considerably more nuance than that. The kaijin, much like the kaiju, seem to be uniquely Japanese in origin; yet, the idea of a human grown to kaiju size isn't included in this definition. In fact, the "kaijin" genre seems to focus more on normal-sized individuals who are infused with new powers and abilities that can allow them to do evil (Weismann's "supervillain"); however, these new powers come at the cost of mutations of the human body that ostracize and mentally disturb the individual experiencing these changes. During the tokusatsu era spawned by the popularity of Godzilla, and, indeed, through many of the early years of the Showa era, kaijin were in abundance, ranging from *Goke, Body Snatcher from Hell*, *Matango*, *The H-Man*, and *The Human Vapor*, among others.†

For films such as *The Amazing Colossal Man*, the fact that these humans have grown gigantic literally makes their already existing problems giant-sized, and held up for all the world to see, and to react in

---

*There's plenty of body horror among normally-sized people during this era of the American horror film: not only works such as *The Fly* but also *The Indestructible Man*, *The Wasp Woman*, and many others.

†To make matters more confusing for new fans, these films are often referred to as henshin ningen films, which Wisemann describes as "other non-rubber-monster sci-fi/horror outings" (103), but can be more faithfully understood as "human transformation" films. Henshin ningen films are popularly understood to be limited to at least *The H-Man*, *The Secret of the Telegian*, and *The Human Vapor*. They all can also be understood to fit in the broader kaijin label.

fear.* Consider the difference in the original version of *The Fly*: in the end, the body horror and the repulsive transformation is revealed in physical form to only a few members of the human cast. Otherwise, the hybrid human/fly issue is one that is almost entirely localized, rarely breaching the edges of the Delambre estate. Manning and Archer can't escape society, and their issues are such that their presence requires entire armies to try to stop them. Of these three works, the only film that deals with a grotesquerie that extends just beyond size is *War of the Colossal Beast*: Glenn Manning is hideously scarred and driven to being more animalistic as a result of the attacks that supposedly killed him in *The Amazing Colossal Man*. In this regard, to borrow Japanese terminology and transfer it recklessly, he's a (almost) kaiju that is also a (almost) kaijin!

This is also where we end up more in the realm of monster theory, the idea that monsters are representative of a society's fears. The edges of monster theory can indeed bleed into discussions about our "big, familiar creature" category because the *true* monster in those films often is not the ape or Yeti or prehistoric creature; it's often profiteers, mad scientists, and malicious people who just enjoy being cruel. So, when we move the lens of what a "monster" is to Glenn Manning and Nancy Archer, the borders become much fuzzier. As we will see, there's a convincing argument to be made that these two characters take us on wildly different paths in terms of who is a monster, and who is not, and, as a result, one of them is much closer to being a "big, familiar" creature (and, thus, closer to kaiju in the hierarchy laid out above) than the other.

So, these are four distinct categories that may provide a sufficient bridge in kaiju studies, a sort of "guideline," if you will, of what makes a kaiju film a kaiju film. Frankly, and as you will see in this text, I think each category allows us to further understand kaiju as a pop culture phenomenon *and* as a reflection of sociocultural concerns and apprehensions. As you'll notice, I don't necessarily adhere to these categories strictly for this book—if I were to "just" write about authentic kaiju films, I feel I wouldn't be able to further discuss certain aspects of them, and would have to disallow some films that I feel are integral to understanding kaiju as a pop culture phenomenon. At times, it's just easier to step outside the boundaries and look inwards rather than to sit in the middle of the milieu and try to define the edges from an inside perspective. That's why you will see me sometimes refer to "kaiju-adjacent" films: films that loosely fit within the same family, even if they are distant, distant fourth cousins.

---

*This theme is explored to great effect in—strangely—*Monsters vs. Aliens* (2009), an animated film in which a young woman, Susan Murphy, grows super-sized and becomes Ginormica. One of the main character arcs for Susan Murphy is her slow embrace of her differences as Ginormica and coming to terms with her being a "monster."

All in all, these are just proposed definitions—the overall idea of these categories is to try to find a way that will assuage and placate most fans of *all* of these films, and, indeed, I think there's arguments to be made that there are at least tangible relationships between these different categories that place them all in the same overall categories. Films such as *Attack of the 50 Foot Woman* and *Trollhunter* continue to delight us today, not only because of the same sort of novelty and camp that we see in the Showa-era Godzilla and Gamera films, but also because they focus on the same issues and anxieties that dominate the sociocultural conversation of the time period ... and beyond.

2

Toys and Dinosaurs and Nostalgia

I've got a lineup of X-Plus 30 cm Godzillas under my television, running from left to right in chronological order, from the 1954 Train Biter Godzilla to the 2016 Frozen Shin Godzilla, with a few notable absences (in my defense, Showa-era Godzillas that are 30 cm in size are hard to track down and deeply expensive on the secondary market), but the row is there, at all times, no matter what I watch. To borrow from *That Mitchell and Webb Look*, they sit there, staring at me, bearing mute vinyl witness to my utter inability to bow to the prevailing taste consensus. These Godzillas spent the entire time I wrote this book staring at me staring at the television. And the reactions from visitors (who, I admit, I often watch like a hawk if they touch them or pick them up) widely varies. Sometimes, it's outright interest, as in the case of a pair of workers who dropped off a new oven and spent much of the time talking to one another, unprompted, about their favorite Godzilla films. Other times, it's someone walking by them on their way to do some quick work in the ungodly basement, filled with the boxes that once held these figures, and laughing and saying "what a zoo!" A plumber once said "build more shelves!" when I said I had run out of space for new Godzillas. And still other times, it's a silent, very judging glare, followed by a slight head shake and thin smile: what a weirdo, they seem to be thinking.

But there's numerous online clubs that follow every new release and gossip and compare notes about kaiju figures with the merciless scalpel-like precision of a mortician. Ask, for instance, about the differences between the 30 cm Yuji Sakai Modeling Collection Godzilla 1984 Shinjuku Subcenter Battle Version and the 30 cm Godzilla 1984 Shinjuku Decisive Battle Version, and you will receive several treatises comparing the look and sculpt of the figure. In fact, there's more than a few YouTube channels out there dedicated to discussing and appreciating these figures, often by comparing different sculpts and "looks" for the same "model" of

2. Toys and Dinosaurs and Nostalgia 27

Godzilla. These shows can last well over an hour and often have guests—fellow collectors and enthusiasts—who engage in considerable detail about how the sculpt looks and feels, even discussing the balancing of the figure and the coloration of the figure. In the above example, those are two different versions of Godzilla from *The Return of Godzilla* in 1984, each of them capturing a pose from a different portion of the film—the Sakai Godzilla can even come with a miniature Super X ship for Godzilla to face off against.

When you buy these figures, you have to make a very basic, but ultimately telling, decision: how "real" do you want your kaiju to be as they sit on your shelf? Some fans tend to prefer figures that are as "movie accurate" as possible, and this provides the possibility for some really neat photo sessions where one can recreate film scenes or create new havoc.* A few years ago, I set a few kaiju in the Christmas village in our home, took pictures of them terrorizing the local populace, and then sent them out to friends and family. The reception to these cards—which, if I may say so, were more creative than the basic formula cards we received, the ones that come in bulk packages of 50—was one of great indifference. Oh well; it's an audience thing, and, like the display of these figures, there is, among many non-fans, the aspect of perhaps "playing" with "toys" that would betray the basic maturity levels of someone in their 40s. Kaiju are for kids! Kaiju toys are for kids! And taking pictures of them are for slightly older kids!

This is really the purpose of the discussion. How a perceived maturity level is the burden upon which many kaiju fans tend to labor under. Horror films? Sci-Fi films? Even Disney films, all cut across numerous age groups. They are marketed and discussed as, generally, for "young and old alike." Kaiju films, including both Godzilla and Gamera, rarely receive much popular attention in the West as something for the masses, either as a genre or a set of individual appreciations that can extend beyond one's own childhood.

Of course, nostalgia and "all ages"–style entertainment has become a veritable bumper crop for corporations over the past several years. I wrapped up my book *The Kaiju Film* before the first episode of *Stranger Things* aired, and immediately after *Star Wars Episode VII: The Force Awakens* came to divorce many adults, looking for their childhoods, pressed between the very frames of the film, from their money. Yes, nostalgia became the fuel for the newest bumper crop of film franchises that either were a part of our collective childhood experiences (for example, one of my first theatergoing experiences was to watch the Ewoks in *Return*

---

*There's no lack of fans who enjoy more stylized figures that feature radically different colorations and more rounded or toy-like features: CCP and Medicom figures, among others.

28   **The Kaiju Connection**

of the Jedi), or to remind us of a place and time where we were ourselves children.* Alongside *Stranger Things* and the *Star Wars* properties, so too have arrived other nostalgia-fueled properties, including *Ghostbusters*, *Ready Player One*, both the book and the subsequent film (which featured a guest appearance from Mechagodzilla), the soundtrack for *Guardians of the Galaxy*, and horror movie *Summer of '84*, among many others.

But what do most casual fans who are in their 30s and 40s remember most from their childhoods about Godzilla or Gamera (or even King Kong)? Most likely: endless weirdness, trapped in their eras without much hope for retrieval and modernization. The adults who consume new *Star Wars* toys because they enjoyed *A New Hope* as kids probably remember Godzilla and Jet Jaguar or Gamera as a friend to all children.

In other words: goofiness. The fearsome symbol of atomic destruction and pain, reduced to a puppylike countenance as he shakes hands with a robot. How pervasive is this mindset? Claire Stanford writes what I feel is the usual response to someone who is exposed to *Godzilla* (1954) with little knowledge other than the pop culture influence:

> Before watching Godzilla for the first time, in the spring of 2021, I had expected a hokey, formulaic monster movie, the kind of breezy entertainment typical of the genre, with its cartoonish plots, B-movie acting, and schlocky special effects. But Godzilla, released in Japan in 1954 and the first of what would become a franchise of 36 films, strikes a markedly different tone. It is a somber and mournful movie, I quickly realized, and distinctly unschlocky [90].

This is the usual response of the "outsider" who rarely, if at all, sees kaiju films. The genre is so supersaturated with cheese and camp that it unduly influences the perception of every film in the genre.

Another example comes to us from Adam Charles Hart, who, in a book about the horror genre, mentions Godzilla in passing:

> From *Frankenstein* and *Dracula* on, we have been deeply invested in horror's monsters in a way that we haven't been in their heroes and heroines. This is true even of figures that don't suggest much of a psychology with which to sympathize, whether it's Godzilla or the xenomorphs […], or Jason Voorhees [196].

On the surface, this is a true statement, but misses the mark in terms of Godzilla. We know the xenomorphs—they don't really change from film to

---

*And this can happen in places where you least expect. *The Americans*, a television spy show/drama set in 1980s Washington, D.C., had numerous similarities to *Stranger Things* in terms of clothing, furnishings, and the like, but because it has a firmer sense of place, it also featured, playing lightly in the background, the commercial for Jhoon Rhee Taekwondo and their instantly recognizable (and interminably memorizable) jingle.

2. Toys and Dinosaurs and Nostalgia

film, even in the oft-maligned prequels, and we know Jason Voorhees, who, setting aside all but a few moments of the first film, is a supernatural killer. Both the xenomorphs and Voorhees, even if the look and the origin change, are emotionless and soulless killing machines, although it's safe to say that an "investment" in the literally faceless armies of xenomorphs is a bit of a stretch. But Godzilla? Firstly, which one? The symbol of nuclear radiation and international hegemony? The goofy dad looking out for his kid? The force of nature? The walking symbol of the Japanese war dead? Hart clearly uses "Godzilla" as a catch-all for "monster" without really quite realizing that there have been, almost literally, dozens of different Godzillas since 1954.

But, even placing Godzilla in the same realm as Jason Voorhees is itself a puzzling comparison. As noted already, Voorhees is a supernatural, unstoppable killer, who as early as his first full appearance in *Friday the 13th Part II*, begins to be cheered by the audience for two distinct reasons: he's a complete badass, and he also is killing generally unlikable people. For Voorhees, he functions as a sort of schadenfreude wish fulfillment, and as the series progresses, it's clear that Voorhees becomes the antihero of his own film franchise, as the characters he hunts become more and more aggravating, morally corrupt, and bothersome (except for the Final Girl, of course, but that's a different discussion).

Yet, when almost any iteration of Godzilla is on the screen, the "killing" and monstrousness occurs in a much more somber, but ultimately distant, way. Hart's comment seems to point to the original Godzilla as the source of his definition, but there's no emotionless death in that film, nor is there any "hunting" of people in *Godzilla*. Throughout the franchise's history, when Godzilla kills people (not aliens, they seem to be fair game), it's a tragedy, and it's often played as such for much of the franchise; even the villains who get their comeuppance are often tragic figures. And when Godzilla kills people without a hint of tragedy, there's a sense of justice— they deserved it!—or comedy.

Okay, so there's two examples of the broad brush with which the general public and much of academia seem to paint Godzilla.

But for the rest of us, who have spent a lot of time watching and re-watching kaiju films more times than we can count, we know that there's multiple Godzillas. To turn back to toys, it would be really cool to collect them all.

The primary question, though, is how Godzilla manages to captivate so many people across the world. I think a part of the answer is simply dinosaurs. It's an easily transferable set of ideas, after all: dinosaurs to dinosaur-like creatures with special powers that battle one another and humanity itself. It shouldn't be too terribly surprising, then, that the first kaiju "versus" film, *Godzilla Raids Again!* is an update of an ages-old battle in the imagination of the general public. In place of battle between the Tyrannosaurus and Triceratops, which dominated depictions of dinosaurs since the start of the twentieth century (Sax 57), we're treated to a battle between a tyrannosaur-like kaiju (Godzilla) and a squat four-legged spiky triceratops-like creature (Anguirus). In this regard, kaiju film can be seen as an almost natural extension of the general adoration of dinosaurs, stretching itself back from the initial popularity to their frequent appearances in films ranging from *Jurassic Park* to *65*.* No less than Ed Goziszewski, one of the leading historians and scholars of the kaiju genre, waxed philosophical about the connection between dinosaurs and kaiju:

> As with most kids of my generation, I had a fascination with all things dinosaur. My prized possession was a set of dinosaur figures with which I staged endless pretend battles against a set of army men. In the summer of 1963 [...] you can imagine my reaction when a trailer for *King Kong vs. Godzilla* came on the screen ... as Godzilla appears, I'm thinking, "Wow! This is the greatest dinosaur I've ever seen!" And when his fins glowed and he shot his atomic breath, little did I realize that I was about to embark on a lifelong journey into the world of Japanese monsters [qtd. in England xi].

The then-nine-year-old Godziszewski made the same connection that almost every dinosaur-smitten child makes: kaiju as dinosaurs, but bigger, better, more exciting.

This isn't a huge logical leap to make, either, as numerous science fiction authors used dinosaurs as central pieces of their fiction to challenge their readers' imaginations. Jules Verne's *Journey to the Center of the Earth* in 1864 and Arthur Conan Doyle's *The Lost World* in 1912 are two of the most famous examples of early science fiction that featured dinosaur or dinosaur-like creatures. But the fascination over dinosaurs that exploded during the Victorian era never quite abated, and they took on new importance as paleontology came out of the "bust" cycle of the Great Depression (Marshall 169). This "second dinosaur rush," which straddled the depression, led to movies and other forms of art based on a newfound and "precise biologic information" that led to dinosaurs being understood—and depicted—as "living" creatures (Sanz 20, 25, 27). This newfound collision of mass culture, postmodernism, and a resurgence in interest in scientific feats—and fears—revived dinosaurs as a topic of mainstream conversation and pop culture creativity.

Of the numerous science fiction writers in the early twentieth century, it's hard to think of many who enjoyed writing about dinosaurs as

---

*Numerous Kong films, including *King Kong*, *Son of Kong*, and *King Kong Escapes*, depict Kong living alongside dinosaurs and often battling them for dominance. By the time we get to *Skull Island*, the dinosaurs have mostly metamorphosed into a wide array of kaiju wearing clear dinosaur influences in their design.

much as Ray Bradbury, whose short stories and poems about dinosaurs ended up in a collected volume called *Dinosaur Tales*. Bradbury's most famous work, in fact, was "The Fog Horn," which inspired *The Beast from 20,000 Fathoms* (which, in turn, partially inspired *Godzilla*). But perhaps the most faithful depiction of the role dinosaurs play in the life of children, especially young boys, comes in the short story "Besides a Dinosaur, Whatta Ya Wanna Be When You Grow Up?" The story focuses on Benjamin, a young boy who lost his parents, and the relationship he has with his grandfather, who grows more and more concerned over Benjamin's obsession with dinosaurs. In the grandfather's mind, Benjamin becomes "lost in time, mist, and sump-water trackless bogs" (30), and he becomes worried that Benjamin is actually turning himself into a dinosaur. The grandfather goes into the boy's bedroom and finds magazines and books open to depictions of

> Dinosaurs grinning, lurching, touching primeval mists with fingerprinting claws. While others rode the kite skies with whistle-drumming membrances or periscope up with long boa-constrictor necks from smoking bogs, or grasped at the teeming sky as they sank to vanish in tombs of black tar [...] [44].

But the story ends on a melancholy note; Benjamin, fast asleep, is told by his grandfather to stop thinking of dinosaurs—to stop willing himself to *be* a dinosaur—and instead to become an engineer. The next morning at breakfast, Benjamin, much to his grandfather's relief, dons an engineer's cap. There's a certain loss of innocence here, as Benjamin's coping mechanism, to literally leave the modern era itself and go back to where beasts roam with their "mad surgeon claws" (44), gives way to the much "safer" and appropriate endeavor of wanting to grow up to be an engineer one day, rather than a dinosaur. No small part of Benjamin's childhood ends as soon as he puts on the engineer's cap.

As noted, *Godzilla*'s inspiration is at least partially derived from the Rhedosaurus of *The Beast from 20,000 Fathoms*, and, so, if we trace the lineage back from the Rhedosaurus through Ray Bradbury, and back further still to *The Lost World* and *King Kong*, creations that Bradbury cited as his lifelong inspiration,* we can find the ideas of living, breathing dinosaurs consistently in the forefront of the human imagination. Entire books have been written about the dinosaur-in-pop-culture phenomenon, but it's not a coincidence that Godzilla is, like the Rhedosaurus, initially

---

*"So, you see, the dinosaurs that fell off the cliff in *The Lost World*, that ancient 1925 film, landed squarely on me, as did *King Kong* when I was twelve. Squashed magnificently flat, breathless for love, I floundered to my toy typewriter and spent the rest of my life dying of that unrequited love" (Bradbury 17).

32   **The Kaiju Connection**

described scientifically as a dinosaur, which will become a constant descriptor throughout the Godzilla franchise, especially in films such as *Godzilla vs. King Ghidorah*, featuring, literally, the Godzillasaurus—which, of course, is a dinosaur with Godzilla-like features—and this term will be used to describe the story arc of Baby Godzilla (*Godzilla vs. Mechagodzilla II*), who becomes Little Godzilla *(Godzilla vs. SpaceGodzilla)*, who becomes Godzilla Jr., and then eventually becomes Godzilla (*Godzilla vs. Destroyah*), replacing his father.

This all comes back to the original *Godzilla*, of course, with the descriptions of Godzilla as a dinosaur and his resemblance to the popularized upright Tyrannosaurus Rex depictions of ramrod straight posture, big teeth and tiny arms, but is driven home by *Godzilla Raids Again*, when a scientist in a meeting reads aloud from Edwin Colbert's *The Dinosaur Book* (originally published in 1945), describing an ankylosaurus to the collected group. "The two must have fought from the beginning," he intones, "and has now come back from Godzilla's past." So, a modern Japan, now inflected with two oversized dinosaurs, one irradiated, the other a "smart" and "dangerous" carnivorous beast. If Godzilla as one dinosaur was awful, then having a second dinosaur join the modern world was easily twice as bad.

But there's also the idea of human intervention in these fictional narratives. As we know, almost every kaiju film (and kaiju-adjacent film) features often extensive human narratives (if we can't agree to call them "plots" in many cases), and this, too, mirrors depictions of dinosaurs. As Boria Sax writes, the juxtaposition of humans and human achievement to dinosaurs allows us to rest just a bit more easily over our obsessions:

> People are thrilled by the primeval fierceness of large predators [...] which evoke a combination of identification and fear. To indulge freely in our impulse to admire them, we must first be reassured that they can be subdued, or at least seriously challenged, whether that is by human hunters or by an adversary [...] [67].

Thus, dinosaurs give way to kaiju and the same follows. In order for, say, Gamera or Godzilla to retain their viability in our esteem, they must be attacked, savaged, beaten, sent away, or we have to otherwise receive assurances that human actions play a role in the eventual outcome, be it the creation of a weapon that could destroy the world, or simply pouring liquids on a control panel. In the end, the human interaction and, at times, intervention, continues the idea of humans asserting some form of dominance over beasts much larger and much deadlier than they are.

To return briefly to *Godzilla Raids Again*: there's some subversion of this narrative for a brief span, as Dr. Yamane returns from *Godzilla* to tell

2. Toys and Dinosaurs and Nostalgia

everyone that his proposed "countermeasures" are essentially to try to lure Godzilla away from the coastlines when he appears, evacuate, and hope for the best. There's no sense of any human ability to stop or otherwise defray kaiju attacks in the film until a pilot, Kobayashi, is blasted out of the air by Godzilla, and his crashing plane explodes on a nearby mountain-top, prompting a mini-avalanche. This gives his friend, Tsukioka, the idea to pass along to the Japanese Self-Defense Forces: hit the mountain rather than Godzilla, and bury him in ice, rock, and snow. The plan works (in fact, director Motoyoshi Oda apparently *really* loved filming missiles and planes ramming into the mountain), but only by accident.

Human ingenuity and problem-solving ultimately doesn't play a key role in *Godzilla Raids Again*, and is one of the few Godzilla films—perhaps one of the few kaiju films—where humans aren't taking an active role in defeating or delaying the kaiju from the very start of the film. Is it any wonder that *Godzilla Raids Again* bombed so massively that the nascent Godzilla franchise went on hiatus for seven years, prompted into revival only by the possibility of a matchup with King Kong, an international superstar? And that revival showed humans directly manipulating many of the events, moving Kong to and fro like children picking up toys and dropping them in front of one another?

Human control. In many ways, then, being kaiju fans, and collecting kaiju figures (re: not toys) is the next step of a natural evolution from childhood: we can still "own" the creations we see on our television screens, but they're no longer quite toys: they're "collectibles," and they bear the price of wearing that name, both in terms of cost and in terms of any possible castigation from self-proclaimed "adults" who stumble upon them. In this way, we can reconcile our childhood enjoyment of kaiju and dinosaurs with being the more adult reality of collecting. And, in these ways, too, we can pick up and enjoy control of our dinosauric entertainment, if only when no one else is around.

3

An Appreciation of *Godzilla Raids Again*

There's a lot going against *Godzilla Raids Again*. It's a cheap cash-in sequel. It has a B-team enemy for Godzilla to fight (sorry, Anguirus). It has a thin plot. It's sandwiched between an all-time classic, *Godzilla*, and two other all-time classics, *King Kong vs. Godzilla* and *Mothra vs. Godzilla*. There's no depth to the characters. And so on. Most of the discussion of *Godzilla Raids Again* is the acknowledgment that it prompted the "kaiju versus kaiju" format that will dominate kaiju films—specifically the Gamera and Godzilla franchises—for the next sixty-plus years. In fact, it's difficult to find much critical commentary on *Godzilla Raids Again* outside of various film guide compilations, such as Mike Bogue's *Apocalypse Then* or John Lemay's *The Big Book of Japanese Giant Monster Movies*. There's always plenty of critical attention on *Godzilla*, of course, and some critical focus on *Godzilla vs. Hedorah*, for example, but, of the Showa films, *Godzilla Raids Again* remains among some of the most neglected in critical and fan circles.

Both Pogue and Lemay seem generally apathetic toward the film, with Pogue bemoaning "superficial characters" and a "threadbare story" that "plays like a standard Japanese giant monster movie" (176, 177). Lemay is a little less effusive, telling readers that *Godzilla Raids Again* is mostly "[w]orth watching for historical reasons" (30). There's little doubt in my mind—despite the title of this chapter—that they are inherently correct in their assertions, especially when comparing *Godzilla Raids Again* directly with *Godzilla*. One is a somber reflection on the damage and long-lived trauma of nuclear attack that happens to feature a kaiju emblematic of that form of suffering; the other features a pair of kaiju, and neither of them really garner much depth beyond being labeled as irradiated dinosaurs, destructive throwbacks to another era. In fact, *Godzilla Raids Again* makes the cardinal mistake of any sequel: it immediately reminded the viewer of a better film, at one point stopping the narrative to show us clips

34

3. An Appreciation of Godzilla Raids Again   35

from *Godzilla*, as if to tell us that, yes, these are coming from the same universe.

But there is more than that, and I would argue that in spite of the weaknesses, all so readily acknowledged by even the most apologetic Godzilla fans, *Godzilla Raids Again* is more vital, more interesting, and more worthwhile as a kaiju film than many people think. There are, of course, plenty of "what ifs" that surround the movie, mostly speculation on the long-term viability of the Godzilla (and, almost by default) Gamera franchises, but I think that *Godzilla Raids Again* remains among the very few Godzilla movies that will attempt to create a human plot around the very basic detail of "two (or more) kaiju fighting" structure. Not only that, but the movie focuses on everyday human characters: pilots, criminals, businessmen, lending a greater "ground level" sense to the suffering—and nascent hopes—of a country unable to get out from under the presence of Godzilla.

So many films that come after *Godzilla Raids Again* tend to forget the humans as actual characters, make them comedy figures, are children, or create humans that are campy or otherwise two-dimensional annoying interruptions in a long string of battles that dominate the proceedings, a trend that continued even through the American versions of Godzilla (both 1998 and starting in 2014). After *Godzilla Raids Again*, the emphasis on human characters seems to drop significantly to give "space" to the kaiju and their goings-on (giving us just enough plot to, as I said in the previous chapter, assure humans that they remain dominant), but *Godzilla Raids Again* is a film where the human plot remains central to the goings-on, something that is hard to say for numerous Showa films after *Godzilla*: *Godzilla vs. Hedorah*, perhaps? There's precious little else.

"But I want to see big dumb fights!" comes the rejoinder, and that's fine. But for those of us who like things such as motivation and emotion alongside a sense of a grounded reality, *Godzilla Raids Again* manages only to touch the dark tinge of *Godzilla*, but then lurches toward a somewhat uneven story of two men, their bromance, and the women who love them. Both Kobayashi and Tsukioka are likable characters, pilots trained during World War II, and are now given over to working for a fishing company, Kaiyo, spotting large schools of fish for the company's boats. It's a job, at least, and Kobayashi and Tsukioka seem to enjoy flying, for whatever reason, and their friendship is evident as they speak to one another and the women in the Kaiyo offices charged with relaying their messages. One of the women, Hidemi, is in a sort of lowkey romance with Tsukioka, and it's so lowkey that neither Tsukioka or Hidemi are aware that Kobayashi has a crush on Hidemi.

This mirrors the sort of understated love triangle that appears in the background of *Godzilla* as well, only, I would argue, it is somewhat more well written. Kobayashi and Tsukioka aren't necessarily the sort of stereotypes that Serizawa and Ogata tend to veer toward at times. Both Kobayashi and Tsukioka are working-class people with a unique skill set; Serizawa and Ogata have, after the war, landed firmly in the upper class of science and academics. So, the often staid and stilted interactions that informed the love triangle of Serizawa, Ogata, and Emiko Yamane are replaced by the jocular, emotion-filled, and warm relationship between Kobayashi, Tsukioka, and Hidemi. There are indeed scenes in *Godzilla Raids Again* that we would never see among the scientists and academics that populate *Godzilla*, especially the drunken party in Hokkaido.

This gives the human subplot a certain amount of warmth and interest that's missing in *Godzilla*. Yes, there's an arranged marriage fueling the interaction between Emiko and Serizawa, but neither of them really seem to be affectionate or otherwise engaged with one another, so when it's revealed that Serizawa is aware of the blossoming relationship between his fiancée and Ogata, it lands with a bit of a thud, especially given that he is literally about to kill himself to save the world. Yet, when Tsukioka finds out that the remarkably goofier Kobayashi is ready to break through and profess his admiration and crush on a mystery woman, and we later discover that it's Hidemi, it's much more interesting and, dare I say, believable. Kobayashi dies almost immediately after, and it's a plot point that's a little too neatly wrapped up (guess we won't have to worry about that little love triangle anymore!), but it seems to bring more spark to Kobayashi and Hidemi, in particular.

Okay, so that's basically the human subplot, and I would argue that the main characters in *Godzilla Raids Again* are probably a bit more relatable and less abstract than in *Godzilla*. Yet, there's still reasons why *Godzilla Raids Again* never quite sticks the landing for many audiences, and it's perhaps a bit too romantic and a bit too formulaic, especially when juxtaposed with the same "forbidden love triangle" plot device that dominated *Godzilla*. Yet, the battle between Godzilla and Anguirus, and the eventual "demise" of Godzilla at the end of the film are creative and entertaining, and the human subplot has its moments as well. It's just not what many would consider a "complete" film, especially compared to the tragic nature of *Godzilla*; yet, that's a pinnacle that few—if any—kaiju films have touched.

There's a sort of ripple effect that is caused by the existence of *Godzilla Raids Again*, especially if we take time to set aside all of the negative associations. Yes, the movie was a quick cash-in. Yes, it was mostly poorly written. Yes, it bombed and is mostly forgotten, save for the trivia answer to "which film came between *Godzilla* and *King Kong vs. Godzilla*?"

Godzilla Raids Again is ultimately a small film, lasting a mere 81 minutes, shorter than almost any other Godzilla film—outside of *Godzilla*

3. An Appreciation of Godzilla Raids Again   37

vs. Megalon (which also lasts 81 minutes), and *All Monsters Attack* (a very long 69 minutes filled with stock footage from prior Godzilla movies)—and this 81-minute run-time includes a very long sequence of a mountaintop getting blitzed ... over and over and over again. But within this sparse timeframe, we get a sense of postwar Japan, a sort of postcard from a country still recovering from a massive war and a pair of nuclear attacks, as well as a near-complete reordering of the society. There's fears of starvation when the fishing trawlers can no longer bring back their loads because of Godzilla and Anguirus. There's a pair of pilots who cheerily try to make the best of their situation as spotters, quite the decline in technical skill and valor from being wartime pilots. And there's a general sense of sorrow that tends to bend toward occasional brightness as well; in *Godzilla* and for the early portion of *Godzilla Raids Again*, there's a pervasive sense of hopelessness, driven home by Dr. Yamane.

But, in the face of this hopelessness, there's a newfound but fleeting sense of optimism. Life goes on, and there's parties and dances and general good cheer in spite of the adversity. After a prolonged sequence where Godzilla defeats Anguirus, and in the process destroys much of the shoreline and Kaiyo's buildings, the head of the company, Kohei Yamaji, simply says: "The damage is much worse than I imagined.... I'm going to rebuild it." And, almost instantly, the company is moved north to Hokkaido and apparently thriving again. This resiliency is further underscored because we almost immediately see a company party, with uproarious laughter and plenty of alcohol to drink. While Pogue would describe this as "convenient scripting" (176), I happen to disagree. The somber tones of the destruction of Osaka in the great fight gives way to a near-immediate declaration of resilience, and, the company party is just one example of this, as Kaiyo and its employees find some form of happiness, even after being relocated to the somewhat more hostile and snowy environment of Hokkaido.

It's a neat switch, to move from the more idyllic climes of Osaka to the more foreboding and isolated Hokkaido, with Osaka being the site of devastation and Hokkaido becoming a refuge of sorts, where happiness may not be permanent, but can be found in simple (and traditional) human connections. This is further underscored by the bashful Kobayashi's growing crush on Hidemi, and by Hidemi's flirtatious relationship with Tsukioka. Even in the face of nuclear-powered destruction and untold violence leading to blackouts, fear, and death, there's still a sense of humanity that pervades the film. The tragic elements that course through *Godzilla* are mostly lost, of course, but it seems almost purposeful. *Godzilla Raids Again* seems to want to picture a country and its people adjusting to a new paradigm and finding a new way of life as they struggle to climb out of the darkness.

There were some historical reasons for optimism in Japan, no matter how slight: the country was on the verge of the so-called "Japanese Economic Miracle," where the country's GDP skyrocketed to prewar levels, defying most economic predictions to that point. There's a lot of economic and bureaucratic background to these changes, including one of the most formative, with Japan entering the General Agreement on Tariffs and Trade in 1955 that increased Japanese participation in the world economy, either via exporting products or otherwise importing any number of other goods. In the end, products as diverse as crab meat, textiles, Christmas tree ornaments, televisions, and hypodermic syringes either arrived in Japan as new items or were exported away, bringing in much-needed cash (Forsberg 145–150). What we see in *Godzilla Raids Again* is the slowly growing economic stability of a country; still struggling, but with some new income on the horizon. Not to sound too sappy, but there is room for genuine love and affection in *Godzilla Raids Again*, something that doesn't really seem to appear in *Godzilla* at all, outside of a few very formalized and stilted interactions.

Of course, the plot of *Raids Again* is more than a bit threadbare, and it doesn't feature the sort of painful introspection that makes this "more" than another monster film—you know, the sort of thing that would attract movie critics and academics. Let's face it: as I said in *The Kaiju Film*, the kaiju genre as a whole outside of *Godzilla* has been mostly relegated to the backwaters of academic discourse. Most of that is because films like *Godzilla* (and *Godzilla vs. Hedorah*, to a lesser extent), are very much "plug and play" for academics. They won't have to work too hard to convince themselves, their editors, and their readership that there's something meaningful and profound in *Godzilla*. That much is obvious, and it's this obviousness that has returned *Godzilla* to some form of critical acceptance; never mind the rest of the Godzilla franchise, nor the Gamera franchise, and, quite possibly, any other film remotely related to kaiju outside of *King Kong* (1933) and the occasional mention of *War of the Gargantuas*, and that's mostly because of a few nods to that film from Quentin Tarantino.

This leads to a much broader discussion on what makes some movies "academic worthy" and others not, and we won't necessarily go down that path, but there's a sense that some form of critical respectability and prestige is derived from the films themselves. After all, no one is marching forward to tenure on the back of a critical analysis of, say, *Hell Comes to Frogtown* or, to return to kaiju film, *All Monsters Attack*. No, *Godzilla* had plenty of fodder for academic discussion lightly buried beneath the veneer of the giant monster genre, and, as such, it has become quite rightfully appreciated, although it could be argued that such an appreciation required not only a few decades to pass (some of that time was the lapse in the original Japanese edit to appear on Western shores), but also the esteem of Ishiro

3. An Appreciation of Godzilla Raids Again   39

Honda as well. In the end, *Godzilla* earned its place in academic prestige primarily because of the critical fodder to be found in it; after all, it's one of the few films to directly address the identity crisis of a country still suffering from the aftereffects of a pair of nuclear strikes. Yes, there have been some films that appeared in the decade after the bombing, such as *Hiroshima* (1953), *The Bells of Nagasaki* (1950), and *Children of Hiroshima* (1952), but these are "in the moment" films that immediately examine the aftermath of a moment in history that is deeply tragic and unique.*

Through this lens, pretty much no other Godzilla movie, or Gamera movie, can reach the critical and historical heights of *Godzilla*, so it strikes me as rather unfair to compare *Godzilla Raids Again* to *Godzilla*. Almost no film in the kaiju genre will manage to reach the critical esteem that *Godzilla* has enjoyed—albeit several decades late—and *Godzilla Raids Again* is, in spite of some of its flaws, a semi-successful picture of a country and its people adjusting to a new paradigm, for better or for worse, and trying to eke out some form of happiness during trying times.

Naturally, my sympathy for this film and the human plot may just be Pollyanna-ish projection through an entirely Westernized perspective, but I feel that *Godzilla Raids Again* is somewhat unfairly maligned or otherwise ignored, either as a historical piece (as *Godzilla* criticisms go), or a part of the franchise itself (as most films focus on the "versus" format pioneered here). The film holds up on its own and seems to me to be due for a certain critical reappraisal, at least among the fans, if not academics, and, I think if one were to hold a poll for "best Godzilla films," *Godzilla Raids Again* would probably come in somewhere in the middle, or, if the poll were limited to just the Showa era, even higher than that. I think that the film mostly struggles with being forgotten, a sort of unnecessary coda to a magnificent and genre-inventing film, but ultimately has some merit, if not as an earth-shattering view of the new postwar world order, but as a decent film in its own rights.

As we go back and re-watch the Godzilla films, it's easy to remember just how difficult it was to establish the Godzilla franchise because of the quick cash-in that was *Godzilla Raids Again*. Let's not forget that, as stated earlier, *Godzilla Raids Again* forced Toho to put the franchise—only two movies in!—onto hiatus for several years. But buried within the sometimes plodding script and the sometimes unenthusiastic direction is a film that brings to us the realities of a postwar Japan: still struggling, but with a certain underlying hope that is slowly building up, seeping through the tragedy and the resentment, if only for 81 minutes.

---

*I have to note that the Wikipedia page that lists Japanese films about the atomic bombings doesn't have *Godzilla* listed at all—but does include *Frankenstein vs. Baragon*!

4

Science and Faith: The Solo Kaiju Adventures

It goes without saying that the bread and butter of the kaiju genre is the "versus" films, established, in part, by *Godzilla Raids Again*. Looking back through the films, there's only a few of them that don't feature some sort of kaiju collision. *Godzilla, Mothra, Rodan, Gamera, The Return of Godzilla, Shin Godzilla*, the *Daimajin* series, *Dogora, Space Amoeba*, and *Shin Godzilla* being the most notable exceptions to the rule. In each of these films, the threat to humanity is the title monster itself: rarely does this kaiju take on the role of hero or savior as it normally does in the versus films, and, on the rare occasions where the title kaiju is "bad," say, in *Giant Monsters All-Out Attack*, there's still a clear reason for battle, and, even, in some ways, a sympathetic glance or two toward the bad guy.

It's quite simple to say that the relative lack of solo adventures for our kaiju over the years stems from a confluence of events. Firstly, the promised battle between two massive monsters tends to draw more eyes and ears to the project, not only leading to funding for production, but also, eventually, to more fans being drawn to the final product. Of course, there's also the basic idea that these films tend to be rather easy to write and produce: one kaiju appears, then another, and then they battle. This can create a series of smaller battles leading to a coup de grace, such as in *Godzilla vs. Kong*, or essentially prompt one gigantic chase sequence, such as in *Godzilla* (2014). Everything else in between these battles is usually secondary, a subplot that's created only for the most dedicated kaiju fans to sit through or tease out.

But when the kaiju stand on their own, they tend to reflect a boogeyman, designed strictly for human consumption, a mirror that's held up to society and reflects back some of our most pressing fears and concerns. That's substantially harder to write and it's substantially harder to draw fans into these films; they're often the source of the "but nothing happened!" complaints for *Shin Godzilla*, for example. And in films like

4. Science and Faith: The Solo Kaiju Adventures 41

Dogora and *Gorath*, you'd be forgiven for wondering, for long stretches, if there were any kaiju at all.

Of course, much of the time, the main kaiju in these solo films are the antagonist and a set of protagonists doing their best to "defeat" the creature, even though it is completely unaware of its existence. In the occasional narrative trick, the protagonists manage to create a kaiju battle just the same by trotting out a device such as the Super X in *The Return of Godzilla*. But, mostly, the solo kaiju adventures focuses primarily on the destruction of large swaths of the city (or, if the budget is too low, large swaths of the countryside) while the humans desperately try to figure out conventional ways to stop them.

These humans are almost invariably, as well, authority figures in society: the learned men (and it is almost always men), and there's no greater representative of that set than in *Agon, The Atomic Dragon*. There's a detective, Yamato, a journalist, Goro, and a scientist, Ukyo. Ukyo's assistant—whose primary role is to either be in danger or to be Goro's crush—is Satsuki. These positions of authority define them as "heroes" to the cause of society, representing law and order, transparency, and knowledge, each of them functioning as totems for the very best of social order. In this regard, the true "heroes" manage to defeat the kaiju with their knowledge, even forbidden knowledge, in order to save the day.

Compare this to the typical "versus" film, where much of the main human-based action swirls around children, the military, or government officials. There are some notable exceptions, mostly those closest to *Godzilla* in the franchise chronology. *Mothra vs. Godzilla*, for example, follows a reporter, a photographer, and a scientist as they attempt to convince the Shobijin to engage Godzilla and save the day. But as the Showa era rolled on, and the "versus" format took over both the Godzilla and Gamera franchises, we see the advent of characters from governmental apparatuses such as the United Nations and Interpol, or military-based characters such as those in the Japanese Self-Defense Forces.*

Yet, over time, thoughtful and ethical scientists give way to mad scientists such as Mafune in *Terror of Mechagodzilla* or Shiragami in *Godzilla vs. Biollante*. In fact, the Heisei era of the Godzilla franchise is dominated by characters in the military playing the primary role; science and scientists

---

*Even *Shin Ultraman*, a film evoking the prime Showa era, focuses on the SSSP, a group of scientists in charge of the JSDF. An opening montage shows numerous kaiju falling, Gomess, Pagos, and the like, all at the hands of scientists, who rush to share their discoveries with the military. This leads to the creation of the SSSP, and, at first, they sit in a military intel center near the newly arrived kaiju, analyzing data in real time and giving orders to the military. Although *Shin Ultraman* is a versus-style film, homages to the early Showa era retain the emphasis—at least partially—on science instead of government or the military.

generally take a backseat to the goings-on, even when they're otherwise fully-fleshed characters. And in those few instances where scientists exist in these later "versus" films, they function as an extension of the military, mere advisers who don't make decisions or win the room. They instead create mega-weapons like the Dimension Tide in *Godzilla vs. Megaguirus*, Kiryu in *Godzilla Against Mechagodzilla* and *Tokyo S.O.S*, or MOGUERA in *Godzilla vs. SpaceGodzilla*. Scientific inquiry and puzzle-solving are no longer central plot points for any of the scientists or journalists; they're instead often just bounced from location to location, engaging the kaiju through their high-tech avatars and hoping for the best.

No doubt that many of these similarities are wrapped up in the fact that these solo films often featured, in some capacity, the talents of Ishiro Honda as director, and Shinichi Sekizawa or Tomoyuki Tanaka as producer, or were properties, such as *Gamera*, directly inspired by Toho's output. Honda himself consistently circled back to themes of faith and science in many of his works, and it's no small surprise to see these themes take center stage over and over again in films he directed. In fact, the roles of religious faith and science are almost a necessity in order to create a film, given how "little faith" Honda had "in politicians to resolve a crisis" (Ryfle and Godziszewski 130). In Honda's world, the politicians were effective only when they listened to scientists and researchers.

All of these solo kaiju films hearken back to *Godzilla*, and back on through to the film's inspiration: *The Beast from 20,000 Fathoms*, in which a physicist and a paleontologist work to convince skeptical military commanders of the beast's existence—and the best way to stop the Rhedosaurus. It's been well established by now that *The Beast from 20,000 Fathoms* was one of the key points in inspiring and facilitating the creation of *Godzilla*, but the basic template of scientists working together to overcome a threat can be seen in *Beast* as well, and, if we are truly honest with ourselves, *Beast* was just one of many science-fiction giant creature films during the early 1950s that featured science in a key role in "solving" the dilemmas, which were often, not ironically, created by scientific ambition and the thirst for knowledge.

As Mike Bogue describes this trope, "Hey, Mr. And Mrs. Average Citizen, trust in good ol' American science to save the day!" (118),* all while ignoring the idea that science also caused some of the very issues meant to solve. *Invaders from Mars*, *The Day the Earth Stood Still*, and *The Thing from Another World* are all examples of films that featured scientists of various disciplines in key roles, unraveling the mystery through good old

---

*Nevertheless, there's plenty of skepticism among scientists in movies such as *The Day the Earth Stood Still* and *Earth vs. The Flying Saucers*. When the aliens ask to be taken to the world's leaders, the scientists almost always warn the aliens that they will have trouble contacting and convincing government officials about what's happening.

4. Science and Faith: The Solo Kaiju Adventures   43

scientific observation and inquiry, and, almost equally as often, restraining or otherwise blunting the military's desire to destroy everything in sight in response to the threat.*

Of course, the first true kaiju film, *Godzilla*, has a narrative propelled by science; when government officials appear, they, somewhat surprisingly for our era, listen to the scientists and follow their advice. Even the rural natives of Odo get fair play in front of the government officials, and, in response, government officials dispatch Dr. Yamane, a paleontologist; the rest of the main cast are representative of rugged hard work, in the form of Hideto Ogata, a ship's captain, and ethical science, in Dr. Serizawa. As the plot seemingly requires, there's a young woman, Dr. Yamane's daughter, Emiko, who is caught up in a love triangle featuring Ogata and Serizawa. Class and esteem issues aside—Emiko's impending marriage to Serizawa is arranged based on her own perceived role in society as the daughter of, and wife to, a scientist—these three men again form a sort of super-team of knowledge and effort that leads them to defeat the kaiju.

There's something to be said for the ultimately tragic ending of *Godzilla*, which purposefully rejects the "mad scientist" vibe that Dr. Serizawa labors under as a product of 1940s and 1950s science fiction and horror films. Replete with basement laboratory and eyepatch, Serizawa initially is presented as a man perhaps detached from the world, and, at one point, even dispassionately kills a tankful of fish to show Emiko his discovery. Steve Ryfle and Ed Godziszewski write that

> Serizawa is different from the mad scientist characters that proliferated in sci-fi literature and film; he is no Victor Frankenstein, and has no God complex. He is shrouded in mystery, disfigured by war, and tormented by the implications of his discovery [...] Serizawa is inherently good. He fears his invention could destroy the world, yet hopes to find a peaceful use for it [91].

So, Serizawa's character avoids the easy Victor Frankenstein (or Dr. Carruthers, or Delambre, or Tillinghast, or …) typecasting almost immediately after he turns healthy fish into bones, because he understands the horror of his discovery, and, in this understanding, he rejects the knowledge. It's a bridge too far; he could easily conquer the world or otherwise tilt the power of nations to his own cause. He could become wealthy beyond his dreams. But Serizawa, who, on the surface is scar tissue and sweat-glistened anger, still has feelings; he still has emotions. And even though he ostensibly has motivations to use the Oxygen Destroyer for evil

---

*Scientists—and generals—abound in kaiju film, but in the films that follow a versus format, the scientist is often relegated to a sort of subordinate role to the military, or provides one singular "aha!" moment. No better example of this is Dr. Serizawa in *Godzilla* (2014), whose role as a leading scientist means he can just stand there and listen to increasingly absurd military plans while providing blunt moralistic lessons and meme-worthy quotes.

purposes, he instead refuses to use it at all, for fear of how his discovery will change the balance of the world, and for fear of how many people will die knowing his name as the inventor of their untimely demise.

So, Serizawa flips the script. He rejects the "mad scientist" label that we're initially led to consider when we first meet him and instead ensures that his discovery is lost to humanity, first by destroying his lab and his notes, and then, ultimately, himself. Serizawa dies, loved. He is appreciated and perhaps even venerated for his choice to save the world, twice, in one simple decision that ends his life.

You see this all throughout the solo kaiju films. Learned and esteemed individuals, whose roles in society represent lofty symbolic ideals, confronting an external threat and winning the day. Hell, in *Gorath*, which features a cameo appearance by Meguma,* numerous astrophysicists appear in front of mathematical equations, scrawled across chalkboards, in front of the United Nations. Astronauts radio back measurements and calculations and everyone in the world of *Gorath* seems to be crunching numbers in unison, leading Ryfle and Godzisewski to note, without irony, that most of the discussion of math "gets a bit dry" (167). This is a part of Ishiro Honda's emphasis as well, because, throughout *Gorath*, he "clearly places scientists and their work on a pedestal" (Ryfle and Godziszewski 131). Discussions among the politicians, whom the aliens roundly ignore for much of the film, about the need to drop all borders and share all research in order to "save mankind" abound, but it's the scientists who take over leadership of the project to save the planet from Gorath.

There are outliers to this phenomenon, but these tend to be a function of their chosen setting; in the case of *Daimajin*, science is replaced by faith, and, really, it's somewhat hard to think that there's not a lot of difference there. This is where I would cite Mike Bogue's discussion of "super-science" as a theme that dots kaiju films (206). This is science that itself tends to strain credulity. The Oxygen Destroyer, for example, which was discovered ... somehow ... and works ... somehow. Or the masers that populate Godzilla films. Or the fact that numerous scientists working together can literally move the Earth in a short time span. These things all require some form of faith on the part of the viewer, but also tend to lurch more into fantasy than science fiction—there's not really a lot of "hard" science rationale, even in films like *Gorath*, just a lot of science-based ideas that may never come to fruition, even decades after they were first introduced.

---

*Save for a very brief appearance from Meguma, I realize that *Gorath* is probably more fairly labeled as a science fiction/tokusatsu film. Meguma falls victim within minutes to a trio of ray gun blasts from a rocketship and dies somewhat offscreen. Still, Meguma's presence not only pads the runtime, but makes *Gorath* a less-than-complete member of the kaiju genre.

4. Science and Faith: The Solo Kaiju Adventures 45

Compare the conversations in *Gorath*, focused on mathematics and stars and measured distances that can't be seen or even comprehended (quick, imagine a light year, or two), to the prayers sent out to a stone god, hidden away within a mountain, that hasn't moved in years and is simply viewed as little more than a massive talisman. The quiet desperation of *Daimajin* for the villagers who have been wronged either breaks them or forces them into a greater and renewed adoration of their long-lost faith. The scientists who try to convince everyone of the coming danger, and how to avoid it, find their suitable echoes in the villagers who call out for Daimajin and warn others of his impending destructive appearance.

This is not to wander too far into the "science is a religion" debate, because it clearly isn't. But the thematics of the solo kaiju film beg the point, and the *Daimajin* trilogy, itself such a massive departure in kaiju film in any number of ways, from time period to the creature itself, still follows the same general perception of the role of the individuals in the story. In other words, the *Daimajin* trilogy, all released in 1966, at the height of the Showa-era kaiju genre, borrows the same ideas of experts leading the blind and the dangers of the unknown and the unknowable. Whereas Dr. Serizawa accidentally uncovers the destructive nature of the Oxygen Destroyer via science, so does Kosaza in *Daimajin* use her worn faith to unleash a being that ultimately destroys everything in its path.

All of the *Daimajin* films focus on ne'er-do-well feudal lords, who usurp peace, destroy families, and enslave humble villagers, and the formula, so tried and true throughout the trilogy, relies on Daimajin's being awakened by a newfound lack of faith; in fact, Daimajin's punishments for those who attempt to destroy his statue or otherwise subvert his godlike role in the villages is often one of retributive justice: you like gold? How about you drown in molten gold?

And so, even though *Daimajin* occupies an odd space in kaiju film because it is a jidaigeki—essentially, a period piece—the trilogy often follows the same pattern of many solo kaiju adventures; Daimajin himself rarely shows any regard for humans, and is considered more of an uncaring natural force.* And it takes those holding on to specialized, esoteric knowledge to save the day, often by convincing others that *their* knowledge is the key to unlocking their situations.

For example, it takes about the first twenty minutes of *Varan, the Unbelievable* to examine how faith and science and tradition all intermingle to provide numerous ways of exploring the world. This entire opening portion of the film functions somewhat as a parable of the penalties of a lack of

---

*It's only really in *Daimajin Strikes Again*—the final film of the trilogy—that the god seems to have any empathy toward the suffering of the villagers, and that empathy is mostly directed at the children of the village.

inquisitiveness and a corresponding dismissal of faith. After two of Professor Sugimoto's students die while traversing the "Tibet of Japan," the distant and isolated region of Iwaya Village, Sugimoto gets together with Yuriko, the sister of one of the men killed, Horiguchi, a photographer, and Kenji, one of Sugimoto's students, to discover what happened to the two men. Rumors abound of a creature called the Baradagi, an idea that Kenji scoffs at openly while talking with Sugimoto. For his part, Sugimoto chastises Kenji, noting that "we know nothing about the biological aspects of the place," and how *they* may think Baradagi is a superstition, but the villagers don't, meaning that there's some sort of reality that exists in which the "superstitious" beliefs have some sort of basis in reality; it's up to the scientist to discover that reality.

The group arrives at the village and watches a ritual designed to keep the Baradagi at bay and generally just to get the big guy to calm down. When the village elder chastises them for arriving at the village, Kenji hands the attitude right back, telling the village elder and the villagers that they are too "superstitious" and have to break away from their belief systems. This back-and-forth continues as a dog runs away and his owner, a young boy named Gen, pursues him, crossing the boundaries of where the Baradagi is supposed to tread. The elder holds the villagers back until Kenji rallies them, again arguing that their beliefs are little more than superstitions, and the villagers, rallied rather easily by Kenji and overwhelmed with concern for Gen, break through the boundaries, literally leaving the village elder behind.

And then: Varan. The kaiju bubbles out of the lake, shocking Kenji and forcing the collected villagers to run back past the elder, who immediately begins his prayers and is roundly crushed in a landslide caused by Varan. There's some deep irony here. The converted skeptic survives but the dedicated believer is killed. Kenji's understanding of the intersection between science and belief occurs as soon as he sees Varan, and he spends the rest of the film actively working through science to try to subvert Varan, alongside the decidedly less skeptical Drs. Sugimoto and Fujimora. For Kenji, his deep and unyielding skepticism nearly gets him killed; it's only when he understands that, like Sugimoto asserts, traditional beliefs and "superstition" have a role in science as well.

If the ideas of faith and belief as substitutes for hard science and scientific inquisitiveness are a bridge too far, I need only point you to *Mothra*, a film which somehow manages to unite the two ideas and manages to somehow hold them side by side. One of the most intriguing things, in fact, about Mothra as a character is her relationship to humanity as well as her "fairies," the Shobijin. There's a considerable whiff of folkloric background whenever Mothra appears on screen, and her character frequently represents the faith of her believers in her attempts to keep a natural order

4. Science and Faith: The Solo Kaiju Adventures 47

intact, often by quashing science run amok in the form of kaiju or humanity's latest mega-weapon. In this regard, Mothra the character is one of the few in the kaiju canon who seems to be remarkably consistent in her characterization throughout numerous films.*

The setup for *Mothra* is pretty much the usual casting for these solo films: a radiation specialist, Harada, a linguist, Chujo, and a reporter named Fukuda. This trio of men form the nucleus of the problem-solving protagonists while their traveling companion, the very American Clark Nelson (although he's officially a "Rolisican" in the movie, hailing from "New Kirk City") is the unlearned businessman, the bad guy, and the one who makes a ton of money from kidnapping the Shobijin and having them perform nightly to sold-out audiences. As the Shobijin sing, though, they are calling out to Mothra to save them, and, as these things go, Tokyo is soon under attack by Mothra's larval form, and military leaders and government officials can do little more than try numerous increasingly (self-) destructive attacks to try to stop the larva.

It's Chujo the linguist who understands what to do, and his ability in linguistics is the key, and provides a merging of science and faith. He summons Mothra to hand over the Shobijin, stopping the rampage, by understanding that she responds to a particular religious symbol. Chujo sets down the symbol at an airport, and he, and we, are left to wonder about the almost magical connection between a pair of "fairies" with telepathic powers, a giant larva that can turn into a gigantic flying insect, and religious symbology. To illustrate how important faith is to Mothra, the Shobijin, and Chujo, we only need to fast forward to another Mothra versus Godzilla film in *Tokyo S.O.S.* To wit, the film essentially unfolds with Mothra being angry that the Japanese government has taken the bones of the original Godzilla and made it into a new Mechagodzilla, Kiryu. Then things unfold in such a way that we can find the brick wall in which faith, science, and competence are kept apart:

Shobijin: Mothra will have to declare war on humanity if they keep doing this. Chujo, tell your government.

Chujo: Mothra will declare war on humanity if you keep doing this.

Prime Minister: We'll keep doing this and then we'll stop when we've won.†

---

*Many of Mothra's changes tend to be physical rather than philosophical. Her most radical changes occur when she brings about Mothra Leo in the *Rebirth of Mothra* series. Even so, the standard trappings and iconography of Mothra continue to abound—belief, a relationship with humans, and ancient temples.
†In this instance, it's Chujo's grandson, Shun, who summons Mothra by using the religious symbol; it's clear that children are more willing to take the leap of faith, as Chujo spends much of his time talking with the prime minister of Japan, trying to convince him to stop the project.

There's a distinct coldness to the motives of the government, and it features a lack of scientific understanding (science is militarized and completely abstract to the politicians beyond "will it work?"), indicating the broad difference in how Mothra and those who believe in her are depicted in society, especially as they face a large, bureaucratic and seemingly dispassionate and illogical government.

All the way at the start of *Mothra*, we're exposed to Mothra's worshippers on Infant Island, and, as such, the juxtaposition of their "primitive" methods and the advanced and dashing heroes (even Clark Nelson, the evil capitalist, is handsome) pushes the audience toward thinking that, much as in *King Kong*, the sympathy lies naturally with those who are the knowledgeable: the scientists, and the capitalists that fund the search for knowledge. Yet, there's the sense throughout the movie that the villagers and Shobijin know things that even the most advanced and knowledgeable people in the film can't know—they exist on the other side of that pierced veil of belief and faith, and it's only Chujo who is willing to follow.

As *Mothra* shows, there's a fine line between the dedication for science and the pursuit of knowledge and, in a world where giant monsters seem to habitually appear and kill thousands, the faith and belief needed to be able to cope with this idea. And it's important to remember that many of the kaiju in solo films—including, in this example, the non-kaiju King Kong—are worshiped as deities or gods, including the original Godzilla, himself viewed as an ancient sea creature in folklore, and, of course, Mothra and Daimajin.

Gamera is an ancient engineered guardian in the Heisei trilogy; his origins in the original 1965 *Gamera, The Giant Monster* are a little sketchier, but we know that the native peoples worship the idea of Gamera through the generations. Even the tagline for *Shin Godzilla* refers to "A God Incarnate." Ryfle and Godziszewski note how important *Mothra* is as a part of Ishiro Honda's canon as well, for he moves away from science, in part, to display "a world [...] without scientific rationalization" (161). The world of *Mothra*, in other words, is one of faith and almost magical, fantastic creatures who transcend scientific inquiry and require little more than an acknowledgment and belief from even the harshest skeptics. It's often, frankly, impressive, how unperturbed the characters in *Mothra* are about the sudden appearance of a massive larva that transforms into essentially a very angry butterfly, itself soothed only by a pair of telepathic fairies.

Even a relatively minor film like *Space Amoeba* examines how faith, skepticism, and science collide. In an early sequence, the skeptical Yokoyama and Sakura go fishing on Selgio Island while mocking the village elders, who have warned them of a creature in the ocean. Yokoyama

4. Science and Faith: The Solo Kaiju Adventures   49

changes his tune dramatically when Gezora appears and grabs Sakura, taking him to the depths. In some rather heavy-handed symbolism, when Yokoyama turns around, the village elder Ombo is *right there* to chastise him, standing on the rocks just a few yards away from shore. All during the sequence of Gezora's attack and Yokoyama's sudden embrace of faith that monsters *do* exist, the tribal drums play in the background, further emphasizing the "real" nature of their folkloric beliefs.

This is all too much for Yokoyama, who spends the next several minutes of the film being castigated by others who have arrived on the island and basically running for his life and screaming at the slightest hint of Gezora's presence. Yokoyama's flight from Selgio Island, which he describes as "hell on earth," is interrupted, naturally, by Gezora, who snatches him up as he helplessly throws files and papers at it.

One of the themes in *Space Amoeba* is how the collision between skepticism and faith can be overwhelming to non-believers, as their former worldview is shattered, and their minds simply can't seem to handle the pressure. At the start of *Space Amoeba*, the photographer Kudo swears he watched a space capsule named Helios 7 land while unmanned; he is quickly questioned and marginalized to the point that even he seems to wonder if he believes what he sees. Rico, who witnesses Yokoyama's unfortunate demise at the hands of Gezora, falls mute after the attack and doesn't remember Gezora at all. And, of course, Yokoyama himself is essentially sent toward insanity by his first encounter with Gezora. There's a distinct notion that disbelief, no matter how slight, is an opening to almost cosmic-horror levels of insanity.

No, a nearly dispassionate scientific inquiry is the way to go when confronted by kaiju versions of mutated and alien-possessed sea creatures rampaging through a nearly empty island. "Anything can happen now," Ayako, the corporate representative who hired Kudo, says as the villagers start a ceremony designed to placate Gezora and stop the rampaging. The rest of the party have different motivations for witnessing Gezora. Kudo, the photojournalist, wants evidence to prove Gezora's existence, and to make a lot of money in doing so, as well as restore his credibility. Obata, a corporate spy, simply wants to escape with a rival company's plans to exploit Selgio Island, and Dr. Miya simply wants to discover the truth, whatever that may be.

Ayako opens her mind to the possibility of Gezora, and even says she would pray with the villagers if she could, while Obata mocks her and says he would take Gezora and put it on display for profit. This is the moment where the viewer knows that Obata will either die or face a test of faith by the end of the film; more about that later.

Dr. Miya, the biologist, uses his knowledge to eventually understand

50   **The Kaiju Connection**

that the creatures are not natural beings,* nor are they gods. Piecing together the evidence and Kudo's eyewitness accounts of the Helios 7, Miya is the first to understand the presence of an alien entity on Earth. It is here, again, where science and faith collide, as the villagers and their ceremony provide the key to stopping Gezora; not through soothing the giant beast, but rather because it shrinks from the heat of the torches at the ceremony. Miya, ever the observational scientist, notices this, and the two ideas, that the ceremony stops the rampage and the heat chases Gezora away, overlap. Miya's sudden understanding that, no matter how improbable, he's observing a slow alien takeover, is the key to winning the day, all the while without impugning or denigrating the faith of the villagers (and Ayako's burgeoning belief system).

But almost all of these films where the kaiju encounter humanity, and vice versa, shows how scholarship, knowledge, and belief combine to help humans survive and ultimately win the day. Science isn't quite as militarized as it is in the standard "versus" film, where scientists exist only to create the next big weapon and are mostly impersonal or struggling with basic ethics. It's ironic, then, that after what was literally dozens of films where the military took the lead over the Showa era that we have a return to science as a decidedly non-militaristic savior in the most Cold War–inspired film of the group: *The Return of Godzilla*.

The scientific investigation begins here with the appearance of massive sea lice, and Dr. Hayashida, whose subsequent investigation allows him to hypothesize that Godzilla has returned. From there, Cold War politics win out, as the Soviets and the Americans both debate just launching nuclear weapons at Japan in order to stop Godzilla. Japan's ace in the hole, though, is the Super X, a superweapon created to respond to just these emergencies. It's a device created by the Japanese Self Defense Forces, and, along with the advanced Maser Cannons from Godzilla lore, they surprisingly manage to knock out Godzilla, in what, given Godzilla's dominance in kaiju film up to this point, should have led to a self-congratulatory pat on the back. The Soviets launch their nuclear weapon, and the Americans manage to blow it up in the atmosphere, reviving Godzilla once more, and, now angrier and more powerful, he quickly dispatches the Super X.

This is all, of course, typical 1980s Cold War commentary that doesn't really need much further exploration: science in this instance, however, has been militarized and is portrayed, alongside government and geopolitics,

---

*There are enough references to *King Kong* in this movie to make one wonder if *Space Amoeba* is meant to be set in the same universe. Dr. Miya believes it is entirely possible that a gigantic version of a "real" animal can exist. Coupled with Obata's laughter at wanting to capture Gezora and bring it back to Japan for profit, and it seems like many of the characters know the "legend" of Kong.

4. Science and Faith: The Solo Kaiju Adventures 51

to be mostly flaccid. The Super X does indeed manage to temporarily render Godzilla unconscious, but then the question: now what? manages to intervene, revealing that neither the military nor the government seemed to have planned out any sort of contingency plan for almost anything that's happening, be it nukes from the Soviets, failsafe plans from the Americans, or ways to finally defeat Godzilla rather than knock him out.

So, what's the answer? Dr. Hayashida already knows how to defeat Godzilla and works frantically to get everything in place. He notices that Godzilla is attracted to bird calls, and creates a device that mimics these bird calls, and decides to place it at the rim of a volcano. The military only plays a relatively minor support role during this plan, and, noticeably, given the nuclear warheads and advanced technology like the Super X, no weapons are fired, or even present, during the finale, where Godzilla is lured into the volcano by the device. The only action that occurs is the dynamiting of the volcanic shelf as Godzilla stands on it.

All along, Dr. Hayashida has the answers. He knows Godzilla is indestructible, and he knows the most convenient way to stop the kaiju, while minimizing casualties, which one would think the government and military would absolutely love to happen and take credit for. Yet, there's a definite feeling that war and violence are the only answers to any problem, at least according to the military, and certainly according to government officials. But this message isn't entirely clear, and the politics of the moment tend to point toward an overall softening of the antimilitaristic and pro-science feeling that overwhelms many of the earlier solo kaiju adventures. As the Showa era progressed, politicians and generals tended to take stronger roles, and long battle sequences between the kaiju and the military were de rigueur. Certainly, by 1984, the idea of military might had grown to the point where the military manages not only to create a super-weapon built for a specific purpose* but also to be successful (if only for a little while) in defeating the kaiju. Over time, perhaps, the

---

*These weapons would arrive hot and heavy soon after *The Return of Godzilla*. Previously, the JSDF or the equivalent militaries would use conventional weaponry or try to hotwire some currently existing infrastructure to attack the rampaging kaiju: for example, using electrical wires as a defense method. But after the appearance of the Super X, there's the Super X-2 from *Godzilla vs. Biollante*, Mechagodzilla II in *Godzilla vs. King Ghidorah*, MOGUERA from *Godzilla vs. SpaceGodzilla*, the Super X-3 from *Godzilla vs. Destroyah*, the Dimension Tide from *Godzilla vs. Megaguirus*, and Kiryu from *Godzilla Against Mechagodzilla* and *Tokyo S.O.S.* The sole outlier to this evolution is the Gotengo from *Atragon*, which, like *Gorath*, is barely a kaiju film, with Manda only appearing for a few moments and relatively pointless to the plot. The Gotengo is "officially" a part of the Godzilla franchise when it appears again as the New Gotengo forty years later in *Godzilla: Final Wars*. This sort of movement is accelerated in the Legendary films as MONARCH starts as a clandestine science and research organization working closely with the military in *Kong: Skull Island* to a near-militaristic organization with super-speed, highly armored aircraft and impressive technology and weapons in *Godzilla vs. Kong*.

numerous battle sequences and crushing of the military over and over again led to a desire to re-integrate the military as a major player in the kaiju realm, and, thus, the speed of the appearance of new weapons and technologies picks up the pace substantially after *The Return of Godzilla*.

Shin Godzilla inverts the formula of competence and expertise, either through science or faith, and in the place of learned individuals, we're presented with government officials. As in *The Return of Godzilla*, it's fair to wonder who the real enemy is in the narrative; Japan is saved from destruction, a devastation "not at the hands of the creature, but rather from the incompetence of the old political order and the self-interest of global rivals" (Green 33). In *Shin Godzilla,* the only scientist who truly knew what was happening dies before the start of the film, which leaves us with long discussions of bureaucrats doing bureaucratic things: holding meetings, signing papers, holding more meetings, interrupting meetings to start other meetings, and generally being completely incompetent in the face of the massive challenge that's crushing the world around them.

It's a film with an arrow pointed right at the heart of the Japanese government's response to the Daiichi Fukushima disaster, roundly condemned by many Japanese as bumbling at best. More than a few times in my interactions online with other kaiju fans, I found that *Shin Godzilla* was one of the more divisive films, with many people pointing to the government meeting sequences as "boring" or otherwise "dragged on."* But that is precisely the point. You're supposed to feel frustration and annoyance (and perhaps outright anger) at the government's inability to think, often literally, outside of the conference room.

Yaguchi is a relatively young government drone working with a large number of other government officials in the upper reaches of the Japanese government, but Yaguchi is one of the few who seems to understand that science is going to be the key to "unlocking" how to defeat, or delay, Godzilla. Yaguchi is the first to embrace the possibility that the tunnel's collapse at the start of the movie occurred because of a sea creature, and is chastised by his superiors for bringing up such an outlandish idea … until, minutes later, he's proven right. The government convenes a meeting (one of many meetings that are called and adjourned over the first half of the movie) of three scientists, but none of them are willing or able to give the government officials much guidance; after all, this creature just appeared and they have no first-hand knowledge, data, or any form of empirical evidence to make any comfortable assertions.

---

*One of the most amusing—and telling—moments of *Shin Godzilla* happens early on, when a meeting starts, a few lines are uttered, and then the screen goes to black with the word "Abbreviated." The scene quickly starts again, but it's clear that the meeting has jumped ahead several minutes. If only all meetings were like that.

4. Science and Faith: The Solo Kaiju Adventures 53

The committee is quickly disbanded and called "ridiculous" and "a waste of time" by the government officials, and that's the last we see of the academic science spectrum; they're relegated to a completely different room in the basement of the Prime Minister's residence. During these emergency meetings, we hear government officials complain that there's no manual for this problem, and there's no precedent, and, as a result, they seem to be paralyzed in the face of the unexpected. These statements remind me of Richard Lloyd's *Ghosts of the Tsunami*, a memoir/investigative report of the near-total destruction of a rural school in Okawa, resulting in the deaths of all but a handful of students and teachers. Parry writes that the teachers and administrators felt a near-paralysis because of the lack of clear instructions in the school's emergency manual:

> Like many Japanese institutions, the operations of Okawa Primary School were governed by a manual [...] One section was devoted to emergencies, including fire, flood, and epidemic. [...] This information was supposed to be updated every year. Kashiba, the headmaster, had not done this, which suggests, at least, mild laxity in disaster preparedness [80].

The sudden uselessness of the emergency manual became apparent as the tsunami warnings began to sound.

> The vagueness of this language was unhelpful. The reference to "park, etc." made little sense out here in the countryside, where there were fields and hills, but no parks as such. As for "vacant land," there was an abundance of that— the question was where? [...] But the Education plan, so minutely prescriptive about other elements in the life of the school, made no clear adjudication about a place of evacuation. In the villages by the sea, [...] teachers and children were ascending without hesitation up steep paths and cliff steps. In Okawa, deputy headmaster Ishiaka stood in the playground and found only these words to puzzle over: *vacant land near school, or park, etc.* [81].

This lack of clear direction not only confounded school authorities, but also created crucial delays in the evacuation of the students, leading to the deaths of a large number of the student body and the teachers. The incident led to much soul-searching in Japan in regards to how the government and governmental apparatus functions in everyday society. Not only the lack of clear leadership in critical moments, but also the general inability of government representatives to make decisions on their own, for fear of consequences or otherwise not following correct procedures. Parry continues:

> In North America and Europe, there is no lack of odious and incompetent leaders; but there is a sense of creative friction and of evolution, of a political

54   **The Kaiju Connection**

marketplace, in which ideas and individuals less popular and effective yield, over time, to those that prove themselves fitter for purpose, and where politics—even if it has wrong turns and dead ends—is at least in constant motion. In Japan, this is not the case; even seventy years after the war, a genuinely competitive multi-party system has still not established itself [110].

If there could be an encapsulation, a thesis, for *Shin Godzilla*, it would be hard to think of something better than Parry's comments here: the stasis in the political environment and government has led to a stagnation of political ideals and political risk-taking of all forms. Barbara Greene also connected Parry's writings to the government inefficiencies and ineptitude, adding that *Shin Godzilla* reveals "the need for enhanced networking and strategic planning of the National Resilience Policy" in Japan (29); the kaiju film as policy wonk! As a result, when we hear in *Shin Godzilla* that "The First Responses Manual doesn't cover this," that becomes the general governmental response to almost everything that happens. It's understandable that there's no anticipation of a gigantic and consistently evolving kaiju appearing, that there's no effective plan for mass evacuations "due to a monster, etc." Interestingly, there's little doubt that the Japanese government in *Shin Godzilla* had plenty of plans for a fast and timely mass evacuation of large portions of the population of, say, Tokyo, but, to highlight Parry's comments, there's no plans for mass evacuations if and when a kaiju appears. The transferability of the idea of mass evacuations is, from the government's perspective, almost nil.

While Prime Minister Seiji Okochi frets about collateral damage and whether his uniform is ready for press conferences, a group described by Yaguchi as "an elite team composed of lone wolves, nerds […] heretics, and enemies of the academic bureaucracy"* begins to pore over the possibilities and the few clues left behind on the Glory-Maru, a boat floating right above the origin point of Godzilla, which had been abandoned by a scientist.

During this time, the government moves from one militaristic response to another, first attempting to attack Godzilla with helicopters (an aborted mission because of potential casualties), to asking the Americans for help, and each time they attempt to stop Godzilla, they ironically force the creature to evolve and become even more destructive. This ultimately leads to the Prime Minister's death, and his replacement is the Minister of Agriculture, Satomi Yusuke, "a man with seniority in government

---

*One of the scientists at the first "summit" mentions that he doesn't want to take any educated guesses on the nature of Godzilla because it could hurt his career, another nod to how the paralysis of decision-making for fear of taking a risk and being incorrect has seeped from government into academia.

4. Science and Faith: The Solo Kaiju Adventures 55

whose loyalty led him to become a minister."* The Minister of Agriculture's first order of business is to order his new Acting Ministers to give him no surprises before looking down at his meal and intoning, gravely, "the noodles got soggy. I knew this job wouldn't be easy."

Of course, *Shin Godzilla* wears the criticism of the government and the bureaucracy on its sleeve. That much is certain, and it's already been the focal point of numerous essays, blogs, and academic critiques in its relatively short shelf-life. But to re-place *Shin Godzilla* in the overall canon of solo kaiju films heightens and adds extra sharpness to the criticism: *Shin Godzilla* is the first solo kaiju film that flips the formula and pushes faith (in this instance, Yaguchi's faith in the answers being present and his willingness to take logical leaps few others would) and science into the background and hypothesizes the outcome of when the government and the military take the lead in these matters, and the answer isn't flattering at all. So while, yes, *Shin Godzilla* can definitely be read as a critique of the governmental response to the Daichii Fukushima disaster, the film's genetic lineage only exacerbates and heightens that criticism. The basic plotline established over so many solo kaiju films is flipped; the government takes control and ignores science and faith and relies instead on bureaucracy and the military, and the country—and the world—suffer greatly as a result. Gone is the optimism of films like *Gorath*, where politicians wonder if borders are really necessary after all, while the scientists get to work and pool their resources to solve the unsolvable problem.

It is difficult to think of a more pessimistic trend.

---

*One of the few compliments paid to Americans in *Shin Godzilla* is a comment on how American culture values work ethic and consistency over seniority and age in the workplace (which doesn't quite hold up to heavy interrogation, but nevertheless)—a clear jab at the exact conditions that will show a government being led by an outmatched and wholly incapable Minister of Agriculture at a time of crisis.

5

"The Third Fire": *Agon, the Atomic Dragon*

The opening credits of *Agon, the Atomic Dragon* are perhaps the darkest (literally and figuratively) in all of kaiju history.* The first frames: a nuclear explosion, as a narrator tells us that the discovery of "the third fire" has led to enormous consequences, and that we have "knocked on another door," presumably creating a new pathway to fearsome destruction. Agon's name in Japanese appears on the screen, written on glass. The glass breaks, shattering the logo and sending it down the screen. And then: we see Agon, who looks maybe not so impressive, but it somehow works, because the buildup in those first minutes has been so spectacular. Agon destroys a building and spits fire at a city while the sparse soundtrack plays in the background. The relative lack of music in this sequence with Agon somehow gives the scene extra gravitas, and we're left only with the sound effects of destruction coupled with a few drum beats.

It's a wholly impressive sequence, and the writer of *Agon*, Shinichi Sekizawa, with whom kaiju fans are familiar for his work on *Varan the Unbelievable, Mothra*, and *King Kong vs. Godzilla*, among many, many others, immediately sets the stage for Agon, almost seemingly daring the viewer. Yes, Agon may look cheap; after all, he was created and produced by Nippon TV, and he may seem a **lot** like Godzilla,† but *I* am taking him seriously, and you should, too. And it works. It's the same notion that fueled *Godzilla*, that "the movie [...] must depict the attack of a giant monster as if it were a real event, with the seriousness of a documentary" (Ryfle and Godziszewski 81). It's a thematic maneuver that few kaiju films have managed to recapture, and the often forgotten *Agon* is one of them.

The opening sequence gives way to a lone pair of headlights in the

---

*Agon was originally a four-episode miniseries; about thirty years after it was aired, Toho edited it into a movie.

†*Agon* was blocked by Toho for around four years because of the resemblance to Godzilla.

5. *"The Third Fire"*: Agon, the Atomic Dragon   57

darkness, a shaky camera, and a pair of very frightened drivers trying to navigate a typhoon, and I realize I'm watching a horror film, or at least a plot setup reminiscent of horror conventions. The storm tosses the truck, which we later find is carrying uranium, into the sea.

There can't be enough said about the sound in *Agon*. The instrumentation is sparse, high-pitched flutes over a few lone drum beats. Synthesizers repetitively spit and rumble. A low drone accompanies traffic and city scenes. Newspaper printing presses roar like massive engines. Lone tones and notes blink in and out of our hearing. Sounds like drips pass like traffic, propelled by a distant rattling drumbeat. Laboratories hum and hiss. Even the car horns seem deafening and dissonant. Portions of the soundtrack have more in common with sections of the *Night of the Living Dead* soundtrack* than it does the sort of loud bombast and orchestral work of *Godzilla*.

Remember, when *Agon* was first conceived in 1964, the kaiju film was still booming and still mostly serious, not quite devolving fully into camp: *Godzilla, Godzilla Raids Again, King Kong vs. Godzilla,* and *Mothra vs. Godzilla,* along with *Dogora* as well as many others. By the time *Agon* entered the arena in 1968, kaiju films as a genre had changed dramatically, often embracing camp, such as *Gamera vs. Barugon* and even the Godzilla franchise had devolved into *Son of Godzilla*. In that way, *Agon,* even only four years later, feels like a relic of a different era. *Agon* is a pastiche, a throwback, and is still wholly relevant as one of the early "serious" kaiju films.

Ironically, it's probably the campiness of the rest of the Showa era that saved *Agon* as a property, and prompted Toho to release it as a film. By mid–1966, the kaiju genre as a whole had become a pop culture phenomenon in Japan, with about six Godzilla films, two Gamera features, a bevy of other kaiju properties such as *Gorath, Frankenstein vs. Baragon,* and *Dogora* appearing in the box office. But, most of all came *Ultraman*. A spin-off from *Ultra Q*, the science fiction anthology show, *Ultraman* was the television show about a man who can secretly transform into a kaiju-sized superhero to battle other kaiju. It broke open the kaiju genre. As Matt Alt writes,

> Japanese entertainment would never be the same. Gargantuan laser-breathing sea creatures. Boiling lakes and flaming forest. High-tech submarines and fighter jets. [...] Human enough to be on our side, monster enough to jude-throw a kaiju into a conveniently placed skyscraper. [...] When *Ultraman* was on, the kids wanted toy kaiju; when they played with their toy kaiju, they dreamed of *Ultraman* [130, 132].

---

*Specifically, the "Feeding Frenzy" portion as well as the end credits.

58   The Kaiju Connection

This sudden upswing in the popularity of the kaiju genre most likely encouraged Toho to drop its concerns about Agon's possible infringement on *Godzilla* (1954), and, so in 1968,* *Agon, the Atomic Dragon* was released as a four-part miniseries. This is why, throughout *Agon*, one is more likely to think of *Godzilla* (1954) and darker shows like *Ultra Q* than they are the often cheerier and more bombastic properties such as *Invasion of the Astro-Monster* or *Ultraman*.

On the other hand, Toho was no doubt right to be worried about the similarities between *Godzilla* and *Agon*. Agon looks a lot like a bargain basement version of Godzilla and the idea of an ancient beast rising from the sea because of radiation and nuclear testing, well, that's quite familiar, too. But Agon isn't quite the same devastating presence; where Godzilla eventually makes his way to Tokyo and causes widespread destruction, Agon is relatively content hanging out in the countryside and doesn't really cause much damage outside of knocking over a few buildings and appearing just long enough to be menacing.

Before Agon appears, we're clued in by his presence through random rumbles and roars coming from … somewhere deep in a cave. At first, the usual group of protagonists, the scientist, the journalist, the detective, and the police officer, mock the local legend that a Tengu sits in the cave, playing a trumpet. As they stand in the mouth of the cave, the voices echo in an almost supernatural manner as they try to determine what's happening. A lone light appears in the darkness in front of them, floating up and down, almost staring at them, and these four men, all skeptics, simultaneously hide. As they wait, the trumpet plays again and again, a long, low, blast.

It's all a head fake. A young boy, Monta, comes out of the cave holding a flashlight, banging a stick on the rock walls. But just as they grow comfortable and even begin to laugh a bit, the Geiger counter erupts to life, indicating that the terror is instead behind them, in the ocean, and *then* we get our first glimpse of Agon, who rises out of the sea and stands there, staring at them.

Okay, so Agon himself isn't that impressive looking, but the reveal, with dissonant chords pounding away and the Geiger counter whirring to life, is brilliant, and captures the unnatural presence of Agon. The creature, explained as a dinosaur reanimated and awakened by A-Bomb and H-Bomb testing, is a malevolent presence, akin to the original Godzilla: alive, damaged, and blindly taking out hatred on whatever happens to be in the way. In fact, Agon can only be sated by uranium itself, and, at one

---

*Alt notes, too, that the kaiju craze permeated politics, and provides a photo of the 1967 Osaka May Day labor protests, where a handmade creature named Amegon—"a monstrous symbol of American influence"—made an appearance (132).

5. *"The Third Fire"*: Agon, the Atomic Dragon   59

point, it destroys a nuclear testing center and takes a nuclear reactor meltdown and explosion to the face before retreating to the sea.

It's safe to say that *Agon, The Atomic Dragon* manages to keep this darkened atmosphere all throughout the four-episode (or ninety-six minute) run. Agon is never dead, nor is it ever injured. It's here to eat uranium and destroy the countryside, and, much of the time, it's all out of uranium. This leads to some of the weakest parts of the film, as Agon painfully battles stock footage in a cheap sequence that was all too familiar to viewers by 1968.

The series takes an unusual turn about halfway through, immediately after Agon is blasted by the nuclear reactor meltdown. The centerpiece suddenly becomes drugs and drug abuse, and, in a neat turn, refocuses itself on a new technological evil that's sweeping the countryside: heroin.* Late one night, a pair of Japanese men are tossed out of their boat during a heavy storm and wash ashore, finding their way to a fisherman's hut to warm up. The fisherman's son is Monta, who already has some misgivings when the two men ask the fisherman to dive to the depths to retrieve a briefcase they lost when their boat capsized.

In some of the creepier segments of the film, Monta's father dives deeper into the sea only to find the case resting on the ocean floor, next to Agon. Agon is mostly still, and the film plays up the *potential* for Agon to awaken as a dreaded moment, and it works. When Agon awakens, there's a distinct sense of fear and doom that pervades the characters. They messed around and found out, it seems, and now there's some retribution in store for the greed of men.

This unfortunately creates one of the more absurd sequences of the film, as Agon simply decides to start walking around with the boat in his mouth, and inside the boat is an unconscious Monta as well as the briefcase. Agon stomps toward a factory, and the scientists and police use uranium to lure him away, for fear that his attack on the factory would lead to Monta's death. Eventually, Agon simply sits down on a hilltop, boat in mouth, and doesn't move, recovering the previously eerie atmosphere, as if he is a god merely tired of being in a world that doesn't worship him anymore. It's one of the many moments where Agon intimidates by simply existing. He doesn't attack, nor does he call out. He simply sits there, an aberration and a disrupting force in the lives of all those who happen to be nearby. He is a scar on the landscape.

Thus, the new plan: drop someone down via helicopter to grab Monta while Agon rests. Of course, this fails, and the rescuer is killed before Agon gets up and starts rampaging again.

*Although they are referred to as "narcotics," it's an easy assumption that this is heroin, as the script was written during the so-called "heroin rampage" of Japan when a crackdown on methamphetamines pushed many addicts to pursue heroin instead (Wada 63).

Lured by the uranium, Agon drops the boat and Monta and the briefcase are recovered, but the bad guys improbably recover the briefcase and helicopter-jack the chopper, and Agon, lured by the uranium on board, eats that ... and the briefcase of drugs. Reeling, Agon unleashes one last attack on a nearby factory before staggering out to the sea, while a narrator wonders aloud if Agon is gone for good ... and then acknowledges that the beast is probably still alive, somewhere, waiting to return. Uranium is good for the Agon. Heroin is not.

The film is a neat little morality tale told in several parts, and its closest cousins, along with *Godzilla* (1954), are television shows such as *Ultra Q*, which managed to get its start as "kaiju episodes with a moral for kids." Kaiju such as Kanegon, created to show the penalties of greed, or Gameron's warning about aging and, perhaps, a too-active imagination. The real-world dangers in *Agon* of drug abuse (and criminal activity) and the "third fire" are a moralistic tale that is more realistic, perhaps even grittier, and don't pull their punches. Agon destroys the countryside, of course, but it's not even really the greatest enemy in the movie; that label belongs to the drug abuse and the nuclear proliferation that makes it possible to, in very little time, scramble a helicopter with a barrel of radioactive material hanging off of it. And, of course, Agon's constant threat and attacks on the countryside are precisely because nuclear waste and nuclear energy are ripe for the picking.

Agon is also very much a product of its time. The film, so long delayed, eventually arrived on television screens as *Ultraman* and *Ultraseven* were dominating the airwaves and popularity, and it must have been a culture shock of sorts for people tuning in to see a kaiju series and finding something closer to *Godzilla* than the much cheerier shows. That's not to say that there weren't darker kaiju or science fiction films about in the late 1960s, but films such as *Gorath* or *Atragon* tended to hover in more world-shattering or galaxy-shattering dilemmas. In many ways, *Agon* remained very localized, eschewing the trends that would take viewers in either fantastic or amusing (or both) directions.

Imagine, if you will: a television series sealed up like a time capsule. One of the most beneficial ways of viewing *Agon, the Atomic Dragon* is as that time capsule, sealed up in 1964, and, in four short intervening years, reappeared into the world of pop culture as an almost antiquated—but still relevant—product. Kaiju films were still all the rage, perhaps more popular than they had ever been before, but the tenor and tone of these products had changed dramatically, shifting their focus to a more family and child-friendly product, and losing sight of the origins of kaiju film. Watching *Agon* now is to expose oneself to a relic, and not a terribly high-quality one, at that. Its close resemblance to *Godzilla* and its overall slow story makes it a difficult watch in spite of the moments of terror and commentary it manages to cobble together. It's difficult for someone to watch in 2023; then again, it was most likely a museum piece already in 1968. *Agon* is a perfect barometer of pop culture and just how sensitive it is to trends and popularity, and the kaiju film and the kaiju genre is no different.

6

The Wor(l)ds Get Stuck in My Throat: Aliens from Sea and Space

In my opinion, there's no more late-night creature feature films than *War of the Gargantuas* and *The X from Outer Space*. Even though *War of the Gargantuas* has enjoyed higher critical esteem, both, to me, have the nostalgic feel of sitting on the couch at 2 a.m., the audio just high enough to be able to be heard (and also low enough that no one else will hear it), with all of the lights off, your skin washed in the pale fluorescent blues of the television.

I've written elsewhere in this volume (to be exact, Chapter 14), about the deft trick that science fiction cinema has played over the years in identifying something as uniquely "alien," and, as such, often an enemy to, if not humanity, then the human body. One of the more interesting things to consider is how making people like Glenn Manning or Nancy Archer, from *The Amazing Colossal Man* and *Attack of the 50 Foot Woman*, respectively, grow, and how that growth makes them foreign bodies in the larger bloodstream of humanity. As such, they must be expelled, extricated, or executed. Yet, in films such as *Fantastic Voyage* or *The Incredible Shrinking Man*, we see the reverse play out: humans shrink, and, as such, *they* retain their humanity, but the surroundings become alien and hostile.

It's this inversion that allows us to take a glimpse at how aliens play a role in the kaiju genre, and how they're almost always juxtaposed against a more humanized opponent, one that we can more easily cheer for and understand—that alone takes up almost the entire basis for series like *Ultraman*.

Aliens in kaiju cinema, however, also abound, and they were frequent opponents for our more heroic kaiju,* especially in the Showa era: Hedorah, Gigan, King Ghidorah, Mechagodzilla. During the Heisei era, Godzilla frequently fought aliens that came to destroy the planet in some way or another: SpaceGodzilla, Orga, and Monster X (later revealed

---

*Gamera even visits an alien planet for a showdown in *Gamera vs. Jiger*.

6. The Wor(l)ds Get Stuck in My Throat 63

to be Keizer Ghidorah, an offshoot of King Ghidorah). In each of these instances, these kaiju are introduced as aliens who are a direct threat to the world, if not the universe, and Godzilla, who is either an ally or a begrudgingly irritated ally, can save the day.

What's fascinating about this theme is that it runs counter to typical alien invasion narratives that appear in horror or science fiction, where the aliens themselves "emphasize difference between the invaders and the invaded in order to justify violence by one side or the other" (Gordon 12). Even peaceful aliens, such as Klaatu and Gort in *The Day the Earth Stood Still* or Abbott and Costello in *Arrival*, are usually deeply distrusted—and often attacked—by the world's militaries and governments precisely because they think or act differently. But in the kaiju film, we often see the alien kaiju mirror, or attempt to mirror, the kaiju they battle. This is a function of a broader theme, and it exists precisely because of the kaiju-ness of Godzilla. He is, in his very origins and by the nature of his existence, also alien to the natural or modern world. As such, Godzilla, in particular, is often asked to battle a version of himself. The difference between Godzilla and many of his alien foes is *minimized* rather than heightened, leading us to realize and understand Godzilla's own changing role in his franchise, as well as his relationship to humans.

Naturally, when we speak of aliens, we don't necessarily need to think of aliens from outer space; they can come from almost anywhere and be labeled as decidedly non-human, a foreign body (sometimes literally) to be tossed out of the bloodstream of everyday life. Before we go much further, there is one perplexing note to the "alien": the creatures who appear from under the ocean waves. When you're in a boat on the ocean, there's a sense of isolation and loneliness. Within the pitch black darkness that surrounds the ship at night, there's a lot of places for the human imagination to roam, and there's a heightened sense of vulnerability, especially the further you get from shore. Little wonder, then, that movies focused on space exploration feature these same tropes, and, impressively, the number of bizarre creatures that we can imagine coming from outer space could also simply rise from beneath the waves of our own oceans, too.

There's a long history in literature of massive and frightening (and nearly supernatural) beasts that come from the ocean, ranging from, yes, *Moby Dick* to *20,000 Leagues Beneath the Sea* and even stretching as far back as various Norse myths, and Leviathan in the Bible. Here Be Monsters; there's always been a deep-seated fear reflected in folklore about the various creatures that exist in the ocean, no doubt fueled not only by the darkness and the solitude of the sea, but also by the appearance of numerous bizarre creatures, wrapped up in fishing nets, that indeed seem alien to us. Japan, as an island country, is rich in folklore and superstition

64   The Kaiju Connection

surrounding the sea; it's little wonder that so many horrifying moments in the Godzilla film franchise feature lonely sailors at sea, confronted with a new menace. Horace Beck, a professor of American literature, writes that

> Descriptions of monsters, unlike those of sea serpents, vary so widely that they defy any attempt at cataloging. Some of them would fit the description of a whale or huge shark, others a giant squid or cuttlefish, while still others suggest a saurian akin to a dinosaur. Some reports describe them as attacking ships and men, while others describe them as placid. A short definition would be: "A large creature of unknown species, presumed dangerous" [293].

I'll avoid belaboring the point from previous chapters, but I will note the use of the word "monsters" and especially "dinosaur" in this passage. So, naturally, there's a considerable presence of not only the sea in kaiju film, but also sea monsters, some of whom happen to be kaiju. See, for example, the massive Shockirus sea lice that attack the sailors in *The Return of Godzilla*, the giant octopus in *War of the Gargantuas*, or the ominous abandoned ship in *Shin Godzilla* with some bizarre creature lurking beneath the surface. These sorts of otherworldly creatures and deeply worrying moments often likewise appear in the works of H.G. Wells, H.P. Lovecraft and then Ray Bradbury, who, in turn, helped inspire *The Beast from 20,000 Fathoms*, and then that, in turn, inspired *Godzilla*.*

There's a certain duality that arises in this instance, specifically with Godzilla and other Toho properties, that's not found in the battles of Gamera or even in *The X From Outer Space*, as we will soon see.† No, Godzilla is far more fertile ground for the nuanced appearance of aliens who do more than simply stand there and look weird. These aliens represent, often, Godzilla himself. Godzilla has, since his origin in 1954, been a dual symbol, the "aggressor and victim, self and other" (Balmain 34), that "provide[s] a multiplicity of interpretations: reptilian, monstrous, god-like, fallen, associated in some readings with Japan and others with the United States" (Miyamoto 1092).

This crucial de-centering of the Godzilla "character" allows not only for different interpretations, but different identities entirely. In the absence of one particular identity, a similar one appears to do battle, a mirrored reflection of an identity that Godzilla has, at least temporarily, shorn. Yuki Miyamoto also argues that a "failure to conjure serious concerns about radiation ironically may have enabled *Gojira* to enjoy its longevity in Japanese popular culture" (1092–1093). But I would argue that this doesn't

---

*Through the 1990s, there were numerous properties that sought to reinvigorate the ocean as an alien wonder, most notably, *The Abyss* and *Leviathan* in 1989, *SeaQuest DSV* that ran 1993 to 1996, and *Deep Blue Sea* in 1999, among many others.

†This theme is still appearing in kaiju cinema. One of the major battles in *Shin Ultraman* is Ultraman versus his own doppelganger, his arch nemesis Zarab in disguise.

6. The Wor(l)ds Get Stuck in My Throat 65

extend solely to the *film*, but it also extends to the *character* of Godzilla. As time passed, the walking message of nuclear aggression became other things, and as such, almost literally routinely battled himself in an effort to employ and cement a new identity.

So, if the original Godzilla represents nuclear anxieties and fear, what do the doppelganger Godzillas represent? There are a lot of different ways to slice this critical pie, but if we turn to critic Chon Noriega, we might be able to effectively answer that question. In 1987, so just before the Heisei era officially began for Godzilla, Noriega wrote that "Godzilla films provide an opportunity to challenge our constructions of the self and the Other," noting that Japanese culture views "self" and "Other" in different lights from Western cultures (64). Here goes:

> While cultural criticism in the West generally acknowledges that construction of an Other primarily defines a self, the Japanese language carries within it the added stipulation that both self and Other remain within the culture [64].

Noriega then quotes Takao Suzuki, who posits that "Japanese culture and sentiment show a strong tendency to overcome this distinction by having the self immerse itself in the other" (qtd. in Noriega 68). Thus, the consistent mirroring of Godzilla through the years, and, ironically, Noriega nearly predicts the future, for the Heisei era consists of numerous attempts to feature a Godzilla and a NotGodzilla,* who are dual identities submerged, sometimes literally, within one another's DNA. This NotGodzilla often mimics—or at times is indistinguishable from—the "real" Godzilla, and the NotGodzilla often replaces the antagonist potential of the 1954 Godzilla in order to oppose the newly "heroic" Godzilla. As the Showa era advanced and Godzilla became more friendly to humans, there was a need to simultaneously acknowledge and disavow the "bad" or "evil" aspects of the original Godzilla. The easiest way to accomplish this was to create a series of NotGodzillas,† a process which accelerated in the Heisei era and through the Millennium era, where a string of kaiju mimicked or fed on, were created from, or attempted to absorb, Godzilla in some way: Biollante, SpaceGodzilla, Orga, Megaguirus, and even Kiryu.‡

---

*I recognize the potential to call them NotZillas, but that's just too cute , and too reminiscent of the horrid Notzilla (2019).

†This duality appears in other forms of media, too. In the IDW comic miniseries *Godzilla in Hell*, one of the first opponents that Godzilla comes across is a demon that takes on his form.

‡In order to further this duality, numerous Millennium films started to reject all of the films that came before, instead acknowledging only the original 1954 Godzilla and "forgetting" the Showa and Heisei era, even though both eras attempted, initially, to create a coherent timeline from one film to the next. Starting with *Godzilla 2000*, the films often reached for the reset button. Only the Kiryu films managed to create a storyline from movie to movie, but only after one more reset, with *Godzilla Against Mechagodzilla*.

66   **The Kaiju Connection**

Perhaps the most Not–NotGodzilla in both fandom and in the film franchise itself is the version that crashed through the streets of New York in 1998. Yes, *that* Godzilla, that was roundly reviled—and still appears to be—by many fans as a decidedly and thoroughly NotGodzilla. This went full circle, just six years later in *Final Wars* (2004), where Godzilla is challenged by the Xiliens to face off against an unknown and all-powerful opponent in Sydney. That enemy? The newly rechristened 'Zilla, who tries to leap over Godzilla, is hit with Godzilla's tail, flies into the Sydney Opera House, and is destroyed by Godzilla's breath in what may be one of the shortest battle sequences in the Godzilla franchise. Since then, 'Zilla has hovered around the edges of Toho licensing,* with a small trickle of licensed toys (especially when compared to almost any other kaiju Toho owns the rights to, including Ebirah and Varan), and has been acknowledged as canonical, becoming perhaps the ultimate and most literal NotGodzilla of them all.

Many of the aliens that appear in kaiju film, both from the ocean, and, as we will discuss later, from space, tend to function as mirror images to one another. They consistently provide an opposite, an Other, that so closely resembles the "hero" of the story in the Godzilla franchise that Godzilla's features appear on his opponent: a problematic portrayal, especially given Godzilla's origins in *Godzilla* (1954), but also one that reveals a heightened anxiety, perhaps, about the movement away from the notion of Godzilla as an antagonist for many of his films, toward a symbol of a protector of Japan in the Showa era, and, later, as a sort of apathetic hero in the Heisei era. 'Zilla, of course, but also Mechagodzilla, Biollante, Orga, SpaceGodzilla. All duplicates, or aliens that are duplicating, Godzilla's original role: the soulless destroyer of Japan, the dangerous outside force that can't be stopped. In some ways, these all feel like attempts to create a sort of "new" Godzilla that can be more easily considered a symbol of nuclear aggression, a facet that can be lost as the years progressed. Thus, Godzilla, the old symbol, destroying a Godzilla-like entity,[†] the new symbol, shows a concerted effort to replace and then destroy the original purpose of Godzilla, as if there's an anxiety in how Godzilla himself moved far away from his origins.

---

*And every time a new licensed toy—er, collectible figure—arrives for 'Zilla, the debate begins anew as to whether or not 'Zilla is to be taken seriously in any capacity, even as Not-Godzilla. There's also substantial confusion as to whether or not the 'Zilla in *Final Wars* is exactly the same as the Godzilla in the 1998 film or the animated television series that followed. Suffice to say, there's enough overlap between the two that they share a common "look."

†Although not an alien, Kiryu, the third Mechagodzilla, should be considered here, as this version of Mechagodzilla is *made from the bones of the original Godzilla* from 1954; as such, there are, quite literally, two Godzillas battling one another: one in the flesh and the other (reluctantly) in a metal shell.

6. The Wor(l)ds Get Stuck in My Throat 67

Lest we forget, too, that Godzilla's introduction in *Godzilla* is meant to frighten. He's a massive beast from the sea, much like his forefather, the Rhedosaurus, and there's a certain unnaturalness to their sudden presence on land. Even in the more kid-friendly films of the Showa era, such as *Son of Godzilla*, Godzilla tends to emerge from the sea. There is, in *Godzilla* (1954), a significant amount of exposition in regards to the ideas of Godzilla's place in the folkloric tradition of the surrounding villagers, and that initial concept fuels much of Godzilla's iconography even today. In the minds of the villagers, Godzilla is not that different from Leviathan or the gigantic octopus that seems to randomly appear in other Toho properties, including *King Kong vs. Godzilla* and *War of the Gargantuas*.*

Yes, *War of the Gargantuas*. That film, interestingly, may be the best place to continue this discussion of aliens, for Gaira is a creature of the sea, and his mirror image is Sanda. Of course, *War of the Gargantuas* shows us two different beasts cut from the same genetic cloth; they're hypothesized to be the offshoots of Frankenstein from *Frankenstein vs. Baragon*. Yet, Gaira, the green one, is far more vicious and destructive than his "brother," Sanda, who wears hues of brown. There's an early swerve in the film where, for a moment, we cheer for Gaira, who saves a fishing boat from the giant octopus. Then, Gaira turns around and destroys the boat himself. Gaira's alien nature is established almost immediately, and it's mentioned several times that he loves to snack on humans, just as any other predator would.

Russ Tamblyn, who plays Dr. Stewart and speaks all of his lines as if he's attempting to invent a verbal soporific,[†] hypothesizes that a Gargantua—descendants of Frankenstein—couldn't possibly live in the ocean, but would most likely move to the mountains to be away from people. He's right, but also wrong. Sanda lives in the mountains, and Gaira comes from the sea. In fact, we're told that Gaira is practically a sea creature himself, in spite of his human shape: wrapped in the same mucous membrane that "covers sea animals," blinded by bright lights because he adapted to the darkest depths of the ocean, and coupled with Gaira's fishy look—as if he is draped in seaweed—all cast him as more fish than human.

Sanda, however, is the true hero, and despite the fact that Sanda and Gaira share the same common ancestor, their "upbringing" couldn't be more different. Sanda, as Stewart hypothesized, lived in the mountains

---

*The connective tissue between these films: Ishiro Honda, who directed each of them. Although *War of the Gargantuas* "helped to stereotype Japanese monster movies as campy, cult cinema" (Ryfle and Godziszewski 190), Honda's approach of treating the subject matter seriously gives the movie a gravitas that is distinctly Honda.

†"What a punk. He pissed me off," remembers Seiji Tani, Ishiro Honda's chief assistant. Ryfle and Godziszewski note dryly that Tamblyn "reportedly showed little enthusiasm for the project and made no friends with his above-it-all attitude" (189)

and somehow adopted a moral system that allowed him to exhibit kindness to others, primarily through his interactions with Akemi, a "surrogate mother" of sorts (Ryfle and Godziszewski 191). He stops the military's electric attacks on Gaira, waving off the military, before helping his genetic brother back to the mountains to recuperate. Later, Sanda injures himself while trying to get in position to save Akemi Togawa, Stewart's assistant. And, to be fair, Sanda is also quite pissed when his recuperating brother stumbles across a hiking troupe and promptly starts eating them.

Sanda's scolding takes the form of whacking Gaira with a tree, and the battle, the war, commences from there. As these things go, there's a prolonged city-crushing sequence before the two end up in the ocean, where Gaira has a distinct advantage. The more sympathetic and humanistic Sanda eventually gains the upper hand as a volcano arises from the sea to swallow them both, a clear homage to their ancestor's demise in *Frankenstein vs. Baragon*.

There has been plenty written on the "nature vs. nurture" debate and how it is portrayed in *Frankenstein vs. Baragon* and then in *War of the Gargantuas*, and, to be fair, the subject is low-hanging fruit, an easily readable content that grants the film some depth on the role of humans and human morals, projected onto kaiju. But the notion falters a bit when we understand that, in the content of *War of the Gargantuas*, at least, that there's little nurturing going on. Sanda and Gaira are isolated and alone for much of their "childhoods" (whatever that may be), and the film makes clear that the natural environment itself played a nearly singular role in their outcomes: the cold, harsh, dark, and unforgiving sea versus the somewhat cheery and plentiful mountains.

Speaking of ocean creatures, there's, of course, Megalon, too, who hails from the deep underground kingdom of Seatopia, a clear homage to the legend of Atlantis, and the less-than-fearsome-but-they-treat-him-that-way-anyway Ebirah,* who, like Godzilla, is a beast whom the local villagers can only hope to avoid or sate. Both of these beasties are alien as well, creatures from down below who look and act different from what we, as denizens of the surface, come to expect. And yes, that includes lobsters, which, when blown up to Ebirah's size, all of the oddities and unusualness of their physical shape take hold, in much the same way that films such as *The Incredible Shrinking Man* highlight the bizarre monstrosities of, say, a blade of grass or a cat. In this way, the battle between Godzilla and Ebirah, too, can be read as a sort of mirroring. Two sea creatures, viewed through a folkloric lens, and warped by radioactivity,

---

*Ebirah, ironically, will later make a cameo in *Godzilla: Final Wars* as a mind-manipulated foot soldier for the Xiliens—evil aliens from outer space!

6. The Wor(l)ds Get Stuck in My Throat

facing off. On one side is the improbably unnatural hero; on the other the improbably enlarged villain.

We're off the beaten path now, so let's transfer from earth-based aliens to the real deal: ones from outer space. Space, of course, has long been the source of many of the same superstitions and traditions, as if we, as humans, simply transferred the depth of the ocean to the depth of the night sky. "Down below" becomes "out there," and we see that tradition run throughout almost all of science fiction, the sort of equating of maritime ideals and ideology to outer space. The voyages of the Starship Enterprise. The Space Marines. And all of the naval nomenclature and iconography that courses through the veins of space exploration, from the Captains and Admirals to the burials at space, where a body is jettisoned into the void, much as they would be at sea. Not to mention the "continuing voyages" of numerous ships in space, from the Enterprise to Babylon 5 to Battlestar Galactica, all reaching out for contact with new civilizations or merely surviving, much like some of the earliest ship's captains in our human history. So, in a way, the "it comes from the sea" isn't as much of a transference from "it comes from space" as we tend to think.

Compared to many of Godzilla's other antagonists, the aliens seem to be unusually powerful and blessed with weapons and abilities that seem to outmatch most of his Earth-based opponents. Gigan has blades in his tummy and massive hooks for claws. Mechagodzilla is loaded to the rafters with missiles, lasers, and numerous space beams. And SpaceGodzilla can siphon massive amounts of energy from crystals and use them to injure and capture his opponents. King Ghidorah has three heads that fire powerful lightning bolts everywhere.*

Let me start with SpaceGodzilla, for his story and background is among the most interesting, although certainly also quite opaque at times. At the end of *Godzilla vs. Biollante*, Godzilla's victory sends the genetically altered spores that contain Biollante and Godzilla cells into space. This somehow eventually spawns SpaceGodzilla, who is first seen encased in crystals and screaming toward the earth. Like Gaira, SpaceGodzilla is a warped and altogether far more evil version of his genetic brother. Godzilla, throughout much of *Godzilla vs. SpaceGodzilla*, is humanized, if not through his interactions with Miki Saegusa, then certainly through the presence of the incredibly adorable Little Godzilla. SpaceGodzilla naturally kidnaps Little Godzilla, making the earthbound Godzilla a de facto

---

*There could be a case made, too, for Biollante, who, like Ebirah, initially appears as a larger form of her original state, and as such, is rendered "unnatural." Biollante's first form, that of a giant rose, soon gives way to a more Godzilla-like presence through the genetic splicing of Godzilla, roses, and a young woman named Erika, who died and is "preserved" genetically by her father by combining her DNA with that of a rose.

hero of the story, a sympathetic figure who has human-like relationships, and, as such, is the far more civilized kaiju of the group.

Gaira, imprisoned in the cold dark sea away from human contact, and SpaceGodzilla, created almost randomly via a batch of cells in the vast and bleak vacuum of space. There's little difference between the two, in many ways, especially when you consider how Sanda has a distinct moral code in spite of not interacting with humans and otherwise seeking isolation; a characteristic that this version of Godzilla carries as well, as he and Little Godzilla set up their tiny family on Birth Island, with Godzilla rising from the ocean to look after his littler self.

SpaceGodzilla, a Godzilla once removed. It's odd to consider how Godzilla's origins made him a prototypical alien creature from the seas, a dire warning and cautionary tale about radiation and nuclear testing, and here, in *Godzilla vs. SpaceGodzilla*, his role is that of a hero, defending one of his mirrored selves—the good one—against another of his mirrored selves—the evil one—and Godzilla stands somewhere betwixt the moral fabric of the story. Yes, Godzilla is still a threat, and that's established by the presence of G-Force, the militaristic science entity tasked with stopping Godzilla, as well as the reintroduction and redesign of MOGUERA—himself a mirror, originally created as an alien from space for *The Mysterians*,* but now cast as a massive robot defending the earth—and the ongoing attempts of Miki Saegusa to "reach" Godzilla telepathically to control him.

Placed within the broader context of the role of aliens in kaiju film, and especially in the Godzilla franchise, *Godzilla vs. SpaceGodzilla* achieves a sort of nuance that is often lacking in the Heisei era films, and, for that matter, many other Showa era films as well. Within the borders of *Godzilla vs. SpaceGodzilla* is a series of events that defines and redefines, often in a rather casual manner, what is "alien" and what is actually not of the world itself. Godzilla is only alien until a more threatening alien comes along. MOGUERA is only an alien until it needs to be reinvented for more human-sympathetic purposes. And even Miki Saegusa, a telepath charged with forming a mental connection to Godzilla, is one of a group of humans who are viewed with some form of suspicion and distrust because of their powers. But she is called upon to defend the very humans who fear her.

The same sort of mirroring occurs somewhat in *Godzilla 2000* as well, for Orga is, at first, a gigantic spaceship, a sort of mirrored cigar reminiscent in some ways of the design of the ship culled, no doubt, from numerous "flying saucer" accounts that appeared in print, both as science fiction

---

*There are actually *two* Mogueras in *The Mysterians*. The first one is destroyed and is replaced by a slightly more robotic version, or at least one with a lot more silver on it.

6. The Wor(l)ds Get Stuck in My Throat 71

and as fact, through history. Unlike SpaceGodzilla, who intrinsically has the same basic shape and design as Godzilla, Orga is wholly alien when we first meet him.

The UFO absorbs Godzilla's cells during an assault and soon becomes a monstrous Godzilla/alien hybrid that has some features of Godzilla, but is ultimately more alien than SpaceGodzilla. As they battle, Orga literally feeds on Godzilla, absorbing his cells and his energy in order to become a new Godzilla. At one point, as Orga attempts to swallow Godzilla whole, he begins to grow Godzilla's dorsal fins. But wait! Godzilla has one trait that Orga hadn't mimicked yet: innate intelligence, and that's enough to win the day, as Godzilla fires his radioactive breath while mostly inside Orga, blowing the alien apart from the inside out.

There's a growing sense of dread in *Godzilla 2000* that Japan might end up with *two* Godzillas when it can barely sustain the presence of one. Like Shin Godzilla slowly metamorphosing into a Godzilla we more readily recognize, Orga slowly changes during the battle to take on Godzilla's form and features as well. Let's consider, too, another alien creature that mimics Godzilla even more successfully than either SpaceGodzilla or Orga: Mechagodzilla, in *Godzilla vs. Mechagodzilla*, who so successfully resembles Godzilla that collected scientists, military personnel, and citizens are all fooled into thinking he's the real thing. Their first clue that this isn't Mechagodzilla is his brutal attack on Godzilla buddy Anguirus, as Mechagodzilla breaks Anguirus' jaw and sends him on a full retreat.

Then there's the "real" aliens, who fail to resemble or mimic Godzilla. Of these, Gigan is the most prevalent after King Ghidorah, and Gigan is perfectly bizarre in his look. A slick visor in place of an eye, massive claws in place of hands, and a buzzsaw that bisect his torso, and it's hard to think of many creatures in our lives who would even remotely resemble Gigan. By the time he appears in *Final Wars*, his final form reveals an alien creature/BDSM hybrid that's as ludicrous as it is bizarre. Apparently wrapped in leather-like skin or armor, Gigan swaps out his big hook-like claws for twin chainsaws.

And, of course, the biggest and probably most frequent enemy that Godzilla has faced during his run: King Ghidorah, who is not "related" to Godzilla or even mimics his presence in any way. Ghidorah is almost always—save for his appearance in *Giant Monsters All-Out Attack* as a spiritual "guardian" of Japan—a massively powerful three-headed alien that often requires numerous kaiju to team up to defeat him. In each of Ghidorah's alien-based appearances, ranging from *Monster Zero* to *Destroy All Monsters* to *Godzilla vs. King Ghidorah* to *Final Wars*, Ghidorah is often cast as a world-ending threat, and is brought to Earth in order to raze society itself. Even in the Americanized Godzilla franchise,

King of the Monsters depicts a Ghidorah who has essentially crash-landed on Earth and then stayed frozen for numerous millennia before awakening and re-molding the world into a more unnatural landscape fit for an alien kaiju.

Ghidorah, in many ways, is the ultimate threat, and is routinely cast that way. In terms of looks, there's little more impressive or daunting than Ghidorah, who often dwarfs Godzilla in size and power, and can fly as well. Like Gigan, he's the ultimate alien; in other words, replete with three heads and ultimately identifiable as Not of This World. In fact, Ghidorah's inspiration—numerous dragons of folklore—adds to the Otherworldly nature of his presence, for his design combines numerous aspects of dragon designs, and so is one dragon and many at the same time: three snakelike heads, upright stance, massive wings, shoots lightning bolts from each mouth. Ghidorah is visually a chimera, and is so cobbled together that the resulting creature is nearly unrecognizable—unlike, say, Godzilla and Anguirus's dinosaurian look, Mothra's butterfly-like design, King Caesar's doglike appearance.

What's to be made of these aliens who work so hard to mimic Godzilla? And what's to be made of the aliens who are routinely chased away by Godzilla or Gamera? There's definitely a sense of the enemy of my enemy is my friend throughout Godzilla and Gamera's battles against aliens, both those who crash-land from space and those who splash ashore from the ocean. But this constant approach to duality, especially across both the Heisei and Showa eras of the Godzilla franchise, reveal a growing sense of unease in the idea of Godzilla being a "good" character, or at least one that is apathetic to humans. It's as if the origins of Godzilla as a parable of loss and suffering, as well as immoral nuclear attacks, were so far gone by these films that a much badder and more evil version of Godzilla needed to take his place.*

Aliens are there to teach us a lesson, or at least that's the way it's *supposed* to go in the absence of campiness. A full accounting of all aliens across numerous kaiju films would take almost an entire book, but I just wanted to point toward *Gamera 2: Attack of Legion*.[†] In the Showa era, the alien was the de facto bad guy, earning very little sympathy and often mocked by Gamera and the children who helped him. But Legion is

---

*It's also worth noting the otherworldly origins of some of the kaiju-adjacent creatures, most notably Clover from *Cloverfield*, whose presence interrupts a "good day" and introduces the city's population to terror and massive destruction. Clover's rampage upsets a going away party and forces our intrepid heroes to traverse a war-torn Manhattan in order to save an ex-girlfriend. Yes, there's a serious bit of navel-gazing egocentrism in this film, where the alien menace never offers a worldwide impact, or really stands for anything in its action. Its "evil" nature is that it really wrecked the plans for our group.
[†]See Chapter 9 for a discussion of the Heisei Gamera films.

6. The Wor(l)ds Get Stuck in My Throat 73

different; the film definitely casts Legion and Gamera as flip sides of the same coin, a theme also explored in *Gamera 3: Revenge of Iris*. The ending of the film points toward Gamera protecting the earth, not humanity, and there's a distinct possibility of Gamera turning on humanity for destroying the world. It's a bizarrely noble proposition—one that essentially fuels Dr. Emma Russell's terroristic actions in *Godzilla: King of the Monsters*—and it makes Gamera an equal threat to humanity as any alien force could choose to be.

It's only a matter of motivation, really. Legion wants to propagate itself and take over entire planets in order to survive. Gamera would eventually, if humanity strays too far off the path, destroy civilization in order to save the planet. For Gamera, his unquestioning faith and loyalty to humanity and to children in particular dissipates during the Heisei era. Gamera, whose origins essentially pre-date modern civilization, is indeed a sort of alien: his creators long gone, he rises from the sea to protect the world from everything, including, eventually, perhaps, the people who rely on him. That *Gamera 3: Revenge of Iris* features government agents who firmly believe Gamera himself is an evil entity from the ancient world, well, it certainly puts a wildly different spin on Gamera than anything in the Showa era.*

I'll wrap up this chapter with *The X From Outer Space*, an extraordinarily bizarre film that is mostly overlooked, and often for good reason: it follows a fairly cookie-cutter formula that doesn't offer many surprises outside of Guilala itself. This kaiju is well-known as a Gigan-like scaly chicken character. The look and style of Guilala, coupled with the hackneyed plot, no doubt drives many viewers away, but the film exists perhaps primarily to provide a neat little bow on this chapter. *The X From Outer Space* isn't a versus film, and it most likely has more in common with films like *Gorath* or *Space Amoeba*, as much of it unfolds around a classic science fiction plot. In this case, it's a trip to Mars for our intrepid group of astronauts, and the dialogue as well as the trip to and from space lasts for over half the film—Guilala doesn't appear in its recognizably absurd form until almost three-quarters of the way through the film.

Yet, one of the few interesting aspects of the film is that the alien threat wins, at least temporarily. The gathered human scientists are initially unable to stop Guilala, and the film would have provided one of

---

*In fact, it feels like the Shusuke Kaneko–directed Gamera franchise went too dark and needed correction, leading to a movie called *Gamera the Brave*, which harkens back to the Showa era of a child-centered plot line and a cuter baby Gamera named Toto. Toto, with the help of his owner, the young Toru, evolves into Gamera and wins the day. The correction to the Kaneko Gamera mythology occurred, and it bombed badly enough that around 15 years will pass before Gamera returns to an anime series on Netflix.

74   The Kaiju Connection

the more haunting sequences in kaiju film history if not for its absurdity: members of the research team huddled in the basement of a mostly destroyed building, listening to Guilala outside. It's only on the screen for a few beats, but the image of a displaced group of people trying to stay safe in the face of an overwhelming threat is a perfect kaiju scenario, one that's been repeated numerous times. But Guilala looks and sounds goofy, and the low budget special effects ultimately ruin the gravitas of the scene.

All of that aside, Guilala is a perfect example of the evil alien that threatens the earth, and is one of many in the science fiction canon, as well as the kaiju genre, who shows up to earth just to destroy things. Guilala is, despite its bizarre design, a parable of the recklessness of science, a sort of "tampering in God's domain" warning for viewers. That Guilala mostly rampages in an effort to seek out different forms of energy—first an electric power plant, then a nuclear power plant, then it heads for a rocket fuel manufacturing facility—reveals the ham-fisted moral of the story about overconsumption. Much like Agon (and like much of humanity, naturally), Guilala actively seeks out energy, and is willing to literally chase any form of energy. Guilala, for example, is lured away from our heroes by a small canister of fuel dragged behind a Jeep. Yet, as in many of these same films, science wins the day by learning how to use Guilalalium to stop Guilala.

Mixed message? Of course, because in order to effectively incorporate an alien into the plot, it must not only reflect our fears, but viewers and the human cast must *reject* those same fears. In other words, Guilala is there only to briefly remind us of our sins, which themselves are easily overcome and quickly forgotten in the ingenuity and quick-thinking of our heroes. Do we consume too much energy, and are perhaps too obsessed with it? Yes, but the *point* is that if we (or the brightest among us) really put our minds to it, we can work things out. And, hey, we may even get lucky and stumble across a discovery that will solve the problem for us! The same is for Godzilla and his various NotGodzilla enemies. In rejecting one "bad" version of Godzilla, we necessarily accept the "good" version of Godzilla, one who is inherently "bad" in his own origins.

It's as if the moral lessons of *Godzilla vs. Hedorah* (and, indeed, Hedorah is both an alien and introduced to the characters as a creature from the sea)* were bludgeoned out of the script of *The X From Outer*

---

*Hedorah can be understood as a larger trend in sci-fi film of the movement away from humanoid shapes—two arms, two legs, head on top of neck—and more of a blobby shape that started to appear in the 1950s with films such as 1953's *It Came From Outer Space* (Stein 122–124). Hedorah is as alien as they come, essentially, as the creature is an alien that doesn't mimic or resemble anything animate (though an argument could be made that Hedorah is a massive oil slick) and feeds off pollution.

6. *The Wor(l)ds Get Stuck in My Throat* 75

Space. Although Godzilla defeats Hedorah, there's plenty of warnings about pollution, as viewers are warned that Hedorah, like Godzilla, can always erupt at any given point in time if we don't change our ways. Guilala? Well, we met the problem, got saved by a random discovery, and shot the problem back into space, so we still have plenty of time for romance. "I now realize that there's someone else who loves Sano," is literally what Lisa says the lesson of the story is, for her at least. It's head-slappingly impressive to see how hollow *The X From Outer Space* is, and much of it is just how it treats the alien menace: as little more than fodder for the special effects. There's no mirroring, no deeper meaning, no morals to be taken away. We stared down the enemy and walked into the sunset, happy in our obliviousness.

This is the same sort of general flaw that haunts the Gamera Showa series. The aliens are external threats and little else; other than Zigra, there's little tie-in to what that threat supposedly represents. Aliens like Jiger are cannon fodder for Gamera and the children: they show up (or Gamera goes to them) and they battle. Eventually Gamera wins, and the enemy is defeated, roll credits. As for Zigra, like *The X From Outer Space*, we're given the lesson; in this case, it's the dangers of unchecked science. But, this lesson is soon lost in the mix, as Zigra is pinned down by Gamera, played like a xylophone, and then destroyed. Gamera saves the day, and there's really not much of a lesson left; it was presented in a haphazard manner and then gave way to ridiculousness. Complain about the oddities in *Godzilla vs. Hedorah*, but at least it stuck to the message, for better or for worse, even if it did moralize quite a bit.

We see aliens all throughout the kaiju genre, but outside of Godzilla, it's rare for these aliens to become much more than enemies to be defeated. There's lessons to be learned here, about how aliens have come to represent the Other others, especially in the Godzilla franchise. Perhaps the primary goal of aliens have always been to arrive on earth just to teach us a little bit more about our own perceptions of the Other … and ourselves.

7

Reigo, Raiga, Ohga: The (Sometimes Loving) Basement of Kaiju Film

Let's be honest right at the start: very few kaiju films will ever be blessed with the money that is thrown at Godzilla, either by Legendary, or Toho, and this era of the "big" kaiju film pretty much lurks under the shadows of those Godzilla properties. So, when there's a new kaiju film, there's going to be some understanding that, barring a revival of the Gamera property, some new and perhaps somewhat not great films will be deeply limited because of their lack of funds. However, there's something to be said for these sorts of passion projects. They don't quite reach the abysmal levels of quick cash-ins as numerous Asylum properties, but there's still plenty of moments in these films that would make the ears of the crew over at *Rifftrax* or *Mystery Science Theater 3000* perk up.

One of the challenges of *Reigo, Raiga,* and *Ohga* is to watch them back-to-back, because they tend to be so tonally different that it's rather surprising. The first of the trilogy is *Reigo: King of the Sea Monsters*, produced in 2008. This one plays it straight, and actually carries with it some interesting concepts by placing the kaiju Reigo in 1942 to battle the famed Japanese battleship *Yamato*. The sequel is a comedy. *Raiga: God of the Monsters* is a somewhat paint-by-numbers kaiju film where a kaiju comes ashore and the military has to fend it off ... but this time, with jokes, and often bizarre ones at that! The third of the films introduces a new kaiju, and follows the standard "versus" format that dominates kaiju film in general. *God Raiga vs. King Ohga: War of the Monsters* arrived a decade after *Raiga,* in 2019.

So, three impressively different films, taking a unique jab at the genre, each of them problematic in their own way. Yet, they stand on their own as kaiju films that bravely attempt to do what they can, all without a budget and with a massive lack of resources, even going so far as to recruit veteran

7. Reigo, Raiga, Ohga

kaiju actors and designers to work on the films. While numerous reviews have razed these films to the ground (one-star reviews for the latter two of the trilogy are very common, while *Reigo* maintains a little more respectability), I can say that *Reigo*, at least, can be appreciated for what it represents: kaiju films made by people who love kaiju films. In this instance, it's Shinpei Hayashiya, who first created an unofficial sequel to the Heisei Gamera films that received some fan acclaim before going on to creating *Reigo*. What makes these films work at even the most base levels is that they manage to avoid the James Nguyen *Birdemic 2*–style* self-referential "we just set out to make a bad film" paradox, where films that are purposefully designed to be bad end up being horrible, whereas films that attempt to be good and end up bad remain (kind of) watchable.

Still, there's little doubt that *Reigo*, at least, was made by a fan of the kaiju genre. From the bombastic and explosive Heisei-style titles to the dire warnings from an elder, the ideas that dominate kaiju film are all there, even if they are sometimes dotted by surprisingly bizarre and sexualized humor. There's even a moment once the Yamato is launched where it is framed by the rising sun. Yes, indeed, the visual shorthand for Japanese "heroes," one often employed by the Showa era to symbolize Godzilla's heroic nature, tells us early that the Yamato is our protagonist. When we learn, then, of the existence of Reigo, we're already aware that the kaiju is the antagonist.

Reigo itself is an unfortunate amalgamation of a series of kaiju visual cues. Called a "dragon" by the elder, that language is quickly passed throughout the ship, and, indeed, when Reigo itself appears, it has the same scaly and reptilian look, and, in fact, seems to be the love child of Agon and Gorgo, only with flippers. Its primary power is to swim really fast and somehow summon lightning bolts.

Like Gorgo and Gappa, Reigo is angered by an attack on its child. The Yamato sees a moving target, and, given the wartime setting and its task to guard an important convoy, asks no questions: it just blows the child kaiju apart without hesitation. This isn't the (kaiju) child abuse we see in *Gorgo* or *Gappa*, where we can easily set aside these kaiju as being righteous in their anger. After all, their children were kidnapped and put on display, all for capitalistic greed. Here, the actions of the Japanese Navy are justified. It's wartime, they saw something suspicious, and they protected their own.

This all sets aside, of course, the sometimes painful CGI, which can

---

*Birdemic: Shock and Terror is one of those bad films created by someone who thought they were making a good film, or at least a decent one. As such, in my book, it gets a pass here, because it sits, in my mind, alongside the *Reigo* trilogy: a labor of love that just turned out awful, no matter how hard the director tried (even though, at times, it wasn't very hard at all).

be forgiven in some ways because of the incredibly small budget for the film. Yet, given the astounding history of low-budget practical effects that run throughout both the Gamera and Godzilla franchises, it's confounding to consider why CGI was a better alternative. Perhaps the practical effects were more expensive, and, if this is the case, it's a depressing reminder of how bygone the "good old days" of rubber suits and tiny ships in pools of water has become. Reigo itself is often practical effects, but the overlaid fires, ships, ocean, and gunfire forms a disconcerting backdrop that continuously pulls the viewer more and more toward disbelief.

The ending of *Reigo*, in which the ship is partially submerged in order to angle the shot better at *Reigo* and ultimately prevails, is bittersweet. The Yamato is sunk by the Americans after the events of *Reigo*, and the pat storylines for a few of the main characters (one is in love, another has a baby on the way*) wrap up in the usual sorrow. It's rare, however, to see a kaiju film directly address World War II and the Japanese role in the conflict, and *Reigo* definitely seems to cast its lot with the Japanese—at least as individuals—as being heroic. As they stare down the American bombardment, the characters perish one by one, before re-entering the frame with large red swaths of paint on their face, reminiscent of kumadori makeup. As viewers, we would come to understand that the choice of the color red is an important one, because it represents heroes and courageousness. Indeed, all throughout the film, the naval officers are portrayed sympathetically, even the drunkards and the low ranking comic relief characters.

This isn't to say, of course, that Japanese artists and directors need to flagellate themselves endlessly for their country's involvement in World War II. There's a sense, however, that *Reigo* arrives at a different place than most kaiju film, and the pride and heroic (though stereotypical) depiction of those aboard the Yamato is found perhaps nowhere else in kaiju film. I'll give the film credit for being unique in this regard, and, certainly, their bravery is unquestioned, as they stare down an unknowable aquatic menace that can reign lightning bolts down on their ships.

One of the more interesting aspects of *Reigo* is how it helps us to understand just how sanitary kaiju films often are, even the American adaptations. Beside the sexualized humor that occasionally appears, there's a moment where the ship is attacked by "bone fish," which are heralds of a sort for Reigo. It's a rather gory sequence, and we're treated, at first, to a bloody hand falling off of an arm, followed by a shocked crew looking above

---

*The kaiju genre embraces many of the same tropes as most films, especially in the Heisei and later periods: when you hear of a character who has small children, is about to retire, or has a baby on the way, it's easier to just mentally start the timer. Most recently, *Kong: Skull Island* has a sequence where the character Jack Chapman talks about his kids back at home. Not much later, he's dead.

7. Reigo, Raiga, Ohga

decks to see dismembered body parts, including a head, scattered across the deck, complete with large pools of blood. Outside of poor Ishida's splattering and the subsequent killing of many of the train passengers in *Gamera 2: Attack of Legion*, this may be the goriest sequence in kaiju film, so far as blood loss and human body destruction.* Gaira chomps on some humans in *War of the Gargantuas*. *Cloverfield* had a sequence where a young woman explodes behind a sheet of plastic at a triage and quarantine area, and, after that, it's hard to think of many other scenes of human violence and gore (of course, we see Godzilla and Anguirus bleed quite a bit in the Showa era). An off-screen death in *Gamera 3: Revenge of Iris*, though, does briefly explore the casualties that result after a kaiju battle: Ayana Hirasaka's parents are killed in a flashback scene. Hirasaka's anger leads to the creation and near-overwhelming power of the Iris kaiju, which almost defeats Gamera.

Sex and (human) violence, sex and (human) violence.† That's really where *Reigo* exposes aspects of the typical kaiju film that are missing. *Godzilla* (1954), of course, addressed real human suffering, and the sequence in the hospital has been mimicked a few times in the Godzilla franchise. Yet, the deaths themselves tend to appear offscreen, and the violence is almost always relegated to the kaiju. Of course, there's humans fighting as well, for example, in *Final Wars* or *Godzilla vs. Biollante*, but it's almost always a completely sanitary experience, even as bullets fly. Those who die or are seriously injured are often faceless and they perish with a minimum of anguish or social connection.

It's rare, then, to see a kaiju film embrace the sort of overarching violence that we see in *Reigo*: disembodied humans, scattered about, with copious amounts of blood. Even one of the most heartbreaking moments in *Godzilla*, where a mother tells her children that they are going to see their father as the city crumbles around them, leads to an offscreen death. Afterwards, it feels like almost every human casualty we see on the screen in the worlds of Godzilla and Gamera, especially, is like bloodlessly turning on and off a switch. A general salutes Godzilla before he gets blasted with atomic breath. The head of a spy agency stares down Godzilla on a rooftop and is crushed by a swipe of the kaiju's hand. And so on.

And in the Heisei era, even the kaiju themselves rarely get bloodied.

---

*Later, in *Reigo*, there is a violent melon attack that's played for seriousness but comes across as rather bizarre. If this makes it sound like the tone of the film is uneven, that's because it is. While someone attacks a melon with a spoon in sorrow, and we are expected to feel sad, a few minutes later, during a deadly serious meeting, someone violently unbuttons their shirt; comical popping sounds are played over it.
†I guess I should say (human) sex, too, because there's several moments in kaiju-adjacent films, such as in *Mighty Peking Man* or *Yeti*, in which a kaiju sized creature behaves lustily toward a human female. It's as disturbing as it sounds, and there's more on those bizarre choices in the "Son(s) of Kong" chapter.

Norman England, who worked on several kaiju film sets, related a time where he encouraged an effects crewmember working on *Giant Monsters All-Out Attack* "to pump the blood like there's no tomorrow." The crewmember, Yamabe, replies that the director of the film, Shushuke Kaneko, instructed everyone "to keep the gore to a minimum" (161). This conversation occurs during the filming of perhaps one of the angriest and most evil iterations of Godzilla. That there's little excessive gore beyond this, even in other Shushuke Kaneko kaiju features such as the Heisei Gamera trilogy, points to a general disdain, perhaps, among more current directors and producers to engage in wholesale depictions of violence.

Of course, the very notion of sex or sexuality is often left unexplored in Godzilla and Gamera films. Sure, there's the chaste romance and pining we see in films like *Godzilla* (1954) or *Godzilla Raids Again*, or the clumsy actions of a smitten guy in *Godzilla Against Mechagodzilla*. The ever effusive Asami in *Shin Ultraman*, for some reason, smacks her own ass when she's excited and then tries to build a team by slapping the behind of a fellow SSSP member. And, of course, the Showa era's positioning of Gamera (and, to a lesser extent, Godzilla) as a friend to the children and targeted primarily to child audiences meant that there was little time for any romance or sexuality. In *Reigo*, the sexuality is often crude and impressively purposeless: a lusty naval officer accidentally grabs a guy's chest instead of his female paramour's, and he reacts in shock and horror. A group of school girls play a prank where their skirts are temporarily lifted up, flashing the audience a glimpse of their underwear. It's quite nonsensical, but it does a great job of showing us how remarkably non-sexual the kaiju film is, even in American productions, which only rarely mention sexuality except in passing one-liners.

There's a lot of subcontext here, and it could be easily explained away, in that the original kaiju film, *Godzilla* (1954), was so deadly serious that all films afterwards have labored on focusing on tragic elements and eschewing humor, sex, and extreme forms of violence. But there's also the slow repositioning of *Godzilla* to the more childlike expressiveness of Godzilla, and the sort of recasting of his presence as a hero, or at least, a sort of heroic force. As a result, Godzilla and Gamera, among others, rarely dip into violence directed at humans, and, when that does occur, it's often violence toward those who "deserve it" (the "bad guys"), or it happens away from our vision. Simply put, the kaiju film regressed and never really had the chance to evolve literally for decades.

The few times Godzilla, for example, has directed his anger directly as civilians who are just going about their daily lives often leads to descriptors of "dark" or "gritty" when discussing the film. *Godzilla* (1954), of course, but also *Giant Monsters All-Out Attack* and *Shin Godzilla* show an enraged Godzilla just indiscriminately killing people. But perhaps the

7. Reigo, Raiga, Ohga 81

most bizarre—and bloodiest—film in kaiju history has to be *Gamera vs. Gyaos*, released in 1967, and, ironically, is really the first Gamera film to be targeted toward children. No matter, because Gyaos is discussed as routinely eating people, and has a thirst for human blood. This leads to the humans intervening to help Gamera by luring Gyaos to a pit filled with artificial human blood, which splashes and spatters as Gyaos approaches and begins to feast. This may be one of the most gruesome and horror-like moments in all of kaiju cinema, but the *human* gore remains abstract and scant.

This is another way in which the kaiju film and kaiju-adjacent films tend to set themselves aside from the genres which no doubt helped found this subgenre. Horror, science fiction, and even adventure films all mixed together to kind of create a creed for all future kaiju film directors: no sexuality and very little human violence. Thus, it seems an integral part, or at least a relatively unchallenged portion of the kaiju genre, is the insertion of excessive gore or blood or sex into the kaiju narrative. Indeed, if we all stood in a room and mentioned the number of times we saw people violently killed on screen in the kaiju genre, we'd be hard pressed to come up with more than a few examples, even in the grittier Legendary reboots, where, again, the films all labor in the PG-13 world of offscreen or bloodless deaths.

And while we're all in that same room, we can spend even less time listing all of the instances of sex or sexuality in kaiju film. It's a facet of the genre that forms its boundaries. Horror, for sure, embraces sex and violence, as do many science fiction and adventure films. I would guess that a film like *War of the Worlds* from 2005 or even *Mars Attacks* from 1996 on their own contain more on-screen and violence toward people than almost all of the kaiju genre combined.

Let's take a breather for a second before moving on, because *Reigo* stands well on its own. The other two that follow in this trilogy simply do not. If there's any sense of challenging the relative abstract nature of the kaiju film's violence, or the genre's lack of sexual maturity, much of that is lost in *Raiga: God of the Monsters*, a film which attempts (heavy emphasis on "attempts") to create a comedic subplot about a father and his three daughters. Raiga is the land-based form of Reigo, apparently, and there's more than one Raiga now. *Raiga*, however, attempts to skewer the seriousness of other kaiju films, so it functions as a head-whipping 180 degree turn from *Reigo* in many ways. While the kaiju film, especially in the world of Godzilla, came to terms with, and depicted such real-world issues as city-wide destruction, heavy pollution, and rampant capitalism, *Reiga* pops each of those balloons, but offers no other commentary.*

---

*Even the relatively un-complex *Shin Ultraman* discusses climate change as a potential reason for the appearance of kaiju, and humanity's own destructive tendencies toward the environment.

82 The Kaiju Connection

Indeed, even the more modern takes of global warming that appears in films as diverse as *Trollhunter* or *Pacific Rim* get their own comeuppance, with their climate change themes quickly dismissed as well. If kaiju aren't caused by humans and human interactions, or if the kaiju doesn't lay bare human relationships with one another, then, really, what's the point? I'm trying to say that it becomes incredibly difficult to parody a genre unless you offer up criticism elsewhere. Otherwise, it becomes a hollow exercise, and *Raiga* seems full of them. Frankly, if a film sets out to fray the edges of a genre, then it should look both forward and back; while *Raiga* is content to provide a series of digs at the kaiju genre, it doesn't really effectively push the boundaries elsewhere.

Let me stop here. I should take a moment to explain that I hardly ever read the reviews of a film before watching it myself. And, after watching *Raiga*, I found myself quite interested to see John Lemay, in his *Big Book of Japanese Giant Monster Movies*, gave the film a relatively glowing review. Lemay writes that the film "spoofs" films such as *Godzilla vs. Hedorah* and *Gamera vs. Zigra*, "and many others," arguing that

> Many other movies, like *Godzilla vs. SpaceGodzilla* (1994), seemed to insert rather arbitrary moments about environmental pollution. As Raiga's characters stand atop a hill, one of them randomly proclaims Raiga came to teach them all about global warming! "Yes, that's it," adds Hajime as one of his daughters ponders how exactly the monster did this. [144]

Let's set aside the conflating of two distinct, but related, issues in pollution and global warming, as, yes, *Godzilla vs. Hedorah* and *Gamera vs. Zigra* were some films that dealt with pollution, while others, such as *Pacific Rim* (itself reviewed by Lemay a few dozen pages later) very astutely "explain" global warming while also managing to criticize the human role in the process. This somewhat encapsulates the issues I have with *Raiga* and the sequel *Raiga vs. Ohga*: they strike out in all directions, and, for every joke that lands, numerous others miss because they're so confused in their execution that they confound rather than amuse. Indeed, as Lemay notes, it's hard to find a more fan-driven set of films than this trilogy, with numerous shots composed to echo sequences from across the kaiju genre. Any sort of depth that the kaiju genre has sought out over the years is instead roundly dismissed and set up for lampooning.*

No, *Raiga* seems to argue that kaiju are simply *there*, as inevitable and destructive as a hurricane, and it does so well before the Legendary *Godzilla* reworked Japan's nuclear angst into a force of nature. The comedic

---

*The role of environmentalism in the kaiju genre is large enough to have produced at least one volume: Sean Rhoads and Brooke McCorkle's *Japan's Green Monsters: Environmental Commentary in Kaiju Cinema*.

7. Reigo, Raiga, Ohga

nature of the film barely rises to a critique worthy of, say, *Kaiju Mono* or *Big Man Japan* (more on these films in Chapter 13), so all we are left with is a film with a few action sequences punctuated by characters who are doing comedy routines. No, no meditations on masculinity or violence, and barely a critique of disaster capitalism—the main character Hajime, and his three daughters Matsuri, Akari, and Hibari, make a tidy profit selling Raiga t-shirts after Raiga and the military response levels a city. But there's so many hit-or-miss jokes (mostly miss) that any sort of trenchant skewering of the growing political nature of the kaiju film falls by the wayside. Yes, kaiju films since *Godzilla* (1954) have been politicized in many ways, but never quite as consistently as they have been since *The Return of Godzilla*. Now, the era of Godzilla, at least, features a Japan struck by the whims of nuclear superpowers, or Godzilla himself is a rewritten text, designed to cast aside American blame for the atomic bombings of Japan.

Raiga, it's safe to say, never goes deeply into these discussions, and merely pooh-poohs the idea of any sort of greater meaning in kaiju film. It's, almost literally, "big dumb fun," and the sole moment where global warming is cited as a possible reason for Raiga's attack—and the subsequent attack of *another* Raiga—is comic as well. If *Raiga* criticizes governmental officials for their ineptitude, it has all the subtlety of a sledgehammer. After the city is destroyed by Japanese Self Defense Forces aircraft, the gathered members of the military and government laugh uproariously at their victory and tell one another jokes while mugging for the camera. This is all at the expense of the thousands of people who died that day, apparently, and so the comedy falls flat.

The nuance of *Shin Godzilla* a few years later finds no purchase here, and, as such, any critiques *Raiga* has to offer collapses under the weight of its own comedy. Some of this is because of the film's ham-fisted approach, but much more of this is because the jokes are garden variety "come on, people am I right, or am I right?"–style jokes. The political complexity, for example, of the sequence in *Shin Godzilla* where the Prime Minister is asked to open fire on Godzilla while there are civilians nearby is not present, instead replaced with the Prime Minister in *Raiga* understanding he will have to resign, to which the Defense Minister agrees, and they hold each other while dramatically sobbing. It's played purely for laughs, in other words, and there's no criticism offered: just a depiction of the government and military officials as slapstick-style morons.

Another moment where the criticism and the deeper meaning gets lost in the fray. A group of people are about to be killed by the battle between Raiga and the military, and they bemoan, as they are dying, that they will never be able to eat their favorite foods. A pair of Americans are in the group and, as they die, they shout out the slogans for Burger

King and McDonald's. A fair dig, and one that does a good job at poking fun at the capitalistic fast food industry and the American romance with fast food, but it happens *while they are dying*, and it's a strange moment to insert into a kaiju battle.* Even so, this stands as one of the more humorous and insightful cuts in the film.

And so, by the time we end up with the final battle of one Raiga versus another, the movie has descended into pure farce. Raiga defeats Raiga (the second kaiju being similar, probably a function of the film's limited budget), and then urinates on the fallen city before going back to the sea. We're not even sure why there are two Raigas or why they are fighting, and the proffered reasoning—perhaps it is global warming!—is tossed aside by the three sisters, who will later appear in the credits as kaiju-sized, playfully kicking Raiga while cheery J-Pop plays in the background. That's the ending.

It's easy to wonder at times if *Raiga* has any sort of affection for any portion of the kaiju genre; it spends most of its runtime caught up in overlong hackneyed and comedic human subplots, with several "big dumb fights" interspersed throughout. Unlike *Kaiju Mono* or *Big Man Japan*, which acknowledges the kaiju genre's flaws while also simultaneously building on, or critiquing, aspects of the genre, *Raiga* lurches forward in such a way that it's hard to imagine that this film wasn't a direct shot at numerous kaiju films, a sort of over-the-top lampooning meant to undermine or otherwise attack the genre for taking itself too seriously and for trying too hard to be meaningful or important, with the numerous homages to other kaiju films placed there simply to defuse any complaints: see, a *real* fan made this!

Alas, *Raiga*, in many ways, points toward a takedown of the kaiju genre for simply not being "fun" anymore, and overloads the points, lambasting numerous tropes, from the serious real-world issues to the emphasis on human plot points and developments that has dominated kaiju film since the 1950s. This begs the question, though. If one truly dislikes the seriousness, the sanitization, the self-awareness of the kaiju genre and all that entails, then what is left other than "big dumb fun," a film with an emphasis on big battles and little more? In some ways, and I know this will get some people fired up, it feels like *Raiga* is the very low-budget predecessor to *Godzilla vs. Kong*, which itself had wooden human characters doing little more than dashing from place to place for often vague reasons, and which eschewed as much "worldliness" as possible in order to focus entirely on the action and the visuals, and little more.

This is a big bridge to build, of course, but the attitude of *Raiga* seems

---

*I genuinely worry—and I hope I am wrong—that the sequence is meant to echo the *Godzilla* (1954) scene where the mother comforts her children as they are about to die.

7. Reigo, Raiga, Ohga

85

to be one that mocks kaiju films for being too serious; as a result, the film seems to argue, the "best" of the kaiju genre are the films that avoid much seriousness at all, instead focusing just on the battles with the human presence being on screen long enough to toss out a one-liner or to give a sense of scale, much like another "big dumb fun" movie, *Rampage.*

As such, it's not so hard to see why it took ten years for the sequel to *Raiga* to be made. The rather impressively named *God Raiga vs. King Ohga: War of the Monsters* is another miss, and one that tends to skirt the same boundaries of *Raiga*, often feeling more like a poor lampoon than a serious attempt, or even a satire or parody. The background for the story is offered by, again, John Lemay, who says that Shinpei Hayashiya was so smitten with the adoration of his first two films after visiting a G-Fest* that he decided to make a third film (197).

Somehow the special effects and the acting in this one is worse than the previous two in the trilogy, so I won't need to spend a lot of time discussing this; it's just painfully bad, and it took me the better part of three sittings to get through the film (it is 84 minutes long). While there's little doubt that this is a labor of love, the limited budget and the rather interchangeable characters—both human and kaiju—make it difficult to invest much interest in the film. Add in the same bizarre tonal quality of *Raiga*, where jokes and massive amounts of death and destruction stand side by side, and the film becomes even more problematic in how it approaches the kaiju genre: a love letter to the genre that also scornfully mocks the genre.

Ultimately *Raiga vs. Ohga* functions like the typical kaiju versus film; as *Reigo* was an origin story set during war time, and *Raiga* a (kind of) comedy that focused on the ineptitude of the government and the military, *Raiga vs. Ohga* completes the trilogy of at least three distinct types of kaiju genre films. It sets itself up in the same way, and like a good number of versus-style films, it has the paint-by-numbers plot. One kaiju appears, then another, and the humans try to find some way to keep the inevitable battle from happening, or at least to minimize the destruction in some way. In *Raiga vs. Ohga*, every character apparently dies during the final battle, including both of the kaiju themselves, only for a weird amalgamation of Raiga and Ohga to appear and join a battle in Hawaii—a clear nod toward *Godzilla* (2014). But that's it; the battles are difficult to see, the jokes fail to land, and the movie doesn't seem to have much purpose.

This isn't meant to take away anything from Shinpei Hayashiya, whose efforts and work on creating not just one, but three, kaiju films on a limited budget and with only a small staff, is an enormous achievement

---

*G-Fest is one of the best stories in kaiju fandom. Put together by J.D. Lees, the publisher of the fanzine *G-Fan*, G-Fest is an annual gathering of kaiju fans as well as some kaiju celebrities. Attendance numbers often rank in the thousands.

on its own. Indeed, in many ways, Hayashiya is rightfully deserving of the adoration he receives from kaiju film fans just for this accomplishment. But, in the end, these films never reach the heights—if they indeed even attempt to strike in the direction—of kaiju film parodies such as *Kaiju Mono* or *Big Man Japan*, and as "pure" kaiju films, they don't quite, with the possible exception of *Reigo*, provide anything new to the genre.

Just to drive the point home, I'll point to *What to Do with the Dead Kaiju?*, a film distributed by Shochiku of *The X From Outer Space* fame. *What to Do with the Dead Kaiju?* essentially carries a simple premise, perhaps borne from the open ending of *Shin Godzilla*: what would inept government officials do in response to a massive dead kaiju in their midst? The answer provides the satire, if not very high-quality comedy, that plays out over an often plodding two hours, which includes odd romantic backstories and a heaping helping of arcane conversations about, incongruously, toilets and Hibachi grills. Essentially, the main plot of the film is that a kaiju arrived in Japan and then mysteriously dropped dead—blasted by a beam of light from the heavens—and its corpse lands in a nearby river, immediately leading to pollution and the potential for an even greater fallout as the body decomposes.

This prompts a series of maniacal, sometimes comic, meetings among numerous government ministers as they attempt to avoid responsibility for their departments to head what is certainly going to be a massive and complex clean-up, and one certainly destined for failure. At one point, a group of ministers, each attempting to escape responsibility, mockingly agree that the Education Minister should take over the corpse, joking that it should become an educational exhibit, an argument that sends the Education Minister into hysterics. But this kaiju corpse football consistently gets kicked around for the duration of the film, as various politicians and their aides come up with solutions, only for other various politicians and aides to try to subvert those solutions so their rivals don't get international credit.

Ultimately, the film boils down to two unique theories for ridding the countryside of the kaiju, which is expanding due to decomposition gasses building up in its body. The resulting potential explosion could further poison the country and the locals, of course. The two solutions are to "flush" the kaiju out to the ocean by blowing up an old dam and using the water pressure to send it away; the other solution is to create a massive fan, compared in the film to a Hibachi fan, which would essentially funnel the gasses up to the ozone layer, where they would break down.

This is all absurd, of course, and *What to Do with the Dead Kaiju?* mostly plays it straight, with the ministers only sometimes acting like children, and the occasional joke or odd moment (the Prime Minister flicks his aide in the

7. Reigo, Raiga, Ohga

forehead with his finger) providing some levity. It's a tonally bizarre film which doesn't quite land as a parody, a satire, or a comedy, and the opening of the movie, with the kaiju already dead, provides some coherent criticism of the modern state of Japan. Reflecting the impact of Covid, the people of Japan are now concerned about "kaiju alarms" that dot the countryside, and they are adjusting to the "new normal" of kaiju and kaiju corpses. The area around the dead kaiju has been abandoned and becomes overgrown, settings reminiscent of the exclusion zones that surround the Fukushima nuclear disaster. And that beam of light that killed the kaiju? Well, the immediate assumption from everyone is that it is the result of American action, forcing an American military official to hold a hasty press conference to deny the involvement of the United States military in killing the kaiju.

These are headier issues, a little more real-world, and they reflect sentiments we've seen in numerous kaiju and kaiju-adjacent films, from *The Host* to *The Return of Godzilla* to *Shin Godzilla*, among others. There are indeed bizarre moments in *What to Do with the Dead Kaiju?*, but they never quite reach the level of absurdity and outright mockery in *Raiga*. Yes, the politicians are inept, inappropriately competitive, and ultimately can't do anything right, but they are (mostly) played straight, and, as a result, we get the full effect of the criticism and the depictions of their ineptitude. Every decision that the ministers make leads to talking, disaster, and more talking, and it's a rather more lighthearted conundrum than the one in *Shin Godzilla*, which itself was filled to the rafters with often sardonic observations about the paralysis of politicians and government officials. No, *Raiga* doesn't feature this at all, and, as such, both *Raiga* and *Raiga vs. Ohga* are somewhat stunning departures from *Reigo*, which bent the boundaries of the kaiju genre without necessarily stopping to mock the genre with a series of increasingly unabashed and often silly jokes.

Maybe I'm overreacting. Perhaps I am taking things too seriously, and, given that I've co-edited a volume of kaiju essays and have now produced two books on kaiju, you'd probably be onto something. But I think some films, even low budget fan films such as *Raiga* and *Raiga vs. Ohga*, move too far away from critiques, criticisms, satire, or parody, and instead reach toward outright mockery. If this is true—and I'll happily admit I'm wrong—then I think the conclusion that follows is a bit alarming: that the kaiju genre has changed significantly enough that the serious topics that served as a hallmark since *Godzilla* (1954) no longer receive merit. Climate change? City wide destruction and the deaths of thousands? Inept government officials? All of these are dismissed or played for comedy, and it's not a good place to be. The glove has to turn inside out. If films such as *Raiga* become more popular, or lurch toward less nuanced social commentary, then the kaiju film itself begins to fade as a genre. Of course, there's

88 The Kaiju Connection

always a film here or there that is absent of weightier topics, such as *Son of Godzilla*, but *Raiga* and *Raiga vs. Ohga* actively dismiss weightier topics rather than dance around them.

This all begs the question: can there be a kaiju comedy? Given that the kaiju film is now approaching three-quarters of a century old if one marks *Godzilla* (1954) as the start of the genre, it's entirely possible that the world is changing enough that there can be a comedic approach to widespread death and destruction; after all, as we noted earlier in the chapter, kaiju films tend to be rather sanitary in their approach. And we know that there are films, both kaiju and kaiju-adjacent, which incorporate humor into them, ranging from *Son of Godzilla* to *Rampage* to even moments of *Godzilla: King of the Monsters*, where characters spend a few moments trying to understand how Mothra and Godzilla's symbiotic relationship "works."

But this is all levity, for the most part, surrounding deadly circumstances, and the mere presence of a kaiju is, literally and figuratively, too big to ignore. Even *Rampage*, which is probably the "jokiest" kaiju adjacent film, tends to feature a significant amount of destruction and action sequences. But the jokes are one-offs—the classic "bad guy gets his comeuppance at the worst moment" style jokes—and they could land in any film, not just a kaiju film, and I suppose that's where *Raiga* and *Raiga vs. Ohga* struggle. They try to mock the kaiju film formula, and perhaps we're just not far enough away from the somber moral structure of *Godzilla* (1954), running all the way through to films like *Godzilla Against Mechagodzilla*, *Godzilla vs. Biollante*, and *Giant Monsters All-Out Attack*. Hell, even Gamera, who promptly descended into goofiness (but never seemed to mock the genre itself) came back to a grittier and darker and much worldlier Heisei version.

It's a fine line, of course, and I'm not saying that *Raiga vs. Ohga* is the harbinger of the end of the genre. It does, however, show us a few cracks in the genre that could fundamentally change how kaiju films are viewed. An emphasis on "big dumb fun" or outright comedy would force the genre away from more nuanced portraits like those in *Shin Godzilla* (even though it is ham-fisted) or *Colossal*. This isn't to say that these films can't co-exist, but for every *Raiga* or *Rampage,* I have to wonder what comes next, and how these films impact the genre as the whole. Maybe they're so unimportant, small, and inept that they would inevitably be forgotten, and that's certainly a possibility, given the dismal reviews *Raiga* and *Raiga vs. Ohga* have received. And maybe *Raiga vs. Ohga* is more readily understood as just another *Zillafoot* or *Atlantic Rim*, and are thus so easily dismissed. Still, it's a massive change in tone from *Reigo* to *Raiga* to *Raiga vs. Ohga*, and, even if they don't "stick" in the genre, they do exist as important works, if only to further understand some of the underbelly of kaiju film, and how they could impact the genre over time.

8

An Ode to Baragon and Barugon

Baragon has appeared a few times in kaiju film, and his "starring" role was in *Frankenstein Conquers the World*, also known as *Frankenstein vs. Baragon*. The only other two times this burrowing beast appeared in film was a quick cameo as a prisoner on Monster Island in *Destroy All Monsters*, and as the first sacrificial lamb for an evil Godzilla in *Godzilla, Mothra, and King Ghidorah: Giant Monsters All-Out Attack*.

Yes, you've noticed by now that Baragon didn't even get top billing in a film where he was described as one of the three "guardians" of Japan. No small part of this lack of billing may be that the battle sequence between Baragon and the enraged Godzilla was somewhat anticlimactic, with Baragon being dispatched with ease, blasted by Godzilla's atomic breath, never to be seen again. In fact, most of Baragon's fighting strategy against Godzilla was to burrow underground, pop up, bite Godzilla on the arm, and then spend the rest of the time getting stomped and tail-whipped. Baragon's somewhat familiar heat-ray attack was even removed to show Godzilla's newfound power levels. The little guy never really had a chance, and he's mostly an afterthought in the movie.

And, going back to *Destroy All Monsters*, Baragon couldn't even get into the final battle against King Ghidorah. While it's understandable that Mothra and Godzilla (and maybe even Minilla) would battle King Ghidorah in the climax, it's hard to believe that Baragon didn't get a chance to show his stuff while other C-List kaiju such as Gorosaurus and Kumonga got to get a few jabs in. No, Baragon is forever stuck on Monster Island, apparently, rarely to return except as cannon fodder.

Baragon, quite simply, seems to be an *Ultraman* kaiju in a *Godzilla* world. His look seems derivative, and even his power set isn't all that unique. A burrowing kaiju? Anguirus. One with a heat ray? Well, that's any number of kaiju, including Godzilla himself. Baragon's puppy-like features are even reminiscent of another fan favorite kaiju, King Caesar.

90   The Kaiju Connection

In fact, take the spines off of Anguirus and send him on a one-night stand with Caesar, and you'll probably end up with something that looks a lot like Baragon.

At least Baragon, however, managed to appear in multiple films and managed to bust some moves here and there. Even Varan, The Unbelievable, who headlined his own film, quickly sank into obscurity, appearing only briefly in *Destroy All Monsters*, and, like Baragon, couldn't even beat out Manda for screen time. Other headliners during that era, much to Varan's shame, I'm certain, managed to be long-lived in the *Godzilla* universe: Godzilla in 1954, Rodan in 1956, Mothra in 1961. Varan, a flying lizard who was also aquatic, has long been ignored or forgotten.

But the ultimate symbol of neglect has to be Kamoebas, who, after a brief appearance in *Space Amoeba*, wouldn't appear again until *Godzilla: Tokyo S.O.S.*, over three decades later ... as a corpse. Indeed, while Baragon and Varan at least had *living* appearances after their initial introductions, poor Kamoebas wasn't even seen alive again, an off-the-screen victim to an underwater Godzilla, washed ashore and left as a harbinger of the destruction to come. And it doesn't look like Godzilla had to do too much work to destroy Kamoebas, as the only visible damage to the big turtle is a series of slashes on his neck.

As we know, shows like *Ultra Q* and *Ultraman* featured "monster of the week" episodes, and, given the limited budget, the creatures often came across as somewhat cheap and hackneyed in design, materials, and execution.* This brings to mind any number of bizarre kaiju creations that barely even reaches the woeful levels of Baragon or Varan: DinoTank from *Ultraseven*, Gango from *Ultraman*, and so on, each of them essentially one-offs that were best forgotten outside of the boundaries of their respective shows. In fact, comparing a kaiju's design to *Ultraman* or a similar television show has become a sort of lowkey insult: "And what a turkey the creature is," John Lemay writes *The X From Outer Space*, "Guilala is the silliest Japanese monster ever designed for a feature film and should've been confined to a TV screen fighting Ultraman and his brethren" (134). Harsh, but understandable; however, the "space chicken/lizard hybrid," as Lemay further describes Guilala, brings up another question (134). Guilala isn't the only "chicken/lizard"; a far more popular kaiju from the Godzilla universe can also lay claim to that bizarre lineage: Gigan.

Yet, Gigan remains ever-present in discussions about kaiju, especially after his redesign in *Godzilla: Final Wars*, where the scaly pale green skin and potbelly is replaced by an almost S&M leather look and much more

---

*Somewhat (in)famously, the kaiju Gomess and Jirass, from *Ultra Q* and *Ultraman* respectively, were cobbled-together and thinly-disguised Godzilla suits.

8. *An Ode to Baragon and Barugon* 91

fit appearance. Gigan's designs have, just as a measure of importance, spawned a number of collectible figures; Guilala less than that by orders of magnitude. Of course, the Gigan in *Final Wars* is also far deadlier, and even though, like many kaiju in the film, he meets his end at the hands of the enraged Godzilla in just a few seconds, he manages to at least *look* dangerous: his long claws instead of hands, eventually turned into twin chainsaws.

And it's important to understand, too, that the Godzilla franchise has been occasionally sullied by a nemesis that was less than inspiring in design and purpose. Megaguirus, for example, who evolves from the Meganulon in *Rodan* ... and that's pretty much the only real purpose for Megaguirus, who looks like a giant mosquito/dragonfly hybrid. Of the numerous disappointing opponents for Godzilla, Megaguirus is perhaps among the worst. Essentially, the main power of Megaguirus is siphoning energy from Godzilla and blasting it back at him. And flying really fast. This all frustrates Godzilla, but the wham-bam, knockout battles we came to expect during this era—this film coming after battles against Destroyah and then Orga—never really materialize, and, at times, borders on the absurd. In fact, the true danger to Godzilla isn't Megaguirus, but the Dimension Tide, a satellite that can theoretically zap Godzilla with a black hole and send him to another dimension.

Yes, Megaguirus is less powerful and less interesting than a satellite.

The only other creature in the Godzilla franchise that is less interesting and less deadly than Megaguirus is Ebirah. The giant lobster. To be fair, however, Ebirah was originally supposed to be the big baddie against King Kong, but Toho lost the rights, and, not willing to sacrifice the work already put into the project, simply slid Godzilla into the script instead.* Ebirah is so weak that a group of advanced superhumans will later easily make it one of the first victims in *Godzilla: Final Wars*. Godzilla didn't really break a sweat in *Godzilla vs. The Sea Monster* against Ebirah, and in the lobster's return appearance, it barely stays on the screen for more than a few seconds in battle against Godzilla

And then there's the spider Kumonga and the praying mantis-like Kamacuras...

But I digress, because we are getting dangerously close to the power scaling discussions that populate social media havens and other such internet back alleys. No, this is an attempt to understand how some kaiju can reach legendary status in our minds, the Godzillas, the Mothras, the Kongs, the Gameras; while others, the Kamoebas, the Ebirahs,

---

*This is why Godzilla gains Kong's already confounding power of being charged by electricity.

even Dinotank, are quickly forgotten and never gain much traction. In fact, most of Godzilla's rogues gallery, to borrow a term from the comics world, features superstar kaiju: Kong, Mothra, King Ghidorah, Biollante, Destroyah ... all of these are well-known and well-regarded beasts in their own right, and some, like Rodan, starred in their own features before joining the Godzilla universe proper.

Yet, it is interesting to consider how Gamera, though, remains the sole darling of his own, albeit shorter-lived, franchise. There are a large number of enemies Gamera has faced, but many of them are remembered primarily because of their absurdity (Barugon), or because of how ubiquitous they are (Gyaos), almost a familiarity bred from just a consistent repetition. I would argue that the only truly memorable standalone kaiju that battled Gamera is Iris, and that was the last effective Gamera movie of the Heisei era.*

In fact, many of Gamera's enemies seem to live in infamy for their outright bizarreness. Guiron, with a massive head shaped like a knife, who crawls around on his hands and knees and chops up opponents and who can summon throwing stars that return like boomerangs from just above his eyes. Or Zigra, a strange bird/shark/alien hybrid with multicolored light attacks. And, of course, one of Gamera's "serious" enemies, Barugon, who commanded most of *Gamera vs. Barugon*'s screenplay, shoots long-distance and destructive rainbows out of his back while also using a freezing mist that fogs out of the end of his very long and extendable tongue.

So what makes a kaiju memorable? What makes them "real" rather than the subject of derision? What is the difference between a kaiju that functions mostly as the answer to a trivia question and one that's given repeat appearances?

The easiest way to approach this is to take a look at the most successful kaiju in the Godzilla film franchise, the ones that consistently appear as enemies or allies, or both; some even command their own films. I'm speaking, of course, of four distinct kaiju: Mothra, King Ghidorah, Rodan, and the various incarnations of Mechagodzilla. Setting aside the numerous cameos in *Final Wars* and *Destroy All Monsters!* these are the only full-grown kaiju (sorry, Minilla, not today) who have appeared in various incarnations in the Godzilla universe. We'll discuss Gyaos in the Gamera franchise a bit later, so hang in there, Gamera fans.

Is it the design of these individual kaiju that wins the day? Although they do have far better design aesthetics than, say, Red King from the

---

Gamera the Brave exists, of course, but it doesn't really "follow" the plot of the previous trilogy and functions more as a standalone family film.

8. An Ode to Baragon and Barugon 93

Ultraman franchise,* there's not a lot there that differentiates them in terms of originality. In fact, other kaiju with far more imposing designs and that are much more unique in the Godzilla franchise didn't even make the cut in *Final Wars*: namely, Biollante, Destroyah, and Orga, among a few others. Rodan, in particular, is pretty much a highly modified dinosaur with wings, and Mothra is a giant moth with a flair for bright colors. In fact, as Mothra has progressed over the years, she has become fuzzier and more toy-like in her look (for a depiction of an aggressively postured Mothra, one needs only look to Battra, all black, with flashes of yellow and red arcing across its wing). King Ghidorah is a dragon with three heads, and Mechagodzilla is a robot version of Godzilla. Nothing spectacular in terms of concept or execution.

No, it's the story of the kaiju that "sells" them most of all, and perhaps that's why so many of the Ultraman-style enemies are so easily forgotten. Not just because of their inherent cheapness or the absurdity of their design,† but because their story is easily adaptable to the situation, and, it's important to note, each of these kaiju have shown that they *can* defeat Godzilla if needed. Thus, their inherent danger to the hero (or anti-hero) is a selling point as well. King Ghidorah, Mothra, Mechagodzilla, and, to a lesser extent, Rodan, have all given Godzilla a run for his money in numerous incarnations—even the Mothra larvae have won a few battles against the big guy.

What makes this phenomenon so interesting is that the design for these kaiju is probably not a foremost concern among fans or creators, and each kaiju enemy is threatening in some way, but, ultimately, they each serve as fantastic creations that stretch into near Godlike territory. They take on—especially Mothra and King Ghidorah—near-mythical status that not only establishes them as threats to Godzilla, but massively powerful creatures of legend. This is the reason why these two, in particular, were cast as "Guardian Monsters" in *Giant Monsters All-Out Attack!*.

And, although Mothra and Rodan's stories have remained somewhat consistent over the years since their debuts in their own film, both King Ghidorah and Mechagodzilla have changed to suit the needs of their creators. Both started as representatives of incoming conquering aliens (a theme which almost always consistently dominates the King Ghidorah origin stories), and eventually evolved over several "versions" of themselves. Just as Gamera and Godzilla have changed over the years to meet the visual needs of an adoring fanbase (making both of them decidedly

---

*The best description of Red King I've found is that it looks "like a genetic cross between Godzilla and a corn cob" (Worthington).
†One of my favorite recent designs in the Ultraman universe is Mochiron, an alien that wears a tiki mask–style barrel around its body that shoots flames.

94   **The Kaiju Connection**

more "badass" in their look than their overly friendly, and, yes, somewhat goofy, look in the Showa era as the kids in the audience grew up),* so, too, have King Ghidorah and Mechagodzilla. In fact, their fates are somewhat intertwined for a few years. The second version of Mechagodzilla is cobbled together by humanity with the remnants of MechaKing Ghidorah after the events of *Godzilla vs. King Ghidorah.*

It's this adaptability, I think, that allows for longer lasting storylines and gives each of these kaiju more of a "final boss" feel; you know that when they show up, the shit's about to get real. Although kaiju can sometimes tax Godzilla—Gigan injures him severely, and Destroyah takes him to the limit—there's always a palpable sense that Godzilla can be severely injured or even destroyed against at least King Ghidorah, Mechagodzilla, or Mothra. Even Rodan gave Godzilla some serious challenges in *Godzilla vs. Mechagodzilla II* after he turned into Fire Rodan, and it goes without saying that Rodan had to sacrifice himself in order to save Godzilla from Mechagodzilla II.

In each of his battles against these opposing kaiju, Godzilla is either knocked down repeatedly, knocked out, severely injured, or outright defeated, and that's something that, I think, contributes to these films' longevity, even more than their design or their backstories. Mothra in her Imago form consistently gives Godzilla fits, but either the Imago or the larva have been successful in bundling up Godzilla and removing him from the situation, often peacefully, by lulling him to sleep and/or wrapping him in webbing. This happens several times. In *Mothra vs. Godzilla,* the larvae cover him in webbing and send him to the ocean. In *Godzilla vs. Mothra,* her Imago form and Battra team up to drop Godzilla back into the ocean. And, in *Tokyo S.O.S.,* the larvae again team up after the Imago form sedates Godzilla, wrapping him up and letting Kiryu—the third Mechagodzilla—crash into the ocean with his unconscious form.

The three distinct Mechagodzillas have all left lasting scars, sometimes literally, on Godzilla, no matter their origins, with Kiryu being the most damaging of the group. With the Absolute Zero mounted on his chest, Kiryu managed to blow a hole in Godzilla's own chest (again with that mirroring—see Chapter 6), sending the beast back to the ocean in a rare victory for the Mechagodzillas. Of course, the very first Mechagodzilla was created with a mean streak, from breaking poor Anguirus's jaw to unleashing multiple bloody salvos on Godzilla across two films and leaving the big kaiju bleeding and injured for much of the film.

Each Mechagodzilla is a unique creation, and they all have in common

---

*William Tsutsui notes that the span from the "goofy, anthropomorphic kiddie Godzilla" to the "angry, frightening looks" and "hostile attitude" is over two decades long (64).

8. An Ode to Baragon and Barugon 95

the absolute ability to stymie and injure Godzilla, often rather graphically. The first Mechagodzilla appears in disguise as Godzilla in *Godzilla vs. Mechagodzilla* and is an alien creation. We first understand something is amiss when the disguised Mechagodzilla promptly stomps on and snaps the jaw of Godzilla's frenemy Anguirus, and, soon, the viewer is treated to a rather fantastic transformation sequence before unloading on Godzilla and managing to keep both Godzilla and King Caesar at bay for much of the battle.

At one point, in one of the gorier sequences in Showa Godzilla films, Godzilla's skin is punctured by several rockets, knocking him down, stunning him, and covering him in blood. In *Terror of Mechagodzilla*, the alien robot manages to drop Godzilla with a single missile to the chest before burying him alive. The second Mechagodzilla manages to stun Godzilla after combining with the Garuda spaceship and becoming (what else?) Super Mechagodzilla. And, of course, Kiryu, built on the bones of the original Godzilla from 1954, also repeatedly damages and defeats Godzilla as well.

This tradition continued somewhat for the fourth Mechagodzilla in *Godzilla vs. Kong*, where Mechagodzilla is a sort of corporate super-creation powered by one of the Ghidorah heads left behind from the battle in *Godzilla: King of the Monsters*. Although the origin story for this Mechagodzilla is spotty at best, it appears to be controlled by that remaining Ghidorah head almost exclusively, and memorably does a number on the Legendary Godzilla, grinding the massive kaiju face-first through Hong Kong and nearly landing a killing blow until Kong intervenes.

King Ghidorah's size and girth makes him a formidable opponent for Godzilla as well, and the Legendary version of King Ghidorah maximizes this difference, showing a massive Godzilla essentially dwarfed by the three heads and massive wing structure as well. Indeed, Ghidorah's role in the Godzilla universe is well established enough that a different form of Ghidorah appears as the literal final boss in *Final Wars*, appearing first as the mysterious Monster X before turning into Keizer Ghidorah. This new version of Ghidorah is overpowered and more grounded, which is apt, as the *Final Wars* version of Godzilla is also extremely powerful, and, as per the norm, Ghidorah manages to stun Godzilla until Godzilla gets some much-needed assistance from humans or other kaiju, or some combination of both.

The best way to illustrate how lore and power work together to make a kaiju more memorable—or profitable enough to make multiple appearances—is to turn to Gyaos. Although the design of Gyaos leaves quite a bit to be desired—he would fit in nicely with many Ultraman kaiju—he is the most dangerous enemy in Gamera's rogues gallery, first appearing in

Gamera vs. Gyaos. Gyaos is immediately established as a threat to Gamera. Even though Gyaos' weakness is to sunlight, their first battle leaves Gamera severely damaged, forcing him to retreat back to the ocean to recover. To add to the general creepiness of Gyaos, it's discovered that the creature has a taste for blood as well, and one of the more bizarre plans in kaiju cinematic history is hatched by the humans: trick Gyaos into staying outside during the day by luring him to a massive fountain of blood surrounded by a rotating platform.

Gamera eventually wins, but Gyaos remains an established threat for the rest of the franchise, something that no other kaiju really does until thirty years later when Iris appears in *Gamera 3: Revenge of Iris*. Forget Barugon and his freeze breath and rainbow-shooting back, and never mind Zigra's somewhat Gyaos-like shape. Gyaos is Gamera's arch-nemesis. In fact, in order to show what a threat Guiron is to Gamera in *Gamera vs. Guiron*, we're treated to Guiron coming out of a pit and quickly dispatching a Gyaos by literally cutting him up into little bits and tossing the chunks of flesh aside.

It makes sense, then, that the gritty Heisei reboot of Gamera would have to start with Gyaos in *Gamera: Guardian of the Universe*. Gamera is no longer the bug-eyed and inherently goofy turtle that performs trapeze acts; he's been replaced by a taller, spikier, and altogether meaner-looking version. But this time, it's a *group* of taller, spikier, and meaner-looking Gyaos that Gamera has to battle, and, eventually one of the initial three survives and eats so much that it becomes a new version of itself, named Super Gyaos, much taller and much more powerful, and again, takes Gamera to his limits.

The Heisei trilogy—setting aside *Gamera the Brave* as a standalone film not related to the other three—ends with a severely wounded Gamera, who, having just dispatched Iris by blowing off his own arm, turns to face a flock of Hyper Gyaos descending on him. It's a wildly appropriate ending, as Gyaos is not only Gamera's nemesis, but quite simply his most reliable foe, one that we know will consistently tax and test Gamera. Gyaos, in its multiple defeats, manages, and I'll loosely borrow professional wrestling terminology here, to give Gamera the rub—he consistently lends the kaiju additional credibility through his challenges.

Like Ghidorah, Mothra, and Mechagodzilla, Gyaos exists solely to give viewers a reason to see Godzilla and Gamera face serious adversity. While, unlike Gamera, Godzilla will occasionally don the antagonist role in *Mothra vs. Godzilla* or *Giant Monsters All-Out Attack*, the danger in those films is that there would be no true challenge for Godzilla. That's why, in *Giant Monsters All-Out Attack*, the ultra-powerful Godzilla, spurred forth as a representation of the Japanese war dead, needs to battle

8. An Ode to Baragon and Barugon   97

successively dangerous opponents. Although he quickly dispatches Baragon, Mothra gives him more trouble, and their deaths eventually invigorate and enlarge King Ghidorah to be able to at least challenge Godzilla on a more toe-to-toe basis.

In some ways, I think, we sort of cheer for these enemies. Not because they are "good" or even the antihero, but because they promise a large, impressive battle that gives us a kaiju pushed to their limits or severely injured. Their presence creates a new height, a new greatness, for Gamera or Godzilla's storyline, no matter how abbreviated. When Godzilla gets a massive hole blown in his chest by Kiryu, the third Mechagodzilla, it resonates with viewers to show not only how dangerous Kiryu is, but also because it shows us how resilient and dominant Godzilla is: when he returns with a massive scar, viewers are given the visual reminder of Godzilla's sort-of defeat at the hands of Kiryu, and the tension ramps up for their new confrontation, especially as Godzilla returns earlier than expected and Kiryu has to race to the battle still severely weakened.

Perhaps this is a function of the aspects of masculinity we tend to project onto kaiju film much of the time (more on this in Chapter 13), but the larger themes of overcoming adversity just don't seem to ring as true in other films where Godzilla is pushed to the limit.* Take *Godzilla vs. Hedorah*: Godzilla suffers a certain amount of damage from Hedorah, including a rather nasty injury to his eye (making Godzilla a reflection of Dr. Yano and his injured eye), but there's never the sense that Godzilla is in much danger. Same goes with *Godzilla vs. Gigan*, when Gigan hits Godzilla with his buzzsaw. Blood spurts out rather dramatically, but Godzilla shakes it off quickly and continues the fight. Fast forward to *Godzilla* (2014), where Godzilla is certainly knocked down and around by the MUTOs, but he doesn't collapse until *after* the battle. In these films, Godzilla never truly retreats or is in much danger for significant stretches of the film's runtime.

Of course, all of this may be that Gyaos, Mothra, Mechagodzilla, and King Ghidorah are now coded in fan's minds as truly deadly kaiju. When they appear on the screen opposite Gamera or Godzilla, we know that there's a serious challenge ahead, one that will tax our protagonist and give it a significant obstacle to overcome. Imagine, for example, that King Ghidorah appeared in a movie and was given the 'Zilla treatment from *Final Wars*: a few seconds of screen time and then blasted out of existence.

---

*Much has been made of the bloodshed in the Gamera Showa-era films, to the point that Eiji Tsuburaya apparently wrote a letter to Daiei asking them to turn down the bloodworks (Lemay 132), but even when Showa Gamera is injured, there's little sense of danger or even long-term injury, even when speared by Viras. Much of the time, even when Gamera is temporarily defeated, the opposing kaiju is equally weakened or otherwise just not all that deadly anyway.

Fans would not only be confused, but would also most likely be irritated that Ghidorah was not treated "realistically" or "faithfully."

Ghidorah, Mothra, and Mechagodzilla, as well as Gyaos, are *supposed* to be the most dangerous opponents (or allies), and these expectations tend to dominate their characterization. They serve as visual signifiers that Godzilla or Gamera are about to face a significant challenge. One of the most important pieces of evidence for this is the Mechagodzilla that appears at the end of *Godzilla vs. Kong*. Despite a relatively uninspired design—having more in common with the Transformers movie franchise than Godzilla—and a rushed and hackneyed origin story (if you blink, you'll miss the fact that one of the "pilots" for this Mechagodzilla was somehow supposed to be Dr. Serizawa's son, Ren)—we *know* as soon as we see Mechagodzilla on the screen that Godzilla is in trouble. Every previous iteration of Mechagodzilla tells us this, and even the barest resemblance in design and backstory does not prevent this connection from being made. This is Mechagodzilla, and Godzilla is about to get whomped.

This lack of any sort of depth or background is why Baragon and Barugon are mostly forgotten, and it's why so many kaiju from both the Godzilla and Gamera franchises rarely make repeat appearances. They exist solely to be beaten, often soundly, by Godzilla and Gamera, to show their somewhat easy dominance (especially in the Showa films). Kaiju like Legion, Hedorah, Rodan, and Guiron certainly test the abilities of Godzilla and Gamera, and may even temporarily knock them down, but their deadliness is never really established. They exist to be cannon fodder; we go into these films knowing that the challenge will be minimal, and so we're left to appreciate their unique look (Gigan) or deeply odd backstory (Megaguirus) before we say farewell to them for decades, if not forever.

Otherwise, kaiju like Varan, Kamoebas, and Ganimes are left with little more than the novelty of their first appearance in our own nostalgia: only *we* truly remember those departed and forgotten kaiju, the ones who once, perhaps, commanded their own film before making a random cameo somewhere else as a captive or a corpse. Perhaps we remember seeing Guilala stomping oddly through the city on a grainy late-night creature feature show, a moment of relaxation and wonder at the end of a particularly bad day. And, as such, it's our own memories and our own backgrounds that give these kaiju just a little bit more life, and gives us just a little more hope that one day, we'll see them again, but this time, they'll be more ready for battle, and they'll perhaps rekindle our nostalgic memories while also giving the kaiju a reason to return, hopefully more frequently, so we can enjoy them again and again and think back to that time when we thought they *almost* beat Godzilla or they *almost* beat Gamera, and maybe the next time…

9

It Turns Out Gamera *Is* Really Neat: The Heisei Trilogy

Shusuke Kaneko should rest comfortably at night knowing that he has won the eternal adoration of many kaiju fans for his revised take on Gamera (and later, Godzilla). Gamera was an overlooked and outdated franchise that had challenged Godzilla during the Showa era, and then buckled and collapsed under its own unusually campy weight. Many of the Gamera films were well-known by the time of the Heisei era because of their appearances on *Mystery Science Theater 3000*. But Kaneko not only returned the kaiju to respectability, but he also created some of the most acclaimed and renowned kaiju films ever made. Yes, the Heisei trilogy of Gamera is just that good, and the recent Arrow box set releases, where you can watch one restored Gamera film after another, manages to show just how deeply Kaneko had to reach in order to pull Gamera back up to mainstream potential.

Like Ishiro Honda, Kaneko made, either consciously or subconsciously, the decision to take Gamera seriously, something that hadn't happened in the Gamera franchise since 1965, three decades earlier. Surprisingly little changes in respect to the basics of Gamera in the Heisei trilogy. Gamera is still a massive turtle-like creature that shoots fireballs and improbably flies by tucking itself into its shell and rocketing around. Gamera is still a friend to … well, *most* children. But, unlike so many of the Showa films, Kaneko plays it straight; the wonderful absurdity is there, but never highlighted, and there's no real attempts to try to "explain" Gamera's oddities.

In place of the campiness of much of the Showa series is a sort of deadly seriousness that runs throughout the franchise. People die, get severely injured, a lot of the country gets destroyed, Gamera struggles to win the day, and some people actually dislike Gamera, even though he's ostensibly protecting them. It's a bold choice and a far cry from the happy "here comes Gamera!" vibe that permeates films such as *Gamera vs. Zigra*.

The Heisei trilogy doesn't quite earn the descriptor of "grim," but it sure as hell reaches for it. That said, the first of the trilogy, *Guardian of the Universe*, is probably the most Showa-y of the group, mostly because it is facing down the task of reestablishing the "rules" of the Gamera franchise and asking the viewer to dislodge and set aside all of their campy notions of Gamera himself.

Most of this is achieved through the breakneck pace of *Gamera: Guardian of the Universe*, as it moves from location to location, character to character so quickly that you don't even have time to question what you're seeing—is that smoke coming out of Gamera's *knees*? But Gamera as a character, a misunderstood kaiju from ancient times, functions well, and we willingly engage in the suspension of disbelief mostly because of the inertia of the film, which is essentially a prolonged chase sequence interspersed with dialogue from researchers and military and government officials.

Where *Guardian of the Universe* splits from its campier forebears is how it treats the ground-level discussions and personnel. We are told, repeatedly, that Gyaos eats people, and we even see that play out a few times, and it is even more gruesome than Gyaos drinking blood in his initial Showa appearance.* Gamera is single-minded to the point that he doesn't necessarily see much of a problem with stomping a straight line through numerous high-rise complexes in order to get to Gyaos. His beeline toward Gyaos resembles the movement of the Mothra larva in *Mothra*. You see, there's destruction, and there's the negative consequences of the destruction, and most kaiju films only acknowledge the former while avoiding the hell out of the latter. Not so in *Guardian*, as we see the aftereffects. All that remains of Mayumi Nagamine's professor and mentor is a pair of glasses sliding down a ball of goo. But not only glasses: Gyaos' bird pellet is filled with numerous human remains.

Gamera himself takes a significant amount of damage in the film (echoing many of the Showa films, where Gamera bleeds profusely), but those wounds are reflected on his human telepathic connection, Asagi Kusanagi. Gamera gets cut on the arm, she bleeds from a new laceration, and so on. This is a new and rather marked departure from the Gamera films of the Showa era; yes, Gamera bled (a lot), to protect and save the children, but this time, the children have skin in the game, too, almost literally. The psychic bond with Kusanagi comes at a terrible price to her. In order for Gamera to defeat Gyaos, she must become physically and

---

*We are told that Gyaos appears because the human destruction of the planet via pollution gave him a better environment in which to thrive, a sentiment which will be echoed in *Pacific Rim* where the characters learn that the kaiju are appearing because humans "practically terraformed" the earth for them.

9. It Turns Out Gamera Is Really Neat: The Heisei Trilogy   101

psychically associated with him, to the point that her own body and psyche are wracked by Gamera's own injuries and turmoil.

By the end of the film, Gamera stands victorious, having gotten a boost from Kusanagi, and, as a sort of reward, he breaks the link with her before going back to the ocean. There's a certain tinge of darkness here. Yes, Gamera protects the children of the world, but there's definitely a sense of danger for Kusanagi as well, as she, too, can only sustain a certain amount of damage. This gives the film a much more foreboding countenance, for it points to the idea that Gamera protects children, but also needs them to survive. Gyaos eats people and other Gyaos in order to survive; Gamera feeds on the energy of children to survive. Think: when Gamera is first "discovered" in the ocean, the team that lands on him finds a charm, and then another, until there are dozens of them, if not hundreds. That charm is how Gamera "links" with Kusanagi, so there's definitely a sense that, for Gamera to fully function, or to become more powerful, he has to, or should, connect with many more children than just Kusanagi.

The theory behind Gamera is that he's a man-made life form, created by the citizens of whatever would eventually become the Atlantis mythology. It's a neat bit of hand-waving away some of Gamera's oddities while also staying true to the original *Gamera* and its notion that Gamera lived on Atlantis. Gamera's being man-made, however, points to the notion that the people who created Gamera not only went completely off-the-wall with the creation (a turtle that flies and spins around and can shoot fireballs out of its mouth!), but that they *also knew that Gamera needed a psychic link in order to become powerful enough to battle Gyaos*. In other words, there's the uncomfortable thought that Gamera was designed to use humans like batteries. It moves the normally happy-go-lucky relationship that Gamera has with children during the Showa era to something more darkly symbiotic. Gamera wins, and so do the children. But Gamera suffers ... and so do the children.

The second of the trilogy, *Attack of Legion*, known in some quarters as *Attack of the Legion*, continues sending the tone ever darker, and adds in copious amounts of realistic violence. Legion arrives on earth as an alien invasion of sorts, and they quickly start burrowing underground, where they run afoul of a subway train. In one of the grislier sequences in kaiju film history, the conductor of the train, Ishida, watches as one of the Legion absorbs the glass barrier between him, and then attacks. We hear his screams and the camera cuts to the door behind him, where a large amount of blood sprays upwards; this, naturally, sends most of the train's passengers into a panic. The individual Legion creatures start to attack, and we see a not insignificant amount of bloodshed, with the camera at one point lingering on a pair of crumpled glasses (shorn of their glass) with blood dripping from the frames.

The Kaiju Connection

Now, this would probably barely earn a PG-13 rating in the U.S., because it's not *really* gory, at least compared to what we would conventionally think of as horror films. Films such as *Predator* or *Friday the 13th* earn their R ratings through multiple on-screen disembowelings, stabbings, beheadings, and eviscerations. But, by kaiju film standards, it's extraordinarily rare to see human-centered violence, especially this bloody.* Kaiju get injured all the time; that's the expectation in a "fair" fight, and Gamera's no stranger to being injured, even if his bright green blood softens the blow a bit.

At one point, Ishida's gruesome death at the hands of Legion is mirrored by Gamera's own near-death. After being covered by numerous Legion creatures, each of them shocking and cutting Gamera, he desperately flies away, spraying a large swath of green blood across the side of a skyscraper. On the other side of that glass stands Obitsu and Midori Honami, who just faced down their own death. Moments earlier, they realized that the explosion that would result from the military's attempt to kill Legion would subsume that very skyscraper, annihilating them both. It's a tense staredown, and Gamera saves them inadvertently, but the mortality of one minor character—Obitsu—and one major character—Midori Honami, a scientist trying to understand Legion—is on display, and there's some tense moments as they wait, staring out the window, waiting for the explosion that will destroy them.

This is all important because the physical link between Gamera and Asagi Kusanagi is abandoned for these remaining films. Gamera takes some pretty gnarly damage from Legion—part of his shell is blown off, his neck is sliced open, and he is punctured several times, resulting in buckets of green blood—after the Legion "mother" appears. There simply would not have been a way to reflect that level of damage on Asagi Kusanagi without going full horror film, and also by opening up some somewhat disturbing possibilities in terms of Gamera's role as a "hero" in his own franchise.

But there's plenty of urban destruction to take its place. "Sendai Annihilated" reads a headline after one of the Legion seed pods blow up; and that's indeed true, as a caption on another newspaper—all of them presented in English with Japanese subtitles—reads "Ruins of Sendai resembilng [*sic*] the bomb wiped state of Japanese cities in WW2."† But, back to Kusanagi, who plays a lesser role in this film. Gamera himself is

---

*More on this in the *Reigo* chapter.

†The newspaper mock-ups are a fascinating part of this film, presented as headlines from major American newspapers such as *The New York Times*. This is clearly a technique that is meant to reach out to Western English speakers—Americans, specifically—to highlight the destruction to them a bit more effectively. If you pause the film at these points, you'll see bizarre turns of phrase and multiple misspellings scattered throughout the articles: Japanese text translated to English.

9. It Turns Out Gamera Is Really Neat: The Heisei Trilogy   103

nearly destroyed by the blast, and it's enough to spark a scene where a father talks to his child, who demands to know why Gamera isn't protecting them. "Gamera is...," the father replies, but doesn't know how to finish the sentence.

Even Gamera's legend as a defender of humanity, specifically children, is nearly destroyed in this film, as his burnt-out form lies prone in the middle of Sendai for quite some time. "Gamera is alive," Kusanagi tells a skeptical Honami, and here, her connection rings true, as children gather alongside the edge of Gamera's form, led by Kusanagi and Honami. In a scene that would make Mothra proud, the combined hope of the children fly like sparks over Gamera and bring him back—a power overload that shatters Kusanagi's stone.* Gamera emerges renewed, and the children silently send him off to battle.

It's all very touching, and Gamera's recovery and subsequent defeat of Legion—with some help from the Self Defense Force—somewhat resets much of the Gamera universe and even rewrites some of the rules established in *Guardian of the Universe*. But, in the end, this film—sandwiched between two films that received much more critical adoration—continues the bizarre juxtaposition of children gathering around Gamera to help revive him alongside sequences where others are brutally splattered. And though we cheer for Gamera, with several Self Defense Force personnel saluting Gamera as he flies away (but noticeably, others do not), we're left with Obitsu and Honami walking down the street. Honami points out to Obitsu that Gamera protects the *earth*, not *people*, which is a good way to separate out Gamera's actions in his films. That he protects the earth, though, ends with a dire warning, as Obitsu notes that people are doing plenty of damage to the environment, and certainly as much as other kaiju. Honami reminds us, "We don't want Gamera against us, do we?"

So, Gamera's recasting is somewhat complete. He functions primarily as the Earth's immune system, rising up to establish wide-ranging threats to protect the Earth. Along the way, as children apparently don't do quite as much to directly damage the environment (notwithstanding overpopulation concerns), well, Gamera doesn't have as much of a beef with them, and their adoration of him allows him to heal and recover. Children believe in Gamera, and he turns into a sort of modern-day deity, an important switch, given *Gamera 3: Revenge of Iris*.

Revenge of Iris is where all of Kaneko's plot beats come to fruition, and we're presented with two very different and very stark Gameras. One is a hero saving the world, the other is a stone cold killer. And, to be honest,

---

*We later learn in *Gamera 3: Revenge of Iris* that *all* of the stones recovered in *Guardian of the Universe* were shattered.

104   **The Kaiju Connection**

Kaneko definitely pushes the viewer into viewing Gamera as a killer for much of the film. Our initial foray into this idea is centered around Ayana Hirasaka, whose parents (and cat named Iris) are killed during the events of *Guardian of the Universe*. Sent away to live in the countryside with a somewhat indifferent foster family, Ayana nurses her hatred of Gamera; her nightmares depict a Gamera not like the friendly-ish turtle we've seen many times before, but is instead what has been nicknamed "Trauma Gamera." This version of Gamera has silver pupil- and iris-less eyes* and is hideously scarred. Instead of the elephantine roar we're used to, this version of Gamera, seen through Ayana's eyes, grunts and growls.

All of this, too, isn't too far of a stretch, and Ayana may have a point. Now shorn of his connection with Asagi Kusanagi and the rest of the children of the world, Gamera's actions are single-minded and completely ignorant of humanity. A pair of Gyaos fly over the Shibuya district, with Gamera in hot pursuit, and we're treated to a spectacle of absolute massive violence as Gamera has clearly had enough of Gyaos' shit: he fires multiple fireballs at them, and lands heavily in the city. Train stations collapse, people burn to death, others are crushed under falling debris, and still others die under falling, flaming Gyaos chunks. In one sequence, an oblivious Gamera stands near Tatsuya, a young boy. His mother has been pulled away from him by the fleeing crowd, and he lies on the pavement, looking up at Gamera. Gamera has cornered one of the Gyaos, who has been beaten senseless and even has an eye hanging out of its socket; Gamera blows a point-blank fireball at the Gyaos, annihilating it. The sequence sees numerous bodies of bystanders flying through the air in front of the explosion.

"Gamera saved me!" Tatsuya cries out to his mother; Kaneko then deftly cuts to a view of the city landscape in flames, and we soon learn that the government estimates that over 15,000 people are dead or injured as a result of the battle. The destruction is so severe that the Japanese Self Defense Force casts their lot and decide to kill Gamera at all costs.

This subjectivity in how we view kaiju was Kaneko's point all along. To some, Gamera is a savior, sometimes by accident; but to many others, Gamera is an object of fear and even scorn. He and his kaiju brethren have traumatized numerous people, including Ayana as well as Tsutomu Osako, who was a detective in the first film and then a security guard in the second. Osako moves from place to place, a refugee in his own country, because of his fear of the kaiju. By the time of the third film, Osako is reduced to selling magazines on a street corner. "Gamera is our friend!" a classmate says, chiding Ayana for her hatred. Her response is prompt and

---

*Kaneko would adopt this look for Godzilla in *Giant Monsters All-Out Attack*, itself a callback to the look of Godzilla in 1954.

9. It Turns Out Gamera Is Really Neat: The Heisei Trilogy 105

justifiable, and it's easy to sympathize with: "Would you say that if he'd crushed your house and your parents?" And so, Asagi Kusanagi's faith in Gamera as a hero across all three films is under assault, and we realize that *she* can worship Gamera because he's never purposefully hurt her or otherwise hurt anyone she loves. Kusanagi's constant belief in Gamera as a force for "good" moves from Showa-like passion in *Guardian of the Universe* to the plaintive and misplaced justifications of a desperate person in *Revenge of Iris.*

And so, the hero of the first two films is cast as a villain while Iris works his way into the plot. A small creature hatched from an egg and distantly related to Gyaos, supposedly destined to kill Gamera so that Gyaos can "reset" the world, is discovered by Ayana. Iris literally feeds off of people. For Ayana, it feeds off of her hate; for others, Iris simply absorbs their life essence, draining them on the spot and turning them into desiccated corpses. It takes a lot of work for Kaneko to turn the somewhat cute Iris into a villain, especially because Gamera is a villain; in other words, in order to make Iris "bad," that kaiju has to outstrip what Gamera has done in the film. As a result, Iris is the cause of several jump scares through the movie, specifically through the discovery—or creation of—the gruesome corpses that Iris leaves behind.

The action of the movie accelerates rapidly, and almost gets bogged down in conspiracy theories, video gaming, mythology, and other side topics that do indeed add some depth to the characters, but ultimately tries to explain too much. To wit: In order to save the world, humanity must be erased from it, and Iris, as a powerful genetic descendent of Gyaos, is the perfect entity to do so. And, because Gamera is keeping this from happening, some people feel that Gamera is "evil," and use Ayana to their own nefarious ends. If Ayana fully bonds with Iris, then Gamera will be outmatched and will surely die.

All of this builds to a nearly 20-minute-long climax, where Gamera and Iris face off, Ayana gets absorbed by Iris, Gamera rips Ayana out of Iris, and Gamera blows off his own hand, absorbs Iris's intended deathblow, and destroys Iris. Ayana is knocked unconscious during this very understandable series of traumatizing events, and Gamera's victorious roar—so different from the Trauma Gamera that haunts her nightmares—wakes her up. Ayana wonders why Gamera saved her, but stops short of becoming a sort of Gamera convert like Asagi. The film ends with Asagi praising Gamera and acknowledging that Gamera will continue to "protect" humanity.*

---

*Mothra, probably the most heroic of all kaiju, has played this card a few times as well, and the Shobijin very noticeably threatens to destroy humanity if they don't stop messing around with Godzilla's bones in *Tokyo S.O.S.*

106   The Kaiju Connection

Kaneko doesn't seem to think so, or, at least, he wants it to remain ambiguous, because the final shot of the film is Gamera walking through a city destroyed and in flames, with most likely another 15,000 or more dead or injured. The implication is clear. Gamera, and, by extension, kaiju themselves, are what we choose to make of them. They are human creations, of course, and they mirror human attitudes and human fears. For Gamera, and for this trilogy, there's a clear divide between localized issues (my city has been destroyed, and/or my family has been killed) and the sort of broader worldwide geopolitical environment (humanity is destroying the planet). This set of films is one of the few films in the kaiju genre that juxtaposes the conflicts between the two, and we see it perfectly in Ayana and Asagi. Ayana's parents (and cat) are dead, killed during a battle where Gamera simply stomps through buildings on the way to hunt down a Gyaos. Asagi, on the other hand, maintains a more intimate connection to Gamera; her home life is stable with a doting and understanding father raising her.* These are human representations of the broader experience of a world inflicted with (infected by?) kaiju.

It's fair to say, then, that no matter the kaiju, there's always going to be a distinct set of human experiences that craft a discussion about what role that kaiju has in the world. Although Godzilla, for example, changed rapidly from nuclear-scarred threat to savior of Japan to an "alpha predator" over the decades, his very kaiju-ness informed all of these interpretations, especially when faced with other kaiju. The Godzilla who battles invading aliens on an empty plain with only a few humans to witness the event saves the world and is a hero; the Godzilla who swims ashore, crushes cities and kills an invading kaiju ... maybe a little less than a hero. It's this duality, somewhat writ large and clear in this Gamera trilogy, that has fueled so many iterations of kaiju, especially in Japan, where the tension between the local (Japan) and the geopolitical (the rest of the world, especially the "superpowers") was foregrounded through the 1960s and well into the 1990s.

Now, you probably noticed at the start of this essay that I referred repeatedly to the Heisei "trilogy" and basically didn't acknowledge *Gamera the Brave*, a somewhat woeful children's movie that more closely resembles the *Rebirth of Mothra* series than it does "adult" kaiju films. Gone is the darkness and the sometimes confounding moral structure of the Kaneko Gamera franchise, and in its place is a Showa-era adherent: bright, colorful, and ultimately hollow and meaningless. It provides a "new" Gamera and one that ignores all of the action of the Kaneko trilogy, instead choosing to pick up in 1973, where the previous Gamera decided to take out a bunch of Gyaos by blowing himself up. It's a rather extreme

---

*There's that mirroring again! Ayana and Iris reflecting Asagi and Gamera.

9. It Turns Out Gamera Is Really Neat: The Heisei Trilogy   107

measure, but the implications of this are never explored. Kosuke Aizawa witnesses this destruction and he and the surrounding population of the blast have slowly recovered. Kosuke has a son, Toru, whose mother (and Kosuke's wife), Miyuki, has died in a car crash. Toru soon stumbles upon a very, well, turtle-sized turtle that eventually becomes magical. The little turtle, named Toto, flies and causes all sorts of mischief, and is, indeed, a baby Gamera slowly growing up under Toru's guidance.

Cue all the usual stuff about childhood loneliness, a distant and harried father, and other childhood issues, and you have a cloying Showa mixture, and—as it completely ignores the Kaneko trilogy—it's hard to shoehorn it into this chapter. This isn't to say that *Gamera the Brave* is a bad film ... well, in many ways it is, especially as it comes on the heels of what is considered one of the best series of kaiju films out there. But it is to say that *Gamera the Brave*, like the aforementioned *Rebirth of Mothra*, is so formulaic and simplified—basically, a film for the kids—that it doesn't really provide much fodder for critical scrutiny. There's some shadows of the themes in the Heisei trilogy in how Toru and Kosuke experience Gamera differently, and, as a result, have wildly differing interpretations of him and his role in their lives. That's it, though. In my introduction, I spoke about how difficult it is to approach some films, and I named the (in)famous *Son of Godzilla* as a sterling example of that concept. Well, add *Gamera the Brave* to the list. Unlike the Heisei trilogy, there's just not a lot of meat on those turtle bones.

Just as an aside, Shusuke Kaneko would go on to direct *Godzilla, Mothra, and King Ghidorah: Giant Monsters All-Out Attack*, which also plays with our expectations for kaiju. Godzilla is a villain of an intensity not seen since 1954, and symbolizes the collective anger of the Japanese war dead, who are tired of being forgotten over the generations. Mothra is a hero, of course, and so is Baragon, but Kaneko re-casts King Ghidorah as a hero as well, and not just *a* hero, but *the* hero, who absorbs Mothra's and Baragon's life essences in order to survive the onslaught from Godzilla. It's a deft move to flip Godzilla from at least "apathetic" to pure aggression toward humanity, and to flip Ghidorah to a hero of folkloric origins, away from the typical alien aggressor background that Ghidorah usually labors under.

This, on a sort of meta level, forces viewers to go through the same sort of examination that Ayana and Asagi go through in their world: which kaiju is the hero? Which is the villain? And what is "victory?," for defeating Godzilla, even temporarily, means a further disconnect from the angered Japanese war dead. Indeed, even though Godzilla is "defeated" at the end, his disembodied heart continues to beat on the ocean floor, a continual warning that the same unaddressed issues will continue to reform and re-propagate, until, finally, there's another battle, and then another.

Humanity will have to change, or die trying, or, more plainly, die in a willfully ignorant state.

A closer examination of the themes and ideas in the run from *Gamera: Guardian of the Universe* to *Gamera: Revenge of Iris* slowly reveals an ever-deepening plot and a question that is rarely asked in kaiju film: what is the human cost, and are we comfortable with it? In some ways, in the Gamera universe that Kaneko created, humans are confronted with morally gray kaiju, even those we normally assume are heroes, and we're asked to pick sides. Is it wrong to wish for the annihilation of (most of) humanity in order to save the planet? Probably. But is it wrong to hope that a kaiju just randomly decides that humanity is "good enough" somehow, and can exist at that kaiju's mercy? Probably not.

It's a theme that's been around science fiction for decades now, from the very moment that Klaatu and Gort zipped away on their flying saucer in *The Day the Earth Stood Still*, with a warning that humanity was headed toward destruction with their warlike ways, and, simply put, don't spread it around the universe. The message has changed only a little; as the Cold War dissipated and wars continued unabated, but continued to be almost wholly localized in various hotspots as proxy wars of a sort, the danger humans pose most on the global level has more plainly become the long-lasting destruction of the environment, and, as a result, the planet. Except, in this reality, there's no kaiju to intervene, for good or for ill.

No, this is a world we have to exist in all on our own. Every day.

10

The Legendary Dr. Serizawa

In my first book, *The Kaiju Film*, I discussed how the portrayal of Godzilla in *Godzilla* (2014) was somewhat sympathetic toward his Japanese origins. I still believe that, because it was truly an international production, and, even as you get American and British perspectives tossed into the mix, you still have numerous nods and ideas culled from the original Japanese property. It's a mélange, in other words, and so there wasn't a complete eschewing of the Japanese origins of Godzilla, although, as Americans have been known to do with Godzilla properties, the origins are often slightly manipulated to give Americans a "pass" for the bombings of Hiroshima and Nagasaki.

Yet, over time, as more Legendary films get released, I've come to the understanding that there has been a slow revision of Godzilla's purpose and origins which has become clearer, and these origins have become much more Western-friendly. This means that Godzilla and Kong, in their respective franchises and team-ups, have basically become overly (and overtly) pro–Western in their stances, and, at times, marginalize or outright ignore Godzilla's origins. Here's the idea: I think that Ken Watanabe's character, Ishiro Serizawa, is a sort of canary in the coal mine throughout the Godzilla films, and, as his character becomes more and more altered to fit into the standard "we didn't do it, and if we did, it probably wasn't that bad" American perspective toward kaiju and nuclear weapons in the Godzilla adaptations. By the time of *Godzilla vs. Kong*, Serizawa and his legacy—his literal son, in a blink-and-you-might-miss-him sort of way—are completely revised and the message is clear: *this* Godzilla is fully American.

Although I enjoyed both *Godzilla* (2014) and *Godzilla: King of the Monsters*, I found myself somewhat befuddled by how Dr. Ishiro Serizawa's role and how his purpose changed dramatically from film to film. I'm loath to be too harsh on *King of the Monsters* because of my own enjoyment of the film (I'm a sucker for Mothra, what can I say?), but the loose portrayal of Serizawa—from his reintroduction to his sudden introduction to the backseat to his somewhat bizarre character turn—continues to confound.

American kaiju films, or their adaptations, have long wrestled with trying—and often failing—to balance the somewhat pro-nuclear messages that dominated 1950s American science fiction with the fact that creatures like Godzilla and Gamera, among others, are clearly borne out of, and destructive precisely because of, American nuclear testing. Thus, adapting a kaiju like Godzilla—a living, walking symbol of nuclear aggression as well as the generalized trauma of a population that are the collective victims of the only nuclear attacks in world history—into American or Westernized ideas is quite the culture shock for all involved.

Americans, after all, and American film companies, have to attempt to reconcile the pain, anguish, and horror of being a nuclear aggressor while also co-opting a certified money-making story into their own worldview. For Japanese viewers, however, an icon that's a symbol of a collective national trauma is co-opted by the very people who created that trauma. As such, repeated adaptations or manipulations of Godzilla by American studios, meant for primarily American audiences, have often attempted to recast Godzilla in a light that's more forgiving to America and its foreign policy decisions, even as Japanese films make no bones about chafing under American influence.*

In 1998, the barely recognizable Americanized Godzilla was indeed the result of nuclear testing, but it wasn't *American* nuclear testing. Instead, it was the French! Blame them! And, alongside that, it's the American military that ultimately saves the day, defeating Godzilla before the creature can cause too much widespread destruction. By the time we get to the Legendary universe of Godzilla, starting in 2014, Americans have actually been recast as somewhat heroic with their nuclear bombing, using the guise of "tests" to send Godzilla away and otherwise keep the secret of kaiju hidden from the world a bit longer. In this regard, Godzilla is a "force of nature," an "alpha predator" that actually requires nuclear energy to survive. And these films—both are direct American "reboots" of Godzilla—share much in common with American re-edited versions of *Godzilla* (turned into *Godzilla, King of the Monsters!*) and *The Return of Godzilla* (edited into *Godzilla 1985*). In almost every instance, Americans, the American military, and American nuclear power are re-cast as heroic, or, at the very least, not as dangerous as they used to be.

In some ways, it feels like Dr. Ishiro Serizawa from the Legendary Godzilla franchise follows the same path over the course of the (thus far)

---

*Even the relatively mild-mannered *Shin Ultraman*, the most recent kaiju film as of the writing of this book, takes a few digs at American hegemony. With the presence of Ultraman causing no shortage of diplomatic travails, we're reminded that "being a dominant country must be fun," as the United States forces Japan to turn over their meager intelligence on Ultraman. Asami is tasked with the chore, and angrily calls Japan a "vassal state," while wondering why the U.S. doesn't just use their own intelligence.

trilogy of Godzilla films. There's some minor resemblances between Dr. Daisuke Serizawa and his Americanized counterpart, of course; Daisuke Serizawa was injured in World War II and sports an eyepatch as a result. He has a passion to use science to explain the world and to try to create knowledge that would benefit the world. Dr. Ishiro Serizawa, too, has ties to World War II as well. His father survived the Hiroshima nuclear attack, and this version of Serizawa continues to hope that science, and, specifically, his research on Titans (the Legendary keyword for kaiju) will help the world.

There's a certain aspect to *Godzilla: King of the Monsters* that makes the film seem to skew more toward a certain conservatism. The "bad guys" are eco-terrorists who hatch a cockamamie scheme to reset the world because of the imminent destruction of the planet through overpopulation and pollution, among other things. In order to conduct this reset, they use a device that brings forward not the hero kaiju in Godzilla, but breaks free King Ghidorah, the "evil" kaiju that is established as completely alien to the planet. As viewers, we're supposed to identify with Dr. Emma Russell's sudden recognition that maybe destroying the planet in order to save it may be quite the daft idea; at this point, she turns more into a hero, but her transgression of aligning with the eco-terrorists ultimately means that she can't survive the events of the film.

Additionally, the portrayal of the American military in *King of the Monsters* is far more sympathetic than in *Godzilla*. Of course, it's expected that the military in *Godzilla* would be at a relative loss for how to cope with the sudden appearance of kaiju; and so, their ridiculous plan to lure the MUTOs with nukes and then nuke them is as untenable as it is wholly American: if you can't solve a problem, bomb it. But the more imperialistic stance of the American military and its quasi-military arms, such as MONARCH, reclaims the standard pomp and righteous destruction of the American viewpoints on an international scale. In *King of the Monsters*, the American military literally backs up Godzilla as he comes to shore, flying past him to launch an initial assault on King Ghidorah. Never mind about the Japanese origins, the American movie makers seem to be saying, he's *ours* now.

"To be clear," W. Scott Poole writes of *Skull Island* and *King of the Monsters*, "the popular films are not kaiju for readers of Howard Zinn" (333). It's little wonder, then, that a spokesperson for an alternative, somewhat non-imperialistic view in Dr. Serizawa is at first shunted to the side in favor of All-American Mark and then given the role of sacrifice by embracing nuclear weapons. Dr. Serizawa, exit stage left.

Of course, one of the benefits of creating a kaiju film is that you can draw in audiences who just want to see "big dumb fun" (a phrase I see

112 The Kaiju Connection

often on social media when describing movies like *Godzilla vs. Kong*) and to simply abandon or otherwise toss the human plots to the background. So, to be fair, in-depth characterization and the politics of the day are most likely secondary considerations for those who work on creating a kaiju film in the United States. Yet, Dr. Serizawa's change in prestige and his overall character arc from film to film is problematic, to say the least, and doesn't hold up to any sort of prolonged examination.

I know. In the introduction, I noted a few reviews of *The Kaiju Film* where I was chastised for being too "political," so, if you're one of those folks, feel free to skip on to the next chapter. But Serizawa's changes in character and perspective only cement some of the worst aspects of the Legendary series, and even more intriguing is that they come in the form of Mark, a supposed "animal behaviorist" hired by MONARCH as a consultant. His qualifications are suspect, especially when compared with Serizawa's impressive resume.

But let's take it from the top. Serizawa is one of the leads in *Godzilla*, and he is presented as a knowledgeable scientist who has been "following" kaiju for decades at this point. He's held in high esteem by his colleagues, but is ultimately shunted aside by the U.S. military.* There's, of course, a lot of discussion about how *Godzilla* would have shaken out as a film if Bryan Cranston's character, Joe Brody, didn't get killed about halfway through the film, and it's mostly because Cranston and Watanabe were the most magnetic actors on the screen. With Joe Brody dead, and Watanabe's Dr. Ishiro Serizawa written in such a way as to make him a side-plot moralizer and exposition engine rather than a true scientific adviser, there's precious little else other than the primary Ford Brody Adventure, with lots of explosions, military bombast, and geographic hopping.

Yet, in *Godzilla*, Serizawa feels like, if only briefly, an important part of the film in the few moments he gets plentiful screen time. He serves as a counterpoint to the American military's "bomb it into oblivion" strategy (or, more honestly, the "lure it elsewhere and bomb it into oblivion" strategy), and reminds Admiral Stenz of the deep moral responsibility and consideration that should be employed while discussing using nuclear weapons. But, to paraphrase Homer Simpson, we see that the American military views nuclear weapons as the cause of, and solution to, all of our problems. It's a sentiment that echoes the 1950s American science fiction film, where nuclear energy in some form saved the day in *The Beast from*

---

*This is a common theme in a lot of "versus" films, and *Godzilla* is no exception: the government and/or the military, or quasi-military organizations, often take the lead roles, tossing the scientists who actually know what they're talking about into the background. This, naturally, leads to often flaccid and inept responses. More on this in the "Science and Faith: The Solo Kaiju Adventures" chapter.

10. The Legendary Dr. Serizawa   113

20,000 Fathoms, It Came from Beneath the Sea, and *The Magnetic Monster,* among others. In this regard, Serizawa's presence is a gentle rejoinder against this thought process, even though he's wholly ignored.

But something dramatic changes in *Godzilla: King of the Monsters.* Serizawa's character gets a bit more screen time, but his previous portrayal is almost completely flipped from the "let them fight" ideal, where the world just stands aside and humans join the chain of natural events and hope for the best, rather than trying to out-muscle kaiju and causing more damage in the process.

Suffice to say, I remain absolutely perplexed by the introduction of Mark as an "animal behaviorist" brought in to consult with MONARCH. I understand that Mark's primary qualification is that he's the ex of the woman who has a device that can communicate, on a base level, with kaiju, and that she's become smitten with a terrorist organization, but Mark's role seems to be extraordinarily outsized. Keep in mind that Serizawa is an established scientist who has been studying kaiju and kaiju behavior for *decades* at the point of *Godzilla: King of the Monsters,* and had access to all of MONARCH's considerable resources while doing so. Yet, there are moments where Serizawa takes a backseat to Mark, often by literally turning and asking Mark what he thinks about behavior that Serizawa *should* already know, having dedicated so much time researching kaiju. There's no more egregious moment in *King of the Monsters* than when MONARCH scientists, including Mark and Serizawa are in the underwater base specifically designed to track and study Godzilla. Godzilla floats around until Mark suddenly brings up that Godzilla is performing an "intimidation display" and then adds an animal leaves its hunting grounds "because it's threatened by something."

That's all well and good, but the character of Mark doesn't really need to say that. Serizawa and perhaps even his colleague, Dr. Graham, should already know this. This begs the question in many ways as to why Mark even exists as a character in the Legendary universe, if only to supplant Serizawa as the "primary" scientist, who is a little younger, much more Western, and more able to engage in the sort of swashbuckling finales we see in, say, *King of the Monsters.**

That's more from a logistical, film production standard; I get that. Here's where the depiction of Serizawa slips a bit: his untimely and almost wholly unnecessary death. *King of the Monsters* is rife with moments where the writers clearly telegraph their intentions, and Serizawa's death, which comes, essentially, at the cost of a jammed door, is one that allows

---

*Also the reason why Bryan Cranston's character dies in *Godzilla* (2014): to make way for the more physically capable Aaron Taylor-Johnson who can more believably engage in numerous stunts and action sequences.

them to write out the character. But in doing so, they completely invert the narrative of Serizawa.

In *Godzilla*, Serizawa frequently intoned the uselessness of mankind's attempts to stop the kaiju battles and was deeply perturbed about the often flip remarks about using nuclear weapons among the American military. "This is madness," he tells Stenz, before showing Stenz his father's watch, frozen on the exact time "Little Boy" detonated over Hiroshima. Much of Serizawa's concern is how their attempts to pacify or kill Godzilla will lead to an imbalance in nature, and, without Godzilla's presence, the world would seriously reorganize itself without the alpha predator.

But Serizawa's disdain for nuclear weaponry is set aside in *Godzilla: King of the Monsters*. Yes, Godzilla is threatened with his own destruction at the hands of King Ghidorah, but it is Serizawa this time who suggests using a nuclear weapon, a massive shift in characterization brought on by desperation, sure, but in doing so, he also disregards a lifelong trauma born out of family tragedy. Frankly, the idea of nuclear weapons—and, more generally, weapons of mass destruction—moves from the more abhorrent stance of the original *Godzilla* of 1954 and more into the realm of the American science fiction nuclear weapon boosterism of films such as *Beast from 20,000 Fathoms* or *It Came from Beneath the Sea*, where nuclear weapons are indeed the cause of, but more importantly, the solution to, the problems that are in front of the audience.

Mark is a somewhat unwilling (and unwitting) participant in MONARCH and the U.S. military's symbiotic relationship, but he ultimately represents the military's balance of power tilting to ally itself with Godzilla and becoming the heroes of their own story ... again. This matches the growing imperialistic stance of *Skull Island* as well, where "U.S. troops can land in an 'un–American jungle' [...] and find themselves welcomed and befriended" (Poole 333). W. Scott Poole places this in the broader context of the political environment running in the background of the years encompassing *Godzilla* (2014), *Skull Island*, and *King of the Monsters*. Naturally, *Godzilla vs. Kong* will follow the same arc: "These popular films don't bother to narrate empire [....] They assume it" (Poole 333). There's a centrality to the American perspective, in other words, that simply can't allow a Japanese character who runs counter to that perspective to exist in the film. As *Godzilla* (2014) turned into the more bombastic *King of the Monsters*, Serizawa's presence as a challenger to the rah-rah American proceedings and outlook was contradictory, and, as such, his role needed to be reduced, inverted, and then eliminated.

In other words, the Serizawa of *Godzilla* was an expert standing on tenuous ground because he is on the outside looking in, not only as a scientist, but also as a decided pacifist and someone who is clearly anti-nuclear.

This needed to change if the American military and MONARCH were going to cast their lots and become active players in the kaiju war zones by the end of *Godzilla* and certainly by the start of *King of the Monsters*. So, Serizawa simply couldn't exist anymore, and there is no better way to allow him to give a tacit endorsement than to have him embrace a nuclear weapon in death.

Of course, in *Godzilla* (1954), nuclear testing is categorically rejected as any sort of solution, and a more powerful weapon, the Oxygen Destroyer, is an even more destructive weapon that is treated with fear; while it is indeed the "solution" to the problem of Godzilla's continued existence, it is also a dangerous, world-ending device that forces Serizawa to destroy not only his lab and his notes, but himself. As if that weren't plain enough, we're told that with more nuclear tests, "another Godzilla might appear," and this is definitely a negative thing.

Fast forward to *Godzilla* (2014), and the same tone is somewhat invoked for the film, and early teasers featured quotes from Oppenheimer, tying destruction, nuclear weapons, and Godzilla into a bundle of negative associations. Yet, the film itself backs off of that tone somewhat, with the American military using nuclear weapons as a part of an overall strategy to defeat Godzilla over the objections of Serizawa, who serves as a sort of moral center for the film. Meanwhile, the bravado of the American military continues to falter throughout the film, and their plan of using nuclear weapons as "lures" for the MUTOs and for Godzilla fails at nearly every turn, ending up with the near-destruction of San Francisco (by nuclear weapons, at least). Yet, even in *Godzilla*, the idea of nuclear weapons' having negative consequences are generally pooh-poohed; yes, they "stopped" Godzilla in the 1950s, but it was no big deal, and the MUTO egg helpfully absorbed the radiation from a nuclear meltdown in Janjira.

Even so, there's definitely a sense of a Pandora's Box that Gareth Edwards, the director of *Godzilla* tends to promote, but that sense is almost completely lost in *Godzilla: King of the Monsters*; it reflects the Heisei period in numerous ways, including in overall tone, darkness, and violence, but, most of all, in its portrayal of the military, or quasi-military structures, as heroic protagonists. Although *Godzilla* features a military main character in Ford Brody, he's generally tossed about by circumstances beyond his control, shorn of any meaningful weaponry, and generally just blown about by the winds of the constantly changing plans. No, *Godzilla* places the military as a relatively ineffectual sideshow, with Serizawa and Joe Brody functioning well as "ground-level" scientists determined to unravel the problem and its causes. We're supposed to assume the ineptitude of the American military in this film, with plenty of evidence to back it up.

But, by the time of *King of the Monsters*, MONARCH has super-weapons, including an aircraft that can fly at ridiculous speeds, massive research bases, and more resources than the world's governments combined. And so, MONARCH and the U.S. military lead the way, zipping from location to location on their super aircraft and generally using numerous weapons at their disposal to try to stop the battle between King Ghidorah and Godzilla. At one point, the U.S. military even breaks out its own Oxygen Destroyer, which has zero effect on Ghidorah, and nearly kills Godzilla. That *King of the Monsters* provides an Oxygen Destroyer—a weapon of unfathomable power in *Godzilla* (1954)—and it's dropped by the U.S. military with nary another thought to the longstanding ethical implications of using it, further heightens the somewhat nonchalant attitude of the Western perspective on weapons of mass destruction. But the military almost kills Godzilla, leading them to hatch a plan to explode another nuclear weapon in front of Godzilla's sleeping form.

This is the plot point upon which the reversal in characterization of Serizawa turns. With Godzilla injured and Mothra floating in the sky above his location, King Ghidorah, Rodan, and any number of other kaiju are destroying the world. The only solution: nuclear weapons (of course!), and it's Serizawa who is not only perfectly fine with the idea, but happily transports the nuclear weapon to Godzilla's underwater lair so he can revive the beast. Not only that, but before he departs the mini-sub, Serizawa turns and physically hands over his notes and his research to Mark, a sort of scientific passing of the torch from a Japanese scientist to an American scientist; it's such a bizarre and cloying moment in what should be an easy character moment for *King of the Monsters*—after all, who doesn't love a heroic sacrifice? But it just doesn't seem to ring true of the character established a film earlier, and it's easy to wonder if Serizawa's slow "Americanization" rapidly accelerated in *King of the Monsters*.

Such a long way from "let them fight," where Serizawa seems to insinuate that Godzilla will win on his own, and, if not, then humanity had a nice run, no big deal. In fact, Serizawa in *Godzilla* repeatedly intones about how small and useless humanity is in the face of the Titans who are now awakening and stomping across the Earth.

I suppose one natural extension of this argument would be that King Ghidorah is established as an alien presence, not of this Earth, and so, we're left with the home team (Godzilla and Mothra) left as defenders of the "natural order" of the planet. This would give Serizawa some reason to be sufficiently more pro–Godzilla than he seemed in *Godzilla*, especially if you take into consideration the fact that he was aware that the MUTOs had *previously killed other Titans with ease*, something he discovered during his research, and a fact that he no doubt reinforced with

10. The Legendary Dr. Serizawa 117

his offscreen research in the span between *Godzilla* (2014) and *King of the Monsters*. Ergo, Serizawa's interference in *King of the Monsters* reinforces the natural order rather than defies it.

But, there's not much to tell us that Godzilla won't return over time: in fact, Mothra is there, trying to summon him, and we know that Godzilla draws radioactivity (the good, natural kind, I suppose) from the Earth. He's on a trickle charger. Essentially, Serizawa's sacrifice is simply a shot in the arm to the proceedings, a jump-start. Yes, if they didn't detonate the nuclear bomb in front of Godzilla's face in his underwater lair, millions of people would have died under King Ghidorah's reign, but … how is that all that different from the MUTOs possibly defeating Godzilla and having a ton of baby MUTOs to take over the planet? Serizawa clearly believes in Godzilla as the alpha predator … until he doesn't.

Just to compare, I encourage you to take a look at *Godzilla* (1954) and *Godzilla Raids Again*. Dr. Yamane makes a cameo appearance in *Godzilla Raids Again*, and his characterization is remarkably consistent. In *Godzilla* (1954), he only chafes against the idea of immediately trying to kill Godzilla, feeling instead that this is a massive bonanza for scientific research. Yet, he changes his demeanor when he sees and understands how Godzilla cannot possibly exist in the world with humans: one or the other will have to go. But Yamane never quite takes an active role in killing Godzilla; he functions as a witness to the proceedings and offers mild advice.

So, when a new Godzilla appears on Iwato Island, this time alongside another kaiju, Anguirus, Yamane flies from Tokyo to share clips of the original *Godzilla* with a gathered group of police, politicians, scientists, and military personnel. We're all screwed, he says. Well, not exactly, but he lays out the reality of the situation. The original Godzilla was killed by a once-in-a-lifetime device that's now lost and can never be discovered again, and the original Godzilla was responsible for untold death and destruction that the country was still recovering from, years later. Add to the mix not only a new Godzilla but another kaiju that's equally destructive, and the only hope that Japan—and the rest of the world—has is to see if there are ways to placate or otherwise distract Godzilla.

Destroying Godzilla is off the table, in Yamane's view; a total impossibility, and with the unknown powers and presence of Anguirus, their return means that Japan has a bitter pill to swallow. Instead of humans taking an active role in "fighting" the threat, all they can do is try to put together some form of evacuation plan and momentary distraction. Then we wait and hope for the best. Anguirus and Godzilla in *Raids Again* are monsters, abominations, and ultimately can be treated only in much the same way as incoming weather events.

118   The Kaiju Connection

In fact, we see Yamane's advice is taken to heart immediately, and the military focuses primarily on self-defense. Godzilla's movement patterns are reported with the breathless fervor that people often reserve for massive weather patterns such as hurricanes or far-ranging blizzards. And, when it becomes apparent that Godzilla is heading toward a particular area, people are asked to shelter or evacuate. The Japanese Self-Defense Force only attempts to use one weapon: flares fired from aircraft, borrowing Yamane's idea that Godzilla is attracted to bright lights. This, coupled with the blackout conditions and the evacuations, create a new paradigm for life in Japan as well as the rest of the world. A sort of Godzilla Watch, with humans permanently (or semi-permanently) consigned to avoiding Godzilla and doing their best to survive his appearances.

This is remarkably consistent characterization and world-building for *Godzilla* (1954) and *Godzilla Raids Again* as well as Dr. Yamane. This *should* be Serizawa's path as well, if Serizawa were written consistently in the Legendary films. Serizawa's main goal in *King of the Monsters* should be to warn others not to play second fiddle to an animal behaviorist— it should not be to actively try to circumvent the natural order that he endorses in *Godzilla*. Yes, in *King of the Monsters*, Godzilla is hurt and sent away by human hands, and, perhaps Serizawa feels that he is rebalancing the scales a bit, but to have a Japanese scientist warning an American admiral about the use of nuclear weapons and then being the first to volunteer on a suicide mission to use a nuclear weapon is quite the head-spinning turnaround.

Interestingly, Michael Dougherty, who directed *King of the Monsters* seemed to, in at least one interview, equate Serizawa's entire character with the sacrifice; he loves the scene "because of what it is saying. The idea of a human being sacrificing his life for Godzilla is something really noble" (Bernstein 88). This gives Serizawa a somewhat problematic end, as if his existence in the film franchise was merely to give way to Mark and then die by using a weapon he absolutely loathed just a few years earlier.

Of course, there's more depth that can be read into it, a sort of "he walks the walk" sacrifice where Serizawa's sacrifice is supposed to show us how desperate the situation is. But that sort of desperation on the part of MONARCH or humanity in general is never quite made clear; Serizawa simply wants to tip the scales and remove the "false king" Titan through his actions. Yet, there's this symbolic sense that an American film company, after employing several side excuses for their nuclear attacks in *Godzilla*, has now had the lone Japanese character rather stoically endorse using nuclear weapons. It all feels uncomfortable.

Ultimately, there's most likely a large series of behind-the-scenes reasons why Ken Watanabe's Serizawa is at first pushed aside (some would

10. The Legendary Dr. Serizawa 119

successfully argue for the word "marginalized" here) and then ultimately killed, and, not only that, willingly killed at the hands of the very technology that he abhorred. For his part, Watanbe said in an interview with *Screen Rant* that he didn't feel Serizawa was "supporting" Godzilla in *King of the Monsters*, stating that "I didn't think about the competition to the creatures. They had the right to live" (Quizon). In a different interview pop culture blog *io9*, Brian Ashcraft asks Watanabe his opinion of Serizawa's sacrifice, and writes that "He replied that when he read it, he loved how the story centers around a scientist and how philosophical the movie gets regarding the relationship between humans, civilization, and science" (Ashcraft).

These are decided non-answers, and, in fact, it seems hard to pin down Watanabe's feelings about not only the death of his character, but also the sudden turn in characterization for Serizawa. Of course, some of this may be lost in translation, as Watanabe, especially in the interview with *Screen Rant*, seems confused by some of the questions, and the translator even steps in for additional clarification. And, naturally, there's also the possibility that Watanabe doesn't want to publicly disagree with the director or writers during the press tour promoting the film (although that didn't stop Juliette Binoche for *Godzilla,* who pointed out the minor roles of women in the movie to Greg Cwik on *Indiewire*).

To go just a step further, it feels like Serizawa is marginalized even more in *Godzilla vs. Kong.** No, he doesn't appear as a character, but his presumed son, Ren, is apparently a bad guy charged with telepathically controlling the remaining King Ghidorah head, and through that, the new Mechagodzilla. All of this information passes like a grounded lightning bolt past the viewer, and Ren Serizawa is soon dispatched with nary an extra thought in the film. On top of this is the fact that we don't even know for sure what relation is to Serizawa, other than an insinuation that he shares some form of "familial" tie to Ken Watanabe's character (Wallace 34). It's as if *Godzilla vs. Kong* simply went out of its way to build on the slow dissolution of Ishiro Serizawa as a character in *King of the Monsters* to completely erasing his legacy in *Godzilla vs. Kong*: not only is he dead, blown apart willingly by the very weapons he sought to admonish people against using, but someone in his family has broken with Dad and has instead decided to use kaiju and technology to rule and reorder the world on behalf of a massive corporation. This heel turn, if we can call it that, based on Ren Serizawa's minuscule presence in the film, essentially deletes and removes the more fully-fleshed and knowledgeable character built in *Godzilla* (2014).

---

*Ironically, Ishiro Serizawa's replacement, Mark, is essentially absent for much of *Godzilla vs. Kong* as well, with his character relegated to the classic kaiju film tropes of "panicked phone call maker" and "concerned starer at the sky"—roles often given over to extras.

120   **The Kaiju Connection**

By the end of *Godzilla vs. Kong*, nearly every lesson, caution, or maxim that Serizawa built in *Godzilla* is completely erased. Humans take an exceptionally active role in the affairs of kaiju, often trying to exploit them for greed and wealth, or, more simply, to try to tilt the balance of power back to humans. Kong is "nobly exploited" by humans and the positioning of Godzilla as a "force of nature"* rather than a walking symbol of American hegemonic nuclear aggression originated in the original *Godzilla*, falls away even further, leading the viewer to actively cheer for Godzilla (in *King of the Monsters*) and then acknowledge the massive kaiju as heroic, positioned alongside the very human Kong as an enemy of capitalistic enterprise (Berkowitz).

Consider all of these changes through a very short-term trilogy, with around eight years spread between the three films, and you can see, through the character of Serizawa, the slow re-absorption of a definitive Westernized view of Godzilla, one that repositions the kaiju itself away from its original purpose. If that's fine—and, in many ways, it's to be expected at this point, given the American-centric views of *Godzilla: King of the Monsters!* (1956), *Gammera, the Invincible* (1966), *The Return of Godzilla*, and *Godzilla*, (both 1998 and 2014)—then a greater sin is the reimagining of Dr. Daisuke Serizawa into Dr. Ishiro Serizawa, and his quick descent into near-marginalization to a comprehensive rewriting of his existence and purpose from film to film.

As I said, I enjoyed *Godzilla* and *Godzilla: King of the Monsters*; yet, if we can set aside the retooling of Godzilla's origins to become, if not pro–American, at least giving America an "out" for the use of nuclear weapons, it's much harder to set aside how the franchise created a sort of alternative Serizawa to lay out the rules of the new universe and then re-work them into even more of a pro-nuclear stance before ultimately symbolically disposing of the character and all of his thoughts. Ultimately, Dr. Ishiro Serizawa remains one of the most problematic pieces of an Americanized version of Godzilla we've seen in the long cinematic history of kaiju film.

---

*The American version of Godzilla as a "force of nature" removes most implications of nuclear weapons; Godzilla has literally existed millennia before the bomb was invented. For many Japanese movies that treat Godzilla as a weather event, ranging from *Godzilla Raids Again* to *Godzilla 2000*, among a few others, the mentions of nuclear energy and nuclear power still exist: Godzilla's creation and existence as a symbol of nuclear attacks and the resultant suffering rarely changes in Japanese productions, even if it is occasionally backgrounded.

11

Kong, Again and Again: The Son[s] of Kong

It's a filmmaking maxim that one of the worst things you can do while making a movie is to remind the viewer of better movies. In the case of *King Kong* and the numerous iterations, sequels (official and unofficial) homages, and parodies that have arrived over the years, there are plenty of reminders of 1933's Kong, and, as a result, there's a veritable bumper crop of films ranging from mediocre to outright awful that use the basic concept and ideas outlined in *King Kong* to often rather poor effect.

There's a reason behind the Kong-based popularity among production companies across the world. King Kong has been the focus of numerous copyright lawsuits over the years, leading to a hodgepodge of legal rulings about the status of the big ape and all of the properties associated with him, from the original book, the 1933 film, and the name and character of "King Kong."

But that hasn't stopped numerous companies from capitalizing on what is probably the second-most famous kaiju in the world (sorry, Gamera), and there's been more than a few attempts at re-writing and re-interpreting the basic plot and idea of *King Kong*. These attempts come from around the world, including Italy's *Yeti: Giant of the 20th Century*, Hong Kong's *Mighty Peking Man*, and England's *Konga*, alongside the more well-known examples, including Toho's own version of King Kong, who battled Godzilla (and was supposed to battle Ebirah), as well as his robot doppelganger, MechaniKong. And, of course, there's the numerous American sequels, reimaginings, and homages, ranging from *Son of Kong*, *King Kong* in 1976, *King Kong Lives* in 1986, *King Kong* in 2005, and simply "Kong" in *Kong: Skull Island* and *Godzilla vs. Kong*.

There's been plenty written about the "mainstream" Kong works, even though many of them are crafted only to slip past copyright laws, so I'll only follow them in passing here; instead, I want to discuss the oddities of the international Kong adaptations before circling around to the

121

new Legendary "Kong" creation. The story of *King Kong*, from the original 1933 movie, has become a cultural touchstone in the United States, with its themes of imperialism, capitalism, and modernity somehow layered so well underneath the surface of a giant ape falling in unrequited love with a young woman. This contextual information is somehow often lost in translation, it seems, and it just boils down to the familiar scenario of a lovely young woman who watches while a giant ape destroys and is ultimately destroyed. The heart of the original is lost, in many cases, replaced by the hollow shell. This, however, leads to new and unique homages to Kong that are, at times, difficult to watch, but also can be enlightening in terms of how large monsters are viewed through a different cultural lens outside of the United States and even Japan. And, if anything, these films often show exactly how *not* to approach the saga of Kong, reinforcing beliefs across the world that *King Kong* is an international classic for a reason.

Of course, there's the direct sequel, titled *Son of Kong*, rushed out just nine months after *King Kong*. It's hard to get a sense of this work, because the dual factors of being a quick cash-in, coupled with the very small screen time of Kong's son, makes it hard to read how Kong's son is supposed to be portrayed. Of course, the fact that Kong's son is still a child (and an orphaned one at that) means that he's smaller than Kong— almost Mighty Joe Young size—and generally not a "mature" version of Kong himself. Almost every time we see Kong's son, who gets the unfortunate nickname of Little Kong, he is in some form of peril; in fact, he's first introduced on the verge of death, drowning in a quicksand pit, and the combined efforts of Denham and Hilda* save him from his doom. In a neat little nod to *King Kong*, and a good way of establishing Denham's growth, Denham bandages little Kong's finger, playing on the sequence in *King Kong* where Denham stabs Kong in the finger, and Kong, confused, realizes that some people can be very dangerous.

This sort of mutual trust and a desire to please the humans around him, especially Denham and Hilda, is what makes Little Kong so different from his father, and perhaps, his character tilts a little more toward inspirational and apologetic glurge than a timeless classic. Little Kong engages in some battles, mostly to defend Denham and Hilda, and, at one point during a battle against a giant cave bear, turns to the couple and seeks approval for his actions ... giving the bear ample time to mount another attack.

This is the way most of *Son of Kong* goes after Little Kong's introduction, and it's quite formulaic, with Little Kong constantly helping

---

*Hilda is only named in the credits, but we'll use that name to identify her. She's known as "kid" to Denham and her stage name is La Belle Helene.

11. Kong, Again and Again: The Son[s] of Kong

Denham and Hilda, whether it be finding treasure they are seeking, or battling off the other denizens of the island to save them, or even, most of all, sacrificing himself so that they can escape the island. Little Kong's final moments are his apparent drowning as he holds Denham in the air above flood waters just long enough for a rescue boat to get to Denham. In many ways, this gives us a happier ending than *King Kong*, one that's free of that nettlesome moralizing about humanity's place in the world. No, *Son of Kong* reassures its viewers that humans are indeed on top of the food chain and animals—even giant ones—exist to serve us, or, well, at least the nicer ones do. In this regard, Little Kong has much more in common with the small monkeys that perform a show earlier in the movie on an almost metatextual level. The monkeys are on a stage and performing for the meager approval of the collected humans who have trained them; Little Kong is on the screen, entertaining the collective humans who have paid to see them.

But Little Kong is simply a pastiche of his literary father, a poorer facsimile that essentially avoids all moral conundrums and seriousness with a more lighthearted, acceptable, and most of all, very human-friendly perspective. There's no long-lasting critiques of colonialism or capitalism here, there's no moralizing about man's place in the world in the food chain or the natural order. All that exists in *Son of Kong* is a happy ending. Denham gets to live (thanks to Little Kong), gets the wealth he seeks (thanks to Little Kong), and even finds a long-term relationship (thanks to Little Kong). Little Kong is merely the axis on which a standard and often trite adventure/romance revolves, and, as such, his thematic hollowness has often left the film sidelined in many critical discussions.

King Kong himself, however, or a reasonable interpretation of Kong, won't reappear until almost thirty years after his debut. So, it's important to consider the Toho Showa version of Kong, as he is the true first "homage" to the original *King Kong* and creates a sort of alternate universe of Kongs and Kong-like beings that will pepper the landscape of science fiction and kaiju cinema for the next sixty years.

The King Kong of *King Kong vs. Godzilla* is cast and described (in the American version) as a more intelligent kaiju, one that can outsmart the more reptilian Godzilla, who relies primarily on brute strength and stamina to win the day. And even though this version of King Kong doesn't necessarily have too much of a direct relationship with humans— there's a brief and forgettable sequence of Kong traditionally and briefly kidnapping a female character—his intelligence makes him more innately humanistic than the original version. While the King Kong of the original 1933 film reacted in a sympathetic way, he never quite achieves getting the audience to view him as human; he was simply a tragic figure that we

124   **The Kaiju Connection**

empathize with and we allow his rampage and destruction to be laid at our feet, accepting the blame as the true destructive forces in the world, masquerading as "civilization."

This King Kong, however, uses strategy to defeat Godzilla, taking his chances at some segments of both battles, and knowing when to retreat and hide. Even so, it's a battle between two rather impersonal kaiju. Godzilla's presence hasn't really been established by this point in his career—his third film—and remains animalistic as well, not quite the family-friendly handshaking-with-my-pal-the-robot kaiju, but also no longer really the force of destruction from the original *Godzilla*. And Kong himself isn't much better, although the film spends a lot of time establishing his characteristics, including his propensity for enjoying red berry juice and passing out while natives worship him.

But this fails, too, somehow, and Kong never really connects with the audience; the battles between Kong and Godzilla were technical mastery at work, but there's no real sense other than "let them fight." The few moments where Kong interacts with a young woman, in this case, Fumiko, seem more like throwaway homages to the original *King Kong* than providing anything of substance. Kong's infatuation with Fumiko is a side plot, never really developed, and quickly forgotten. Unlike other young women we see Kong and Kong-like creations interact with, Fumiko doesn't fuel the plot or even really has much of an impact; she gets picked up by Kong, and the collected heroes save her by knocking him out.

Add to this the odd power scaling we see with Kong, and he becomes even more divorced from any sort of empathy on our part. He not only brushes off numerous blasts from Godzilla's atomic breath—which has been established as terribly deadly in the previous two Godzilla films— but he also manages to become more powerful when exposed to electricity, even storing it and then zapping Godzilla with it.* This somehow makes Kong, who already perhaps looks a little silly, into just another depersonalized kaiju with no real backstory to speak of; he exists, and the people in the cast tend to treat him less as an animal *or* a person and instead talk about him as either a sideshow attraction or a walking weapon of mass destruction. In fact, the final battle between Kong and Godzilla is simply cast as "let's hope they kill each other." We, as viewers, can enjoy the battle and all of the requisite silliness that leads up to the battle, but this version of Kong is significantly more hollow and "flat" than the 1933 King Kong.

King Kong Escapes, however, continues the tradition of Kong being smitten with a young woman, but adds a new twist. This time, this woman,

---

*Maybe it's the purist in me, but these sorts of bizarre power upgrades can be distracting in kaiju films once the character has been established. Mothra suddenly shooting laser beams in *Godzilla vs. Mothra: Battle for Earth* seems like anathema.

11. Kong, Again and Again: The Son[s] of Kong 125

a Navy nurse named Lieutenant Susan Watson, who can seemingly "control" Kong. When he first discovers her on his new island, Mondo, she is immediately cast as the hero. Watson is threatened by the goofy and mostly powerless Gorosaurus, whose main attack is a jumping kick reminiscent of a kangaroo, and Kong wakes up and intervenes to save her. Even so, she remains frightened of him until she understands that he has some form of feelings for her ("he's a male," Carl Nelson explains), and she is able to interact with him using simple commands.* At one point, Kong, who has been captured and hypnotized so he can mine a rare element, is enraged by Watson being placed in danger. He breaks free from his cage and begins to rampage,† saving the day and rescuing our heroes.

This all leads to Kong being somewhat more relatable than the version that battles Godzilla; he's humanized almost from the start, with humanistic motivations and desires, but, as we will see, it's important, too, that these base desires don't really cross any lines. Kong is also significantly de-powered from the fight against Godzilla. He seems much more vulnerable, and his battle against his rival MechaniKong shows him essentially getting pummeled and beaten while trying to rescue Watson and keep her safe. And Kong doesn't even win the day; MechaniKong is defeated by the humans, as Madame Piranha (seriously) damages MechaniKong's remote controls, essentially deactivating him and sending him tumbling to his death, where he breaks up and explodes upon impact.

Kong then, at Watson's prodding, destroys the ship of the mad scientist Dr. Who (seriously), before deciding that he's essentially had enough of humanity in general, and begins to swim home. As Watson calls after him, Carl Nelson declares, rightfully, that Kong has had his fill of "what we call civilization." It's not exactly a closing line on the level of "it was beauty that killed the beast," but it does sum up the events nicely. Kong was fine living on Mondo Island and occasionally kicking the stuffing out of Gorosaurus, but his brush with humanity showed him the worst of their existence: greed, madness, power, and violence, just to start. In this regard, as human viewers, we can identify with Kong and his desire simply to leave humanity behind and while away the days without the sort of base desires that fuel human motivations. This is, interestingly, a Kong that will be, as we will see, the closest iteration for quite some time to the original *King Kong*: primitive, but aware, and occasionally frightened, by humanity's cancerous and destructive nature. For many of the remaining Kong

---

*One of the challenges of watching *King Kong Escapes* is Susan Watson's dubbing, and her constant pleas of "Kong? Koooooong! Kong?" can be taxing at best.
†In one of the symptoms of a fast and inexpensive shoot, Susan Watson screams for help, Kong starts to break free, and the next scene, with the panicked men, *doesn't show Watson at all* before she reappears back in the same place as Kong escapes.

126   The Kaiju Connection

and Kong-like films we will explore, there's not going to be much of this nuance.

The most impressive aspect of *Yeti: Giant of the 20th Century*—besides, perhaps, a helicopter that is the most adorable* miniature in cinematic history—is just how much the cast and crew seem to genuinely believe that no one in the audience has ever seen any iteration of Kong, ever. Created as a "fill in the gap" sort of production after another rights battle erupted over King Kong in 1976, the joint Canadian/Italian venture has been largely forgotten, revived only by the offbeat film aficionados at Code Red DVD. The film's ponderous run-time of just over an hour and forty minutes† features long sequences of the Yeti staring at Jane and her younger, silent, brother, Herbie.

In fact, the slow, dubbed dialogue coupled with the almost zen-like pacing at times makes the film feel otherworldly in places, like a Dario Argento film with kaiju, and at other times, almost laugh-out-loud funny precisely because of unusual timing and odd character beats, like a Dario Argento film with kaiju. One of the oddest beats in the film occurs early on, as Jane is talking with Cliff, the dashing scientist, and casually mentions the source of Herbie's condition: he's been mute since both of his parents died in a fiery plane crash. It would be a tragic moment if it didn't have the heights of absurdity. The flat, emotionless dubbing, coupled with people randomly moving trucks in the background, with scenes of a work crew blasting a block of ice with flamethrowers while large Yeti feet begin to appear just a few yards away.

The Yeti himself is at times large, a human "giant" of seven to ten feet, and, other times, an actual giant of about seven to ten stories, and makes sounds not unlike Sanda and Gaira from *War of the Gargantuas*. In all of the pastiches and probable parodies found within the film, the mimicry of the basic idea of Kong remains. Yeti is "discovered," Yeti falls in love with a young woman, Yeti is brought to civilization and hates every second of it, Yeti rampages through the city, Yeti is asked to leave for his own safety, abandoning a heartbroken young woman (and Herbie, and his dog, who fantastically gets an opening credit at the start of the film) to mourn, and wonder how and why humanity has gone so far adrift.

The Yeti is also strangely sexualized throughout the film, almost more than Jane herself (although, compared to other Kong and Kong-like movies, she remains modestly dressed throughout). At one point, she and Herbie are being carried away, and she places her hand next to his sunken nipple; within seconds, the nipple pops up, and Yeti looks down at her like

---

*A *very* close second is the hover car in *King Kong Escapes*.
†The West German cut of the film moves the length from 105 minutes to 81 minutes, which feels like a much better runtime.

11. Kong, Again and Again: The Son[s] of Kong 127

the Fonz on a Saturday night. To Jane's credit, she is immediately repulsed, and the odd, one-way sexual attraction almost immediately dissipates, but ultimately colors their relationship as a kaiju-sized creature with inappropriate feelings and his younger and attractive female "friend."

In *King Kong* (1933), the giant kaiju protects the young woman from the world, perhaps a bit obsessively, but in *Yeti*, and as we will see, in *Mighty Peking Man*, it feels like the world needs to protect the young woman from the kaiju—this insertion of sexuality we see in these pastiches of *King Kong* subvert the original narrative, and not in a good way. Is this symbolism of the dreaded "male gaze"? As we know, any sexuality in kaiju or kaiju-related films is almost impossible to find, and so, when it happens in these films, it's quite jarring. We're used to our big kaiju being curious, perhaps, but mostly sexless. But, in *Yeti* and in *Mighty Peking Man*, the kaiju is in competition with a potential or realized male partner for the romantic attention of the young woman. In the case of the Yeti, his most direct competition is the swashbuckling and acerbic Cliff Chandler, who playfully and inappropriately prods at Jane, noting that she "might have some duties" with the Yeti when the professor opines that the Kong-like creature views her as his wife.

It's important to pause here to think of the "newer" Kong of 1976, who may have been just as randy as the Yeti in some instances. Dwan has little interest in Kong, and their first and lengthiest interaction has Dwan rambling somewhat incoherently about the Zodiac and her fear of heights before getting angry and punching Kong in the nose. This both angers and impresses Kong, but he refuses to let her escape. From there, a decidedly one-sided romance erupts, with Kong washing Dwan off in a nearby waterfall and then blowing her dry with his breath. At this point, Kong, who is benefiting from special effects by Rick Baker, appears considerably more human than his 1933 version, and the camera places the audience in the same position of admiring Dwan. Jessica Lange wasn't a trained actress at the time of her appearance in *King Kong*, she was a model, and the camera reminds us of this, as almost every sequence with Dwan, especially the waterfall, seems to be plucked out of a fashion spread.

Kong, in fact, even as he attempts to undress Dwan, barely reaches the level of a curious preteen. There's not really any sexual excitement from Kong that's palpable beyond him merely being smitten with a new toy. In fact, his attempt to undress Dwan, although girded with romantic musical cues, has all of the dispassion of a high schooler trying to dissect a frog. It feels like much of the romance isn't Kong being encouraged to feel smitten with Dwan; instead, it feels like the romance is supposed to be the *audience* feeling smitten with Dwan. Kong is just a conduit.

For Kong, he's cast as curious toward Dwan, but there's little to indicate anything that goes beyond that, even as he tries to remove her clothes.

128 The Kaiju Connection

Yes, there's some romantic language from Dwan: "hold on to me," she implores Kong as he meets his incredibly bloody end, but it's more of the affection of some form of sympathy or partnership. When Dwan miraculously teleports to the street below the World Trade Center where Kong lies dying, she turns away from Kong and calls out for Jack, her true love interest, a subplot that develops evenly throughout the movie. This version of Kong is, of course, more human, and thus more readily understood, through better special effects, to have some affection for Dwan, but it doesn't extend toward the Yeti's level of "husband and wife."

One of the oddities of *Yeti* is how this centralized "romance" doesn't quite succeed in any form of believability. This is odd, because the Yeti is played by a de facto human, the wonderfully named Mimmo Crao, and, as a result, the Yeti has a variety of facial expressions that Kong, for much of his existence as the proverbial "man in the rubber suit," does not. He leers, screams, cries, grimaces, and acts surprised, even in the 1976 version. Yet, the relationship between Herbie and his dog is almost given more emphasis than the Yeti's relationship to Jane, or anything else for that matter. After Jane, Herbie, and a group of police officers shoo away the Yeti, who recognizes that he's not fit for society, the collie, thought to be dead, suddenly reappears with blood on his chest. Herbie somehow sees the dog from a rather great distance, and the two run toward each other in slow motion *for the better part of three minutes* in run-time.* Thus, the story of a prehistoric Yeti and his love for a modern woman seems to take a backseat for a love story of a boy and his dog.

This general lack of focus, and there's a lot of lack of focus throughout *Yeti*, seems to highlight where Kong succeeded most. In spite of the Yeti's ability to show human emotion more clearly, we, as viewers, connect to Kong because there's fewer distractions in the way of our relationship with him. Unusually, even films where the humans are kaiju (more on that in Chapter 14), there's still a decided lack of emotion and emotional connection between the kaiju and the audience. In *War of the Colossal Beast*, for example, we already have a well-established character, Glenn Manning, from *The Amazing Colossal Man*, who should be wholly sympathetic. And yet, his first full appearance in *War of the Colossal Beast* belies an animalistic nature, almost creating Reverse Kong: primitive on the inside, human on the outside.

Manning, whose face is partially destroyed by the attacks that closed *The Amazing Colossal Man*, his skull socket showing and burns eclipsing a significant portion of his face, does little more than cry and moan and eat truckloads of food. The gigantic man is clearly in misery, but there's

---

*And the swath of blood on the dog's chest grows in size between shots. Indio the collie just nonchalantly perseveres through the injury, though.

11. Kong, Again and Again: The Son[s] of Kong

little for the viewer to latch on to. Sure, there's Manning's sister, Joyce, who believes her brother can still be reasoned with, but he's as animalistic a kaiju as they come, having more in common with, for example, Sanda or Gaira from *War of the Gargantuas* or Frankenstein from *Frankenstein Conquers the World*. In fact, if one compares Sanda, Gaira, Frankenstein, Glenn Manning, and Kong, the most clearly human of the group in terms of emotions and maturity is ... Kong.

Just to drive this point home, we can briefly consider *King Kong* from 2005. About thirty years removed from the previous 1976 reboot of *King Kong*, the technology for this version of Kong allowed for a much more humanistic portrayal. Andy Serkis, who seems to be the CGI actor for nearly every film out there, portrayed Kong, and the motion capture technology that director Peter Jackson used gave Kong an even greater range of facial expressions. But, as in 1976, it feels like Kong's relationship, this time with Ann Darrow, seems to be one of mutual curiosity and friendship rather than outright lust or even love.

Kong, in fact, initially toys with Darrow, who entertains him by juggling and doing some dances, but when she refuses to do anything more, he simply leaves her. He returns to save her, but he isn't reacting to her as a love interest, but, again, as a sort of friend or plaything that can keep him entertained. In a bizarre sequence, she and Kong hang out on a frozen lake in Central Park, with Kong sliding around while she laughs. He dies soon after, of course. Yet, there's little to suggest Kong has anything but an affection for Darrow, and certainly doesn't rise to the level of sexual interest for Darrow as the Yeti does for Jane ... or, especially, how Ah Wang responds to Ah Wei in *Mighty Peking Man*.

As if to further exploit the "disgruntled giant" themes, the Shaw Brothers, based in Hong Kong, brought their own unique style of frenzied filmmaking to the kaiju genre as well in *Mighty Peking Man*. If you've ever seen a Shaw Brothers film, you know what to expect, which is a generalized and very colorful chaos that spans several genres in a single film. In *Mighty Peking Man*, there's an opening *Daimajin*-style kaiju attack, followed by a sort of travelog that embraces some uncomfortable stereotypes derived from primitivism as our adventurers, based in Hong Kong, travel to India to search for the "Giant Gorilla," who will eventually be known as Ah Wang. There's an elephant stampede, a wild tiger attack, and a climbing accident that kills several explorers, our main character abandoned by the rest of his group, and then the sudden appearance of a blonde woman in a very small cloth bikini swinging through the trees. And that's all in roughly the first 15 minutes.

And soon after, the film devolves temporarily into a love story between a young blonde woman, Ah Wei, and the lone explorer who was left for dead in the middle of the jungle, Johnnie Fang. There's a long sequence of Ah Wei and Johnnie Fang engaging in slow-motion romantic interludes often best included in late-night *Top Thirty Romance Hits of the 1970s* CD collection commercials. They cavort, chase each other around, and playfully pick up and swing around a jaguar, who, for its part, looks like it is seriously questioning its role in this world, all while the incredibly cheesy music plays. There's even a flashback of Johnnie Fang's previous girlfriend cheating on Johnnie with ... his brother, a sequence that only adds to the fantastic soap-opera-fueled stylings that seem to undergird much of *Mighty Peking Man*. And, as we will see, the love triangle that's spurred on here between Johnnie Fang, Ah Wei, and Lucy, Fang's ex-girlfriend, soon becomes a love quadrangle, with Ah Wang in love with Ah Wei.

The movie opens, though, with the initial appearance of Ah Wang, who, because of an earthquake, comes out of a mountain and absolutely destroys the local village. We can assume, perhaps, as viewers, that this has happened before, because the villagers bring a variety of weapons immediately to bear: spears, catapults, and so on, all to no effect. Ah Wang responds by killing them indiscriminately and causing their temple to collapse as they cower, crushing dozens more of them and burying the rest alive. Like Daimajin, Ah Wang is awakened, he's in a bad mood, and he instantly begins to crush the first people he sees.

Unlike Daimajin, however, there's no clear sense of justice that fuels the attack; in the *Daimajin* films, he's a lost god, mostly forgotten by his former worshippers, and, after they're abused by cruel overseers or invading armies, they then dare to call for his help. So, we're not too terribly upset when, after Daimajin administers some ironic justice to the bad guys, he turns on the villagers, too, at least temporarily. After all, they asked for help from a deity they had ignored up to that point. Ah Wang, however, just kills because he's there. Yes, the villagers attack him on sight, but he immediately attacks them before they can even rouse themselves to arms.

After this opening sequence, it's clear that Ah Wang is going to be very hard to sympathize with, and the Giant Gorilla rarely gives the viewer any sort of glimpse at his humanity—even though the actor doesn't have eye black around his eyes, showing clearly a portion of the actor's face behind the mask. Additionally, the few attempts at humor or humanization falls flat before Ah Wang even gets to Hong Kong to wreak havoc. It turns out that Ah Wang adopted a young blonde girl who apparently re-named herself Ah Wei after a plane accident that killed both of her parents. The issue with this scenario is that the film never quite spells out Ah Wang's perspective on Ah Wei; we're led to believe the Giant Gorilla is a

11. Kong, Again and Again: The Son[s] of Kong 131

father figure of sorts: he takes care of her, teaches her the ways of the jungle, and generally protects her.

But Ah Wang is also clearly jealous of Ah Wei's romantic relationship with Johnnie Fang. At one point, the Giant Gorilla peers into Ah Wei's cave and watches as she and Johnnie Fang have sex.* Frustrated, Ah Wang steps away and promptly starts ripping trees out of the ground and throwing rocks through the air in what should be a comedic moment, but ultimately comes across as somewhat disconcerting. The relationship between Ah Wang and Ah Wei flips at this point, and Ah Wei seems to be completely in control of Ah Wang; in fact, when Johnnie Fang asks if Ah Wei can have Ah Wang come back to Hong Kong, it's simply a matter of her asking. No drugs, alcohol, or knockout gas needed.

Ah Wang is enslaved immediately, and this provokes an unearned sense of attempt for sympathy; Ah Wei is upset by his being chained, but it's never quite a point of contention. Ah Wang seems relatively okay, at least, with being chained on the boat. The Giant Gorilla struggles and moans against the chains,† but generally remains agreeable. When the ship runs aground, after all, they loosen his chains so he can keep the boat from being run aground in a storm and Ah Wang is fine with helping out, if Ah Wei tells him to do so.

And Ah Wang is eventually imprisoned in a cage in a stadium, but what forces him to lash out isn't his loss of freedom, or a lack of food, or general abuse. No, he instead witnesses Ah Wei being sexually assaulted, and her cries for help motivates him to bend the bars to his cage, escape, and then crush her rapist, throw him to the ground, and then stomp on him. Now *that* is an action, a sort of justice, that we, as viewers, can appreciate, even if the aspect of summary execution may make some of us uncomfortable.‡ After all, Ah Wang has killed the bad guy, and we rejoice and cheer for his triumph in doing so; but his escape is anti-climactic,

---

*There's just a weird relationship with sex in this movie; Johnnie Fang saves Ah Wei from a cobra bite by sucking out the venom. She was bitten on the inner thigh, and her moans of pain ... well, it's best to say that watching this scene, coupled with the apparent sexual frustrations of Ah Wang, makes you wonder if you've accidentally crossed some sort of moral threshold.

†In another scene apparently designed to test our comfort levels, Ah Wei is given a new outfit because she's "civilized" now, but the outfit is tighter and more uncomfortable than she likes, so she instead strips off the clothes, throws them out the porthole, and happily reclines naked on the bed—a visual callback to Ah Wang chafing under his chains and attempting to be free of them. Neither of them want the trappings of "civilization" after all.

‡Audiences are very quick to go into the "they deserved it" mode, especially with kaiju films, and the death of some characters are a quick dose of schadenfreude based on a sort of wish fulfillment for viewers. In *Godzilla vs. Kong*, Maia Simmons gets her deadly comeuppance at the hands of Kong. Yes, she was one of the "bad' characters, but I found myself pleased mostly because of the cheesy lines ("Dump the monkey!" and "My father gets what he wants.") she delivered throughout the film up to that point. Thanks, Kong!

132   **The Kaiju Connection**

and his coming rampage pushes us away from that brief moment of identification.

In fact, when Ah Wang begins to rampage through the populace, he stomps on two other innocent civilians, harkening back to the elephant stampede and the tiger attack all the way at the start of the film, reminding us that the humanity that we found in King Kong seems to be sorely lacking in Ah Wang. Ah Wang is fully animalistic at this point, with no real relationship to people, either viewers or the cast, and when he starts to be attacked, there's no real sense of loss or sadness. He's an animal on the loose, and so, when the local military leader tricks Ah Wei into getting Ah Wang to drop his defenses so he can be attacked, it provokes, at most, a shrug. I mean, the Giant Gorilla did just kill numerous innocent people in a sequence that lasts several minutes. Along with stomping on innocent civilians, he crushes apartments *after* seeing people inside them, and he picks up cars and flings them away, causing numerous more deaths.

In many kaiju films, there's little regard to the supposed human cost of a city being destroyed. Godzilla and Gamera routinely kills hundreds, if not thousands, of innocent people,* and there's little moral judgment attached to it; in many of these battles, the hero kaiju is simply fighting. Human death is collateral damage. It's just a long, long way from the sequence in *Godzilla* (1954) when a young mother huddles with her two children as the city burns around them, reminding them that they'll be meeting their dead father soon. The people of Hong Kong who are crushed, stomped, thrown, and buried alive by Ah Wang are merely props, so there's no sense of deeper meaning. They're just an incidental body count. But the time it takes to show them on the screen as well as their deaths, forces the viewers to understand the death and destruction Ah Wang brings to the city.

Eventually Ah Wei is shot accidentally while planes attack Ah Wang, and both die, leaving behind Johnnie Fang as he holds Ah Wei's corpse, staring at the destroyed Hong Kong skyline. And that's it; there's no additional commentary, no moral to the story, really, and certainly very little sympathy for any of the characters outside of, perhaps, Ah Wei. Almost every other character suffers from some sort of moral corruption, and even the noble Johnnie Fang is ready to ditch Ah Wei after reuniting with his old girlfriend (the one who had sex with his brother)

---

*One of the most perplexing moments in *Godzilla* (2014) is when the stadium full of wounded and suddenly homeless people because of the near-total destruction of San Francisco by Godzilla and the MUTOs ... cheer for Godzilla when they see him on the big screens in the stadium. Hooray for the giant creature we didn't know existed until a few days ago and was just partially responsible for thousands of dead and billions of dollars in property damage!

11. Kong, Again and Again: The Son[s] of Kong

because it turns out that, according to her, his brother manipulated her into sex. This new information reunites them even before Ah Wei's corpse grows cold.

So, through all of these bizarre romantic interludes, somewhat racially charged adventures abroad, and the destruction of numerous buildings throughout Hong Kong, there's very little sense of what is "right" and what is "wrong" in the movie; even Ah Wei, in all of her innocence, tends to be unlikeable at times, as she quickly manipulates Ah Wang to get on the boat because Johnnie Fang asked nicely. She's quite willing to expose Ah Wang to danger if it makes Johnnie Fang happy.

Although *Yeti: Giant of the 20th Century* focused on mostly flat, uninspiring, or just plain insipid or annoying characters, *Mighty Peking Man* pulls off another feat entirely. Almost none of the characters earn our empathy or our sympathy throughout. And the ostensible "hero" of the piece is alternatively a mass murdering beast, a randy pervert, and a mass murdering beast again. By comparison, there are questions left about the role of King Kong in the world, because in the humanity that Kong presented, we found that most of the other characters in the cast were sorely lacking that same humanity. For Ah Wang, he's strictly an unlikable beast, whose sole motivation in the one instance of being a hero even comes across as selfish, or at least self-serving.

His role as a "father" to Ah Wei routinely takes a backseat to the Giant Gorilla's leering and jealousy, and so his one moment of heroism comes across as less of him doing the right thing, and more of him just essentially acting on his jealousy. What comes after this "heroic" moment in saving Ah Wei from being raped makes him even more distant from the viewer. Ironically, even the group that made *Yeti: Giant of the 20th Century* knew when to pull back from the general uncomfortable "romance" aspects of the relationship, but Ah Wang's depiction of his relationship with Ah Wei is simply too disturbing to overcome.

Thankfully, the film *Konga*—and I know it barely qualifies as a kaiju film, but bear with me, and I'll keep it short—manages to avoid these sort of disturbing relationships, instead focusing on the destructive relationship between Dr. Charles Decker and Margaret, his lab assistant *cum*-lover *cum*-wife. You see, Decker spent a year stranded in the jungle, where he learned of a plant that, when administered to an animal, can make it grow larger. He also learned from the local medicine man how to hypnotize people, which is quite a set of outcomes given the circumstances.

When he shows up in London, looking remarkably well-groomed, he has a chimpanzee with him, and we immediately draw the connection, and soon, Decker, played with unhinged menace by Michael Gough, uses his mad scientist chops to turn the small chimp into a human-sized gorilla (an equally miraculous change that no one remarks on); he then nefariously hypnotizes Konga into killing his enemies. The first Konga kill is the dean of the biology department where Decker works—the dean threatens to shut down Decker's research. The next is a rival botanist (who knew botany was such a cutthroat field of study?), and, soon, Decker's ambitions begin to grow in size as well, for he decides to try to conquer the world.

During this entire setup, which informs most of the film, the woman who is often cast as the object of adoration in Kong pastiches everywhere isn't an object of admiration for Konga at all; in fact, their working relationship seems to be completely professional, as Konga, still in moderately-sized chimp form, is happy to bring her tea on request. No, the toxic relationship is between the humans. Dr. Decker's cold mania set off by her desire to be married and become a "respectable" woman free from the gossip that apparently follows a botanist and his attractive lab assistant. Each of them feed off of each other for much of *Konga*, and it's a relief to see a "real" relationship, no matter how toxic, play out during this marathon of Kong-like films.

But, what of Konga? We're certainly, as viewers, asked to sympathize with the chimp, mostly because we're introduced to it as a baby, and then we hear its screams when Decker first injects it with his growth serum. In fact, we know Konga is in danger if he is the subject of a failed experiment. After Margaret accidentally knocks some of the serum to the floor, the house cat licks some of it up. Decker, in full Hammer Horror angry villain mode, goes through the drawers of science equipment until finally finding his revolver—yes, he keeps a loaded revolver among the test tubes and beakers, apparently—and promptly shoots the cat. Not once, but twice.

Decker's cruelty to the cat only temporarily registers with Margaret, but we, as viewers, are left to draw the easy connection: if the experiment fails, Konga is next. Of course, the experiment doesn't fail, and Konga becomes an unwitting instrument of Decker's destruction, a hypnotized ape assassin (which would make an excellent band name), asked to kill, repeatedly, at Decker's commands.

Konga is indeed a killer of many, but the kills were under duress, or at least, under extreme suggestion, and the one kill that doesn't come under duress is Konga picking up Decker and squishing him. For all of Decker's lunacy, it comes across as an entirely plausible and sympathetic murder. Konga, though primitive, carries a sense of justice, or at least, retribution. Where the plot changes though, is in how Decker becomes fond of his student assistant, Sandra, and his fondness soon turns to an obsession.

Sandra's boyfriend, Bob, cottons on to this new dynamic, and Bob and Decker get into a fistfight, which Decker promptly loses, because he's an older, brainy scientist and Bob is a young, virile man. Completely

11. Kong, Again and Again: The Son[s] of Kong   135

emasculated by this easy defeat, Decker orders Konga to kill Bob, which is really the impetus for our switch from "that's unfair" in the murders to "this guy's gone crazy," and, indeed, at the climax of the film, Decker forces himself on Sandra while Margaret watches. Perturbed, Margaret goes to the lab and gives Konga a megadose of the serum, hypnotizing him to become her weapon of revenge. The hypnosis fails, and Konga kills her and then snatches Decker away, heading deeper into London.

Decker remains alive for much of Konga's rampage, held in Konga's hands in a neat inversion of the classic *King Kong* formula; in this instance, the giant ape isn't protecting (or feels like he is protecting) a young woman. Instead, Konga is keeping prisoner a crazed, middle-aged college professor. Strangely, other than Decker's home and laboratory, the rest of the rampage is free of property destruction and murder. As Konga heads toward Big Ben, people run through the streets, and Konga politely stays on the road and almost refuses to cause any damage or kill anyone. There's a decided loss of sympathy, though, because the justice we seek for Decker, who has a body count and has been revealed to be a lecher, stays alive, and it's initially hard to tell if Konga is seeking revenge or if he's still somewhat hypnotized.

The remaining shreds of sympathy are lost, however, when Konga arrives at Big Ben as the police officers and a few local army units arrive, and Konga ... just stands and watches. It's safe to say, after watching this sequence a few times, that Konga, who shows no rage or, really, any emotion of any sort at the gathering storm, is a complete and abject moron. Of course, the soldiers and police officers open fire, ultimately killing Konga, but not before Konga throws Decker at them, killing Decker in the process. There's no real sense of retribution here, and it's not difficult to imagine that Konga didn't kill Decker out of hate or justice, but rather out of a sense of protecting himself. Soon, Konga is dead in the hail of bullets and rockets, and the giant ape reverts back to the baby chimp we saw at the beginning of the movie, in a rather callous attempt to tug at the viewer's heartstrings, before the closing shot of ... Big Ben.*

So, we learn more from the film *Konga* because it casts the main creature as almost wholly animalistic, and lacking in anything that would resemble humanity outside of a vague physical shape. The giant primate is a victim so much as it is a bona fide killer, and Konga's turn at the end, when Margaret attempts to hypnotize him, only for him to break the spell entirely, leads us to wonder: exactly *how* hypnotized was he when he murdered Decker's enemies? For some reason, it's hard to think that Konga

---

*The classic British resolve is on display in the film when a detective from Scotland Yard answers the phone and says, without a hint of irony or humor: "Fantastic! There's a huge monster gorilla that's constantly growing to outlandish proportions at loose on the streets."

carries zero complicity in the attacks, and it's hard to say why. Perhaps waving a small flashlight in the eyes of an enlarged primate and speaking more slowly than usual doesn't seem like a very effective method of hypnosis ... and, besides, if we put aside all of the scientific gobbledygook about growth serums and plant/animal cell interaction, do we truly have any reason to believe a human can hypnotize a primate?

There's just some ideas that tend to stretch too far. It's hard to shear off Konga's roles in the killings and proclaim him completely innocent, although it is fair to admit that when he finally goes on an enraged rampage, he simply wanders down the street. Of course, we also expect Decker to get his comeuppance, but even Decker's murder makes us wonder if that was purposeful. Are we to assume, then, that Konga can only kill under hypnosis? And if so, then why was Margaret killed? She was quite friendly with Konga, and only wanted to use Konga to smite her enemies (Decker, and possibly Sandra). It's a huge morass of conflicting motivations and ideals, and Konga the character seems to hold the viewers far apart from any sort of comprehension, understanding, or sympathy.

Unlike *Konga, Yeti,* or *Mighty Peking Man*, Joe Young from *Mighty Joe Young* (1949) arrives for the viewer in an already deeply humanized form. He's generally smaller than the others, usually depicted about 15 to 20 feet in height, and even his name belies his innate humanity as presented to the viewer. From the start, Joe Young and his young friend, Jill, form a partnership shorn of the bizarre romantic interludes, and focuses almost entirely on business. After Joe is "discovered," Jill agrees to take him to perform in a sideshow, and Jill immediately enjoys the benefits, wearing fancier outfits and spending some time making case-fulls of money. Meanwhile, for his performances, Joe sits in a cage just twice as large as he is, and, after ten straight weeks of performing, refuses to eat and is generally completely miserable.

Joe's "humanity" is established during these earliest performances because he is, in fact, willing to play. He seems to genuinely enjoy the playfulness of the shows, which includes spinning Jill around on a platform while she plays piano, and playing tug of war with the "world's ten strongest men," a performance which leads to Joe playfully boxing with a former heavyweight champion.* These are all harmless activities, but the overall grind of show after show wears Joe down into a depression—another characteristic that human viewers can readily identify with. Unlike Kong, who retains his more "primitive" nature throughout the movie, prompted only to disaster by his sudden exposure to a strange world, Joe Young tends

---

*The real-life Primo Carnera, who stood 6'6" and eventually transitioned to professional wrestling after his boxing career ended.

11. Kong, Again and Again: The Son[s] of Kong   137

to exist just fine, with the usual human complaints about poor working conditions.

It's only when Joe comes across the worst of humanity—three drunkards who abuse him by teaching him to drink liquor and then burning his fingers with a match—that he responds with violence. In the annals of giant-sized primates attacking men, Joe's lashing out at the three drunkards is probably among the most justified and sympathetic, but the three men escape back into the audience, and, as Joe chases them, he rampages through the audience (complete with requisite fainting women). Even so, his focus remains mostly on the man who burned him, and he chases a man up a fake tree, knocks down a gangway, sending several band members plummeting, and destroys the set.

Of course, those who saw *King Kong* knew the rampage was inevitable, but the spark that lights Joe's fire makes him *more* human rather than less. In fact, Joe's attack doesn't seem to injure many humans; they escape while Joe is distracted by lions in an exhibit in the amphitheater and resoundingly thrashes them. At one point, he even saves the man who burned his fingers from a lion attack, although it's unclear if Joe himself makes the connection at that point. And Joe's rampage doesn't end in his own death or his own injury. Although police arrive loaded for bear and willing to shoot, Jill, with the help and distraction of the show owner, O'Hara, and Gregg, O'Hara's animal wrangler, lock Joe back in his cage, foiling the police plans for a summary execution.

After the rampage, *Mighty Joe Young* takes an even deeper turn into "civilization," as it fast forwards to … a trial! The court orders that Young gets shot, so his reprieve is only temporary, and his humanity needs to be further established at this point. Joe's path tends to wend toward a wholly sympathetic and humanistic portrayal (in fact, the police officer tasked with shooting Joe, leaves with the rather unfeeling statement "Let's get this done, I've got a date tonight"); his only strain of aggressive behavior comes at the hands of abusive behavior on the part of people, and his rampage is relatively small and confined, compared to almost any other giant primate film that we've discussed so far. In this regard, Joe Young is wholly a victim. Where we can look at Kong and notice it is his primitivism clashing with technology that causes his rampage, we can only really identify with his tragic end as a sort of beast out of time.

With Young, however, we have the ultimate human-sympathetic motivation: he doesn't like assholes. This is also a theme in films like *Mighty Peking Man*, but the resultant rampage is time that doesn't fit the crime, so to speak, because the widespread and indiscriminate murder isn't targeted to just the offenders. Young is embarrassed and humiliated by three drunken men, loses his temper and is quickly talked down

138 **The Kaiju Connection**

again. That Young's death sentence is commuted is a function of the ultimate act of heroism. He's taken from his cell not for an execution, but to be rushed to the scene of a (quite melodramatic) burning orphanage. Young burns himself and exhausts himself saving the children, and he is, instead of being shot, sent back to his home in Africa with Jill and Gregg, a place where he "belongs." Like the Toho Kong, Mighty Joe Young would simply prefer to be left alone and away from much of humanity.

What are we to make of these films, then? Quite simply, that our identification with gigantic primates can only carry us so far. The more "human" they are in outlook and destruction, the more likely we are to reach out in sympathy for them. This all fits in with W.J.T. Marshall's assertion about *King Kong* that Kong is the Other until placed against a greater Other (or series of Others) that ultimately humanize or "ally" Kong with the human protagonists, and, by extension, the audience themselves (171–173). A quick re-view of each of these other creatures reveal that many of them fail to successfully "humanize" or otherwise de–Other the giant creatures: Mighty Joe Young is perhaps the only one that receives much sympathy from us because he arrives, as we have said, pre-packaged as humanistic. *Son of Kong* follows the same pathway of a tragic demise after battling dinosaurs. Even MechaniKong provides a wholly alien and bizarre Other for Kong to battle. But Yeti, Ah Wang, and Konga retain their general primitiveness, and they're never successfully juxtaposed against any sort of non-sympathetic creation that could somehow out–Other them.

As a result, we're left with creations that simply don't ring true for human audiences. Any hints of excessive violence, outrage, perversity, stupidity, or, simply, too much "primitive," keeps us at a far remove, unable to identify with the creature. Also as a result, films like *Yeti* and *Konga* tend to be mostly forgotten, and, when we do watch them, we tend to view them with the immense skepticism granted to us by the inherent distance the film keeps in front of us. No, there is nothing in *Konga* that makes us readily identify with the beast, and Ah Wang's rampage makes him too bloodthirsty for our tastes. Even though the original *King Kong* showed Kong chomping down on a guy and then casually tossing him to the ground, there's still a sense of justice and sympathy, for Kong has clearly been manipulated and wronged, and his final tragic death only heightens that sense of injustice.

And so, we're carried far into the future to the newest Kong, this time in *Skull Island* and *Godzilla vs. Kong*. The Legendary version of Kong tends to hold adults at a distance and has the very sympathetic trait of just wanting to be left alone. In *Skull Island*, Kong is a generally peaceful giant ape consistently provoked into action. Helicopters come out of nowhere to attack him, so he fights back. He doesn't even "finish the battle," leaving

11. Kong, Again and Again: The Son[s] of Kong — 139

the various human survivors behind. He understands—at the moment—that they pose little danger to him.

At several points in the movie, we, as viewers, are given symbolic representations of Kong's "human" nature, and possibly the most blatant moment is when one of the soldiers named Chapman, injured and thirsty, strides to a river to wash out his wounds and fill his canteen. Chapman hears a commotion and sees Kong, not battling, but washing out his wounds and drinking the water. Later, the photographer, Mason Weaver, attempts to save a massive buffalo-like kaiju trapped in the wreckage of a helicopter, and fails. Kong hears the cries of the buffalo and arrives to rescue it.

Skull Island consistently uses Kong as a mirror to show the best and worst of his own humanity; his actions often directly mimic the humans as they attempt to interact with him. He is peaceful when greeted peacefully, and violent when greeted violently. Although there are nods to the original *King Kong*, such as Kong's passing interest in Mason Weaver—founded more by curiosity rather than romance (*King Kong*), friendship (*Mighty Joe Young*) or outright lust (*Mighty Peking Man*)—this version of Kong, at least for the duration of *Skull Island* tends to lack a certain primitiveness that we have come to expect from other Kongs through history: his anger is measured and his violence rarely vengeful. He doesn't rampage or otherwise kill indiscriminately; much of his violence is geared toward those who would challenge his position as the alpha predator on Skull Island.

And, all throughout *Skull Island*, Kong is sympathetically cast *against* Others: be they Skullcrawlers, overly aggressive military men played by Samuel L. Jackson, or any variety of other beasts in the strange menagerie that inhabits the island and the caverns below. As a result, Kong achieves the same sort of humanization and de–Othering that permeates much of *King Kong* and *Son of Kong*, as well as any number of *King Kong* reboots.

It should come as little surprise, then, that the same Kong that appears in *Skull Island* is wholly "human" by the time he arrives on our screens for *Godzilla vs. Kong*. This version of Kong is an older, much smarter, and altogether humanized version, at one point even stopping to restfully scratch his ass before continuing on his way. Kong, even though he is trapped in a pretend world meant to mimic Skull Island, only occasionally chafes at the simulation, as he is fully enraptured with a young girl, Jia, with whom he can communicate in sign language.

And so, Kong battles Godzilla, who is slightly redesigned to appear more reptilian* and also becomes a much more powerful version of himself. Although Godzilla himself receives some mild humanization

---

*We actually see a sort of proto–Godzilla during the Hollow Earth sequence. It's simply called the Scaly Quadruped. "It's like a lizard from the Galapagos Island, but huge," says John DesJardin, VFX Supervisor for *Godzilla vs. Kong* (Wallace 110).

(Wingard famously spoke about making Godzilla "smile" during one sequence), he is largely absent for large portions of the film, making his presence more of a supersized cameo in a Kong-centered film.

As if the juxtaposition against a re-worked Godzilla wasn't enough, Kong displays almost wholly human emotions and characteristics during the length of the film, from his facial expressions to his apparent ability to feel uniquely human emotions of hatred, revenge, panic, and fear. Thus, enter Mechagodzilla, which exists less as a foil to Godzilla in this film than it does to position Kong as the sole "true" hero of the film. Yes, Godzilla is in the title, and yes, he does play a rather bizarre role in ultimately defeating Mechagodzilla, but the ultimate symbol of the unnatural: a robotic being piloted by an autonomous and apparently still-functioning head of an alien kaiju, is vanquished, with some ease, by Kong himself, with Godzilla (and a pair of teens) providing only an assist.

In fact, Adam Wingard, with all of the subtlety of a sledgehammer, uses an Elvis Presley song to emphasize the point. Kong lies, prone, on an aircraft carrier as he's taken to explore a potential opening to Hollow Earth. The presence of an Elvis Presley love ballad in a film featuring multiple kaiju battles is, to say the least, terribly incongruous,* but "Loving Arms" opens with the verse

> If you could see me now
> The one who said that he would rather roam
> The one who said he'd rather be alone
> If you could only see me now [1974][†]

We're encouraged, of course, to draw inferences between Kong and his newfound mission in his life to avoid his loneliness and to try to reunite with his ancestors. See, he's been misled by the folks at MONARCH into believing that other Kongs may be hiding out in Middle Earth, and we're meant to sympathize not only with the fact that he's been lied to, but also with the fact that he's leading a ridiculously lonely life without other Kongs around him. Kong may understand he's being lied to, but a part of that is being willfully misled, in the hopes that he may, on the off chance, at least learn about his roots and where he belongs.

There's little more that's effective in the "humanizing" and "non–Othering" playbook than a romantic ballad with song lyrics designed to

---

*But not nearly as incongruous as the *Godzilla vs. Kong* trailer, which drops the beat with the hip hop "Here We Go" by Chris Classic while Kong and Godzilla slap each other silly.
[†]There's also a somewhat anti-romantic line later on in the song where Elvis sings about "looking back and longing for the freedom of my chains." Although it's quite the paradox, it carries with it the bizarre possibility that Kong is wishing for a return to captivity in the facsimile Skull Island. We see Kong being irritated and distrustful of this captivity, but also enjoying an extremely comfortable and Skullcrawler-free environment.

11. Kong, Again and Again: The Son[s] of Kong 141

tug at the heart strings, especially an Elvis Presley romantic ballad, and it just piles onto the somewhat heavy-handed and completely repetitive nature of *Godzilla vs. Kong*'s attempts to make Kong a de facto hero and savior of humanity.

But, in the end, Kong is so humanized that it's nearly impossible not to root for him. He becomes a veritable action star, even popping his shoulder back into place like Martin Riggs does in *Lethal Weapon*. Kong gets numerous moments where he goes through more in-depth thought processes that we, as viewers, can identify with. An example: when Godzilla steps on his face and roars, you can see Kong's expressions changing from confusion to outright anger as he essentially refuses, upon pain of potential death, to submit, and he essentially goes "you know what? Fuck you, too!" before roaring back at Godzilla. Yet, there's something primal that's missing in this version of Kong: no deep well of anger, no feats of bravado or derring-do that make him any different from any low-level superhero in the Marvel or DC cinematic universes. He swings from place to place, narrowly avoids getting blasted, gets blasted, dies, comes back, and then wins the day.

It's all somewhat a little too on-the-nose in terms of making Kong some sort of fully humanized kaiju. By making Kong almost exactly like a super athletic and supersized human, there's something lost, and a lot of it is his ultimate rage and his animalistic nature, things that made him unique throughout his franchises, and, not only that, also gave us some sympathetic moments to ponder. As human viewers, our identification for Kong was played for empathy and a sort of (perhaps begrudging) awareness of our humanity's flaws. He was somehow more primitive, but also somehow *better* because of his inherent innocence; he represented nature and natural processes in an unpolluted and pristine wilderness, and, as such, he seemed to, no matter how "human" he became, be something uniquely different.

And, as we will see in Chapter 11, there's also the loss of Kong's vulnerability: his general inability to be injured or even permanently killed makes him more superheroic than heroic, more superman than man, and, as a result, there's some jading there. We know he can't be hurt for long, and we know that he'll be perfectly fine. There's no long-term physical trauma like we see even in the Gamera series or the Godzilla franchise at times. Our ability, as people, to identify with Kong begins to slip a little because he's just a little *too* good.

Think about Kong in *Godzilla vs. Kong* as the final arc of the loss of this unique aspect of Kong; he's first portrayed in a human environment that is completely man made and completely synthetic, and although Kong chafes over this, he remains, and casts his lot with humans, even as they displace him and mislead him. He is besties with a young girl and communicates directly to her through human-based sign language. He is, overwhelmingly, a human in an ape's body. Frankly, there's no room for much depth to this iteration of Kong, and it is hard to believe that the Kong in *King Kong vs. Godzilla*, as goofy as he looked, somehow came across as a stronger and more unique character. And there's little room for sociocultural commentary through Kong in *Godzilla vs. Kong*. He's fully our superheroic representative, and that ultimately strips away what has made him a unique and iconic figure for almost a century now. In humanizing Kong to this extent, and then going even beyond those boundaries into super-humanizing him, we lose any sort of base relationship with his actions or his personality.

Despite these missteps, we can see that Kong and most of the Kong reiterations, including *Son of Kong* and even *Mighty Joe Young*, tend to manage Kong as a sympathetic, nearly humanistic non–Other throughout his history, especially when compared to the lesser films that follow the same general plotlines, such as *Yeti*, *Konga*, and *Mighty Peking Man*, all movies which never quite land the same way as the Kong franchise(s). These films lack the depictions of romance in place of lust, intelligence, and sympathy, and, as a result, the title creations tend to be completely forgettable.

No, Kong is just right. Is the giant primate in *King Kong* the same as the Kong in Toho's universe, the Kong we see in the Legendary universe? Clearly not. But the general thematics of *King Kong*, of a de–Othered humanistic creature just stuck in the wrong time, and simply seeking peace, quiet, and friendship, is a genetic strain we see lacking in almost every other Kong homage (or "ripoff," if you're not feeling generous today). Ultimately, it's why Kong tends to return cyclically as a box office bona fide: it's a familiar story, upon which we, as human viewers, can relate to a massive ape who just wants to be left alone.

12

Toward the Past and the Future at the Same Time: *Colossal* and *Godzilla vs. Kong*

There's a fair argument to be made that comparing a small film like *Colossal* to a major blockbuster like *Godzilla vs. Kong* is unfair, and it really is in many ways. One's more of a domestic drama focused on two broken individuals in a small rural town; the other is a massive, world-spanning (and world-blowing-a-hole-through) battle between a pair and then a trio of massive kaiju, with humans and human connections only providing an often nonsensical breather in the action. But I'm going to compare them anyway, mostly because I feel that they are two different poles that show us how kaiju films are evolving in the past ten years or so.

Each film takes its own creative path toward understanding what a kaiju film is, and what a kaiju film can be. Where *Godzilla: King of the Monsters* was an homage to the darker and grittier Heisei era, *Godzilla vs. Kong* was a pure paean to the cheesier films of the Showa era. And *Colossal* stands somewhere in left field, a new approach cast against older approaches. And I'll wear my opinion on my sleeve here: I liked *Colossal*, but I continue to think that *Godzilla vs. Kong* must be among the most disappointing Godzilla films I've seen. So, grain of salt.

Before we discuss *Colossal* as a kaiju film, we'll need to discuss the ways that *King of the Monsters* and *Godzilla vs. Kong* pay homage to their individual eras, for better or for worse. *Godzilla: King of the Monsters* was a massive departure in tone from *Godzilla* (2014); no small part of that tonal shift was that Gareth Edwards, who tends to favor pacing and plot dynamics over action and expansive casts (see: *Monsters*) directed *Godzilla*. *Godzilla: King of the Monsters*, however, was directed by Michael Dougherty, a horror director whose films include *Trick 'r Treat* and *Krampus*. Both *Trick 'r Treat* and *Krampus* tend to favor significant action to move the characters from point to point, and often rely on expansive casts.

Trick 'r Treat is an anthology film and features around a dozen characters. *Krampus* focuses entirely on an extended family trapped in the house for the holidays; at full strength, the cast features almost as many characters. This is all reflected in the hectic place-to-place dashing across a huge cast of characters in *King of the Monsters.*

Of course, Edwards had the unenviable task of creating the new universe of Godzilla for Legendary, and, as such, he needed to set the "rules" of the universe and provide an origin story for Godzilla. And, of course, Edwards was most likely still very aware of the negative impact of the last Americanization of Godzilla in 1998. Doughtery didn't necessarily need to rebuild the new universe; just expand on what Edwards had already established, and, as a result, many of the nods to the original *Godzilla* (1954) that are present in *Godzilla* (2014) fall by the wayside and are replaced by the more action-packed and fantastic-technology–driven tones that we see in numerous Heisei Godzilla films.

So, it's not a surprise, really, that MONARCH has tons of high-tech and costly bases across the world and under the ocean, nor does it come as a surprise that they also command an aircraft, the Argo, that can nearly outfly Rodan at full speed, but also ferry them from destination to destination at tremendous speed. This is somewhat of a far cry from MONARCH's capabilities as depicted in *Godzilla*, where their technology and understanding of kaiju seems only moderately higher than decades before, in *Skull Island.* Perhaps governments gave MONARCH a ton of money in those few years, but the technological leaps that the organization makes rival almost any leap made in the Heisei era, from the Super X in *The Return of Godzilla* and the Super X–II in *Godzilla vs. Biollante* to the creation of Mechagodzilla II and then Kiryu.

And, just to differentiate from what's about to come in the discussion of the Showa era, there's precious little advanced (re: fantastic) technology that humans create. Much of the time, in fact, outside of Jet Jaguar, the humans generally find themselves utilizing already existing technology, such as telephone wires or helicopters to try to solve the problems. They instead spend a significant amount of time *subverting* advanced technology. The aliens almost inevitably have control centers, mind-controlling devices, or spacecraft that need to be disconnected or otherwise blown up. Yet, the only "enemy" device in *King of the Monsters* is the ORCA, a device created by Emma Russell, and it's something that is essentially completely dependent on the intentions of the people who have it in their hands. It can soothe kaiju, distract them, awaken, or lure them, among other things, but it's not necessarily a technology that needs to be destroyed, and much of the conversation about the ORCA is about retrieving it or getting it back into the so-called "right hands."

12. Toward the Past and the Future at the Same Time   145

Stepping beyond the thematics, the look of *King of the Monsters* is also an homage to the Heisei era. The monsters are big and mean, snarling at one another, and the colors are mostly muted. Battles occur in the rain or at night, and there's plenty of fog and smoke that moves around the humans and the kaiju. Like the Heisei Gamera series, the Heisei Godzilla series is covered mostly in darkness; there's very few bright colors and even fewer moments of daylight. In fact, Mothra's appearance in *King of the Monsters* as she tries to summon Godzilla from the depths to rejoin the battle is almost refreshing: a blast of light in the seemingly unending darkness that dominates the color palette of the film.

The director of *Godzilla vs. Kong*, Adam Wingard, mentioned his vision of *Godzilla vs. Kong* as being a natural extension of the more colorful Showa era:

> The MonsterVerse films have kind of followed this natural trajectory that the original Showa era Godzilla films did, which was the very first Godzilla movie, for its time, was very grounded and real and depressing and tragic and very much a disaster movie. Then they slowly got more psychedelic and trippy and cartoony and colorful as time went on. I'm kind of the *Destroy All Monsters* era, I think those type of films, if I had to pick one. A film that's very colorful. [Pearson].

Naturally, the best evidence of this is that, unlike *Godzilla* (2014) and *King of the Monsters*, *Godzilla vs. Kong* is bright and colorful, not mired in heavy rainfall, nighttime scenes, or smoke and destructive fallout. While the primary color palette for *Godzilla* tended to hover in the grays and darker hues, *King of the Monsters* brought out blue, gold, and red, with occasional daylight scenes (though most of the battles still happened in the darkness). *Godzilla vs. Kong*, though, emphasizes tonal brightness, and there's few moments where a viewer will struggle to see what is happening, as the kaiju are lit by city lights (the battle in Hong Kong), the setting sun (the aircraft carrier battle), or the morning sun (the final battle with Mechagodzilla).

As you've no doubt noted, I somewhat disagree, however, with Wingard's assertion that *King of the Monsters* also comes from the Showa era in terms of inspiration. The Heisei era is dotted with incredibly dark films with muted colors, and rarely does any kaiju action occur during the day. Compare this, however, to numerous lighter (and lighthearted) films, where the major battles almost always occur in full view. *Destroy All Monsters*, of course, as Wingard cites, is one of the brightest and easiest to witness films in the entire Godzilla canon; each monster—and there are a lot of them—is easily discernible, and each monster, outside of random cameos, has a relatively large role to play in the buildup to the final battle. Even Kumonga gets a piece of the action, teaming up with the Mothra larva to help web King Ghidorah!

And the kaiju in *Godzilla vs. Kong* are almost as emotive as the dancing Godzilla in *Invasion of the Astro-Monster* or the nose-wiping Godzilla in *Ebirah, Horror of the Deep*. In both cases, these instances are direct homages to human fictional characters. The "shê" dance from the cartoon character Iyami, and the nose wipe from the heroic character Yuichi Tanuma, of the popular *Waka Daisho* series of films. Godzilla and Kong in *Godzilla vs. Kong* are also unusually expressive, and Godzilla, in particular, overtly adopts human mannerisms for the first time in the Legendary series. Although Godzilla's light redesign makes him more reptilian, he, too, has moments of human authenticity, in spite of Toho mandates to the otherwise; Wingard claims to have been able to "get around" the edict by leaving Godzilla's smile open to interpretation, but it's clear to anyone who watches the film that Godzilla sneers in an authentically human manner (Raymond). And, even though Kong was more humanistic in *Skull Island*, this version of Kong has numerous facial expressions: fear, distress, happiness, contentment, that tend to make him more humanized, especially compared to, well, almost any other version of Kong.

But the worst of the lighter Showa-era films is on display in *Godzilla vs. Kong* as well. At the top of the list have to be the nearly pointless human characters, who engage in often improbable tasks, or otherwise just stand there, dumbfounded. Mark spends much of his time in *Godzilla vs. Kong* doing little other than talking on the phone and looking up, a task that many of the adult actors perform with some aplomb; the plot instead follows a pair of teenagers, Madison Russell and Josh Valentine, as they try to unravel the mystery of why Godzilla is suddenly attacking people, unprovoked. It's a plotline straight out of *Godzilla vs. Mechagodzilla*, and Josh's role as a podcaster is a twenty-first century update on the standard Showa-era role of the journalist as main character.

Jun Fukuda, director of five Showa-era Godzilla films, including *Godzilla vs. Gigan* and *Godzilla vs. Megalon*, said of his work in an interview that all of his films earned, in his view, a "minus score" because "the monsters became the stars, and the human characters were put into the background. The human story was cut down" ("Jun Fukuda"). For *King of the Monsters*, the human story was indeed cut down; in *Godzilla vs. Kong*, it's practically nonexistent.

As *King of the Monsters* captured the best and the worst of the Heisei era, *Godzilla vs. Kong* managed also to underscore some of the triumphs and frustrations of the Showa era. There's little doubt that the Showa era, especially the span running from *Invasion of the Astro Monster* to *Terror of Mechagodzilla*, was dotted, if not overwhelmed, with outlandish plots, ridiculous dialogue, and instances that beg the forgiveness of even the most relaxed viewer. During some moments of *Godzilla vs. Kong*, I

12. Toward the Past and the Future at the Same Time 147

began to wonder if we were going to see the physics-defying dropkick from *Godzilla vs. Megalon* or the flying backwards maneuver from *Godzilla vs. Hedorah*. We did get some definitive physics-defying stuff: Godzilla using his atomic breath to blow a hole miles deep through the Earth's crust, along with quick transport portals for teenage podcasters to zip through from city to city with nary a care in the world.

And although *Godzilla vs. Kong* did feature numerous battle sequences, they all felt almost as hollow and purposeless as many of those from the Showa era. With Godzilla *and* Kong as the ostensible heroes of the movie, we already know neither of them can lose (despite the film's tagline teasing just that outcome), and so, at best, we can only get the sort of stalemate that ended *King Kong vs. Godzilla*.

If only. Instead, Godzilla and Kong battle, Godzilla (kind of) wins and then (kind of) loses to the newly minted Mechagodzilla, before a revived Kong comes back and teams up with Godzilla to win the day and defeat the new menace, who, outside of a few minutes scraping the ground, literally, with Godzilla—Godzilla! Who, we should note, can blow holes through the Earth's crust with his breath, but only singe Kong and not even really damage Mechagodzilla—may be a threat in some way. We never know. We just know the very sparest details of Mechagodzilla, and, in the end, the two human teenagers manage to subvert Mechagodzilla's systems by pouring whiskey on a control panel, allowing Godzilla and Kong the seconds-long break they need to apparently regroup and win the day.

Their begrudging and somewhat respectful alliance aside, Godzilla and Kong seem to be as hollow as the Earth they tend to trod, moving from place to place just long enough to set up the battles that we're asked to enjoy. Much like the Showa adventures, conflicts between kaiju, and the sometimes unbelievable alliances that result, are set up by lengthy arcs where the humans stand around and discuss their discoveries and try to figure out what's going on. It's all empty pageantry, I'm afraid, and *Godzilla vs. Kong* takes its rightful place alongside movies like *Godzilla vs. Megalon* and *Godzilla vs. Gigan*: bring on the copious amounts of cheese. What's most interesting about *Godzilla vs. Kong* is how the complaints about Godzilla films—especially the Legendary series—from fans about too many people talking is somehow heightened in this film. The humans are barely likable, shorn of any reasonable motivation, and just barely manage to form any sort of coherent plot.

And yet, one of the hallmarks of *Godzilla vs. Kong*, and, to a lesser extent, is just how much humans interact and manipulate the events of the kaiju themselves when they do actually appear. Of course, this happens on a much grander scale in the Heisei era, where humans build giant mechs and flying machines and are essentially almost all militarized or

148   The Kaiju Connection

government officials, but it's the average ground-level children and scientists in the Showa era who consistently interact with and influence the events.

Take, in *Godzilla vs. Kong*, the initial battle at sea between the two. Kong is trapped in chains as the ship he's on capsizes, and someone swims over to a panel to pull on the lever that will unchain him. The human, nearly drowning, screams out, and, in return, our next shot of Kong is him screaming out, too—a clear symbolic link. Later in the battle, Godzilla is dragging Kong deeper and deeper into the ocean to drown him, prompting one woman to yell out that they need to use depth charges, and, indeed, the plans work in disrupting Godzilla (but strangely leave Kong unaffected).

They save Kong's life here, and in several other moments throughout the movie, as if to not only show the viewer that Kong is somehow humanity's true champion (after *King of the Monsters* worked so hard to make Godzilla the humanized kaiju, now Kong is the new beau), but that Kong *also constantly needs assistance from humans* in order to win the day, and in doing so, he comes across as somehow superhuman but also completely inept at the same time. It's a way of making representative humans kaiju-sized, if not physically, then at least in terms of the plot.

This isn't too far off a philosophy—this sort of mirroring—from what we see routinely in the Showa era. Perhaps the most blatant example is in *Godzilla vs. Hedorah*, where Godzilla's injured eye mirrors the injured eye of Dr. Yano. More obvious examples would be Ichiro and Minilla in *All Monsters Attack*, and Jet Jaguar in *Godzilla vs. Megalon*, who not only resembles Ultraman, but is the result of a contest held for fans to determine a new battling kaiju. In Jet Jaguar's case, he's a humanoid robot, clearly crafted by humans, and comes complete with human-like intelligence.

We see it all throughout the Showa era. Humans, everyday citizens who are scientists, journalists, children, laymen, and so on, not only narrate and comment on the action as if they were professional wrestling announcers, but they also directly interfere in the events, or otherwise are equated with kaiju. Gengo Kotaka and his friends in *Godzilla vs. Gigan* prevent the Godzilla Tower from destroying Godzilla, and King Caesar is awakened by humans to help Godzilla in *Godzilla vs. Mechagodzilla*. And, of course, in *King Kong vs. Godzilla*, the collected cast brings Kong to Godzilla for the final battle.

This process of humans influencing the events of the film happens in fits and spurts throughout the Heisei era, too, but not to the extent of the Showa era. In *Tokyo S.O.S.*, for example, Dr. Chujo and his grandson, Shun, successfully summon Mothra into the battle, but that's outstripped by Dr. Chujo's nephew, Yoshito, who pilots Kiryu, and whom much of the film's

12. Toward the Past and the Future at the Same Time   149

human arc centers on. Yet, constantly, within the Heisei era, we rarely see non-military or non-governmental characters directly influence the events and the outcomes. You could point, of course, to *Godzilla vs. Biollante*, where Dr. Shiragami's research and experiments lead to the creation of Biollante, but Shiragami isn't a "mad scientist," nor is he involved in anything other than the accidental creation of Biollante; his theories about heating up Godzilla so the military can strike him with their latest weaponized scientific idea, the Anti-Nuclear Energy Bacteria, is simply a subplot that does little other than to provide a break in the action, giving Biollante enough time to regenerate and mutate into a more imposing form.

Otherwise, the military/science (and there's significant overlap between the two in the Heisei era as well in the Legendary film series) "solutions" end up being more trouble than they're worth. MOGUERA, Mechagodzilla II, Kiryu, Super X … all weapons that have some moderate success before being destroyed by Godzilla or his enemies. The Heisei era of films generally depict humans as primarily spectators, with their attempts to interfere in the proceedings or to try to tilt the balance in one direction or the other often end up in abject failure—in fact, in *Godzilla vs. King Ghidorah*, all of the tampering with the timelines reveals only one thing: Godzilla is inevitable.

Thus, it's easy to see how *Godzilla vs. Kong*—as if the multiple throwbacks to Showa-era scenes and sequences weren't enough—tends to mimic the Showa era with plodding characters who somehow successfully tilt the scales in favor of their intended hero, who is, in this particular film, Kong. The destruction of the control panel in *Godzilla vs. Kong* by a pair of teens and a conspiracy-minded adult, who manage to "pause" Mechagodzilla by … pouring whiskey on a control panel, a clear echo of Gengo Kotaka's trick to blow up the control room for Godzilla Tower. The short circuit—which somehow interrupts a robot whose brain is powered by the decapitated King Ghidorah head from *King of the Monsters*—gives Kong and Godzilla the upper hand, and they win the day.

There's a weird, almost self-centered bravado in the Showa era that is reflected in *Godzilla vs. Kong*. The humans are rarely desperate, out of sorts, or simply unable to cope. They aren't resigned to their fate; the presence of aliens is just as predictable and shoulder-shrugging as the idea that the world itself is hollowed out and contains numerous kaiju who just may wander out at any time. Pollution can indeed create a massive kaiju, and a corporation can smuggle a kaiju head into their base by hitherto unknown quick-travel tunnels spread across the Earth. Of course an ancient God can be summoned to help Godzilla, or perhaps it can be a robot that can grow ridiculously huge in size; of course humans can shock a kaiju's heart into beating again by blowing up some fancy and magical technology on his chest.

It puts the "dumb" in the "big dumb fun" idea, and, I have to admit, it's not without its charm. It includes *us*, as everyday people, helping out kaiju and participating in the massive events spread across the screen, and we don't even have to think much about it; we just accept it, sit back, and wait for the next explosion to shatter our eardrums.

And this is where *Colossal* purposefully breaks free of kaiju history; although, like every kaiju film, there are distinct nods to the genre, *Colossal* manages to invert the kaiju violence we see in *King of the Monsters* or *Godzilla vs. Kong* and shoot it through with a disturbing subcontext of abuse and manipulation: very human elements, but also ones that show humans at their worst rather than their improbable best. For the kaiju who fight in *Colossal* are mere representatives of two very broken individuals. In fact, *Colossal* is so human-focused that kaiju fan complaints about *Colossal* not focusing on the kaiju, or kaiju battles, feel very valid. However, there are kaiju (or kaiju-like) creations that dominate the film's plot and feed the interactions of the humans, as their faults literally become larger than life. Few films have managed to milk so much tension, and, later, victory, from human feet stomping across a playground, and human feet walking down a sidewalk.

Nacho Vigalondo, the director and writer of *Colossal*, sets out a group of nifty "rules" for the kaiju to follow, and each of these "rules" plays with the genre to create something unique, much to the frustration of many of the "I just want to see big monsters fight" contingent of fans. And really, it's not surprising that Vigalondo, who also wrote and directed the incredibly intricate *Timecrimes*, would also put together a cohesive universe for *Colossal*, where a sort of interior logic slowly reveals itself as the film progresses.

Rule Number One: The Humans Are the Key to the Action and Are, in Fact, Actually Kaiju

As Matt Zoller Seitz rhetorically asks in his review of *Colossal*, "What if Godzilla was a projection of your issues?" It's a pretty fair assessment of the engine that drives the movie. If we accept that kaiju is, at the very base term, a giant creature, then we see two poles of the same people in *Colossal*. Their kaijus aren't opposites, however; in fact, their kaiju forms initially seem to be much friendlier and caring than their human counterparts. Gloria, in particular, finds something other than wayward and aimless drunkenness in her life when she understands that she is, in fact, also a kaiju on the other side of the world. She genuinely cares about the accidental destruction she causes, and works to avoid it as much as she can; in

12. Toward the Past and the Future at the Same Time   151

fact, she's initially horrified by the duality of her own personality, pressed into a massive kaiju form. It's as if someone took her and, instead of turning her into the 50 Foot Woman, simply transmogrified her outer form; the deeply flawed interior, however, remains in place.

As for Oscar, her foil for much of the film, he finds that the power he has long sought in his life is finally his, if only across the world. He is a deeply flawed and possessive individual, filled with sorrow and hatred, and his realization that his life is confined to a small town rather than primed by his ambition (as Gloria's was before she relapsed), and his realization that he, too, controls a massive robot somewhere in Seoul, fills him with a sense of real power he's never had before, and, while his avatar causes untold death and destruction on the other side of the world, Oscar gets what he really wants, which is a completely submissive group of people around him, especially Gloria. His understanding of his Other form is that it manifests the true power that he seeks; while Gloria is somewhat ashamed by her Other's drunken stumbling and accidental murder, Oscar is emboldened by it. He admits that his discovery that he's a massive, murderous robot in another world gives him a sense of importance and power that far outstrips what he expected, and, perhaps, what he feels he deserves. As such, his newfound power not only gives him domain over, almost literally, every move Gloria makes, but also over life and death itself.

As with Glenn Manning and Nancy Archer, their sudden change in size—even though they don't even witness their avatar kaiju personally—heightens their grotesquery, and their responses form (and eventually inverts) the intricate power play that fuels the climax of the film.

Rule Number Two: The Action Between the Humans Takes Place Primarily on or Around a Playground

One of the most frustrating moments that fans tend to bring up in *Godzilla* (2014) is when Godzilla appears in Hawaii, and we, as viewers, are on the verge of seeing Godzilla and the MUTOs battle for the first time. But, just as that is about to happen, we cut away to the Brody home, where Sam plays with his dinosaur toys in front of a newscast showing Godzilla and the MUTO finally engaging. It's a moment that shows the movement from "big screen" to "small screen" and yet pays homage to the reality of kaiju being, in part, children's playthings. For director Gareth Edwards, it's a moment where he can pay tribute to dinosaurs and imagination, and their role in the creation of the kaiju we see on the screen. Nacho Vigalondo heightens that metaphor by literally placing the domain of the humans within a playground.

The playground—just an average, run-of-the-mill, somewhat down-trodden small town municipal playground—is the site of massive battles that take place in an exotic location. In this way, Vigalondo echoes Edwards's homage by quite literally having the adults act like children on the playground, summoning forth their "real" creations in a place neither of them have ever been.

Another moment that matches this idea is the "origin story," if you will, of the playground itself. It is imbued with the nostalgic meaning of both Oscar's and Gloria's shared past: while walking to school with a diorama of Seoul, a jealous Oscar (her diorama is far superior to his), destroys it. Their collective anger draws a mythical lightning bolt from the heavens, and we see their two future avatars: children's toys. Oscar's is a robot and Gloria's is a dinosaur. In this way, *Colossal* not only provides a bit of magical fantasy to the proceedings, but very uniquely ties together childhood and kaiju in an inextricable link coated in trauma.

Oscar is severely depressed and aware that he is slowly growing into the same small-town nothing that his father had become, and Gloria is a raging alcoholic who alienates everyone she meets, specifically so she can be lonely and miserable. To both of them, the origin story of the diorama, and the sudden shift of their toys from playthings to future living kaiju, is a part of the last happy and naive days they will feel. Their wholly toxic relationship fuels the appearance of the kaiju (although, technically, I supposed Oscar's robot would be a jaeger), and provide a literal battleground that echoes the "you're it" games and challenges that fueled their childhood.

In this way, Vigalondo successfully, in my opinion, merges the ideas of childhood nostalgia and kaiju by presenting two very flawed characters, with Oscar, in particular, slowly devolving from odd to outright sadistic and controlling. *Colossal* essentially focuses on three distinct locations: playground, bar, and Gloria's house, and they each show the failures and vulnerabilities of the adults, as each of them are somewhat trapped in the past. The playground, of course, didn't even exist when their "origin story" occurs, but it's fitting that it's a mostly abandoned playground, given over to adults reenacting every childhood fantasy, for good or for ill, within its geographic confines.

In fact, one of the visual cues Vigalondo uses to show the viewer that it's time for the action to take place on the playground (the exact time is 8:05 a.m., and lasts only as long as the initial conflict between Oscar and Gloria when they were children) are large groups of children walking to school. Yet, every time we see the playground, there are no children there, none to be chased away, and none that apparently even use the seemingly brand-new equipment. This playground, like the bar itself, is a refuge for

12. Toward the Past and the Future at the Same Time   153

adults, a place to be freed from the drudgery and apathy of everyday life. Within the confines of the playground, just as in the confines of the bar, is a small social group that tacitly agrees to reflect the larger surrounding community.

As we see frequently in *Colossal*, Oscar has a small group of friends and acquaintances that surround him at the bar, and each of them agree to leave their issues at the door, a characteristic that Oscar readily exploits when he calls Garth a "junkie," which sends Garth almost completely out of the film at that point.

Finally, there's Gloria's house, which fails as a sanctuary for her, because, over the course of the film, it is slowly filled, more and more, with symbols of Oscar's oppression. He constantly sends over furniture as a sort of power play. Each time new furniture arrives, it functions as a means to further subject Gloria, tying her more and more to Oscar.

Rule Number Three: The Death and Destruction is Felt Worlds Away

In a geopolitical sense, there's a certain acidity to the notion that a few Americans are responsible for—often ignorantly responsible for—widespread destruction and death in an Eastern country. In this case, it's South Korea, specifically Seoul, and the ignorance of the American characters regarding everything about … well, any other part of the world … is clear. Ironically, and *Colossal* may be a direct nod, this motif also appears in *The Host*, a South Korean kaiju film. In *The Host*, a single American military doctor orders his South Korean subordinate to empty hundreds of bottles of formaldehyde into the nearby Han River, leading to contamination that eventually spawns the creature that kills dozens, if not hundreds, of South Koreans. There's a sort of malicious butterfly effect here, where an individual American's problems trickle out of their own personal lives and begin to affect—and kill—numerous innocent people in the East.

We see something similar in *The Return of Godzilla*, of course, when Japan is caught in a nuclear showdown between the Americans and the Soviets; although the American re-editing (*Godzilla 1985*) makes sure that the viewer knows that the Soviets are the aggressors, the Japanese cut definitely points to the Americans as having an equal, if not slightly heavier, responsibility for the idea of again bombing Japan.

But *Colossal* does what no other kaiju film does. It makes civilians and their flaws the centerpiece of the film. Yes, we can root against a corrupt military and we can see how geopolitics lead to awful decision-making for almost anyone but a few lone superpowers, but with Gloria and Oscar,

154 The Kaiju Connection

there's no easy transference and no one, really, to root for. Gloria's drunkenness causes a significant amount of destruction, and her impulse to show off for her new friends leads to dozens of more deaths when she stumbles and falls. Oscar, of course, is the ultimate baddie in the movie: a power-hungry, gaslighting, malicious, and mean-spirited alcoholic; when juxtaposed against Gloria, it's easy to forget that she, too, isn't necessarily a hero in the conventional sense. But there's no doubt that she enjoys some mild redemption within the narrative; as Kathi Maio writes:

> Identifying herself as an ugly, lizard-skinned behemoth is an unusual but potent path to personal empowerment. Gloria realizes that even a monster can be a protector and a positive force in the world. That is a role she eventually embraces, without reference to a romantic solution to life's travails [182].

It's important to note that she rejects both toxic relationships while in human form. She rejects Tim and she also travels across the world, literally, to confront a gigantic robot all on her own.

What's most telling about their arcs is how Gloria and Oscar internalize—or don't—the death and destruction they cause. Like many Westerners, they seem blissfully ignorant of geopolitics and geography; yet, Gloria's discovery that *she* killed hundreds of South Koreans leads her to panic and depression. However, Oscar's journey is almost militaristic: he sees South Koreans, and his power over them, as extensions of his power over Gloria, and, as such, he feels no moral qualms about murdering them and causing untold property damage to get what *he* wants. When Gloria rides with Oscar to find the nearest Korean person in New Hampshire (which seems to take them a while), Gloria is struck with guilt over seeing the older Korean couple console one another while watching her avatar cause destruction on the screen. Oscar's response? Well, he talks about how hungry he is.

Both Gloria and Oscar seem to be the typical Ugly American, with only an abstract sense of others around them, and the further away those others are, the less they seem to understand, empathize, or sympathize with them. Although Gloria sees the innate humanity in the situation she is in, Oscar obstinately refuses to do so, and, as such, becomes the other half of the foreign policy coin. He's the guy who is quick to anger and ready to resort to violence to get the power he craves, and will often do so happily.

Rule Number Four: It's All a Matter of Perception

In this way, *Colossal* seems to look forward to new possibilities in the kaiju genre; no, they aren't strictly "kaiju," and *Colossal* may barely qualify

12. Toward the Past and the Future at the Same Time   155

as a kaiju film in the eyes of some academics and critics. Yet, the kaiju in this film tend to expand the plot rather than narrow it. The ideas within *Colossal* follow a neat trick of using giant monsters manifesting on the other side of the world to go from macro to micro. While the monsters do the typical stomp and battle routine, the more serious—and frightening—aspects of their existence plays out among the humans. Gloria seems barely redeemable in her decision-making ability and her clear alcoholism; Oscar slowly becomes more and more maniacal and possessive until he clearly turns into the worst kind of manipulative stalker. The kaiju are damned near friendly and peaceful on their own; it's the *people* who make them anything other than completely neutral.

In fact, it's mostly accidents at the start of the film that lead to the destruction of large swaths of Seoul; Gloria stumbles drunkenly through the city, and then she falls over when she finds out that Oscar has a kaiju avatar as well. Before she falls over, however, we realize that a happy, well-adjusted Gloria, who is keen to show off her newfound identity, can dance and playfully motion toward the citizens of Seoul, and no destruction will result. Later, after she falls over, she feels guilty enough to convince Oscar to take her to the nearest Korean he knows and she reappears as her kaiju, only this time to transcribe her apology into a nearby field for all to see.

This "casts" Gloria's avatar as the "good" kaiju after an initial burst of destruction, not unlike Gamera and Godzilla's story arcs, and, as such, that means that the "good" kaiju will eventually need an enemy: the very robotic opposition in Oscar's robot form, which is appropriately (for him) inhuman and emotionless. What is horrible violence to one person is delicious mayhem to another.

It's important to note that kaiju in *Colossal* were pretty much initially dismissed as conspiracy crank theory. When the first Gloria "attack" occurs, the world reacts in shock, but we soon understand that a glimpse of her kaiju first appeared a few decades earlier when it was first created in Gloria's mind. And we see a world soon after that reveals a bizarre community atmosphere. I'd like to think that people were getting together to support one another during this paradigm shift—and it appears Gloria expects the same—but, in actuality, Oscar's bar gets packed with people to watch numerous big screen TVs, as if they were watching a World Cup semifinal. This all happens *somewhere else*, so it can be viewed with intense detachment and fascination.

And that fascination doesn't last very long. As the townspeople get more "used" to the kaiju appearances, there's no clear need for the townspeople to support one another, or at least to exchange notes or discuss their ideas. This is made obvious by the relative lack of people who go to the bar when we revisit it over and over again during the film. The novelty of the kaiju wears off; after all, it's perfectly distant from New Hampshire, and, once it becomes relatively clear that there's no direct impact for many of their lives, then it's time to go about their daily lives. It's a fair portrayal of a typical kaiju question: we always see the people running away from the beasts as they stomp through the cities that they live and work in, but how does that impact people who are further away? As Shin Godzilla plows from Kamakura to Tokyo, how does it affect the daily lives of those in Sapporo? How does it affect them to know that a massive frozen kaiju sits in Tokyo? How do people in a small town in Kentucky, for example, respond to Godzilla's appearing in Hawaii to battle MUTOs? And so on.

What *Colossal* seems to posit is that, after the kaiju appear and the initial shock wears off, those who aren't immediately and directly affected simply adjust to the paradigm and then move on. The world changes, until it doesn't. The perception of a threat, the perception of a new world order, is rarely felt in the kaiju genre … if the battles happen in a rural area, it's usually somewhere devoid of population (often, the battles take place around villages, such as in *Daimajin* and *Varan*), and if it happens in a city, we rarely understand—or refuse to consider—the fallout that occurs. In films as diverse as *Cloverfield* to *Shin Godzilla* to *King of the Monsters*, entire cities are laid to waste, and we, as viewers, are rarely invited to consider these consequences, and are, at times, coaxed into not even seeking out the reality: outside of *Godzilla* (1954), *Gamera 3: Revenge of Iris*, it's difficult to think of extended sequences of refugees or casualties. Even *Godzilla* (2014) attempted to show us the displacement of a huge number of people, whose homes are lost or threatened, and they are gathered into stadiums or into impromptu refugee camps. But, at the same time, those refugees cheer for Godzilla as he awakens and swims away. After all, Godzilla is a "force of nature" in the Legendary series—for at least one film—but he isn't a natural disaster. No hurt feelings; it's just a byproduct of his existence.

There's a metanalysis available here. In every decision made during the production of a kaiju film, we're asked to inhabit the same space that people who are unaffected by disasters tend to inhabit. We might feel bad if we're shown the results, and we may even volunteer or donate. But, generally, if the impact isn't directly felt, then we're safe, sound, and perfectly able and willing to turn away after the initial shock and continue on with our workaday lives.

And so, with *Colossal*, there's also very much the sense that this film, if it isn't feminist, at least is one of the first films that focus in-depth on a female main character (in fact, for much of the film, Gloria is the *only* female character) and her slow understanding of her role in the world. While we all no doubt cheer at Gloria's inversion of the kaiju process,

12. Toward the Past and the Future at the Same Time   157

which leads to her literally throwing Oscar away, I think there's a much deeper moment that occurs in the film that gives credence to this sympathetic portrayal and the depth of her character.

As we know, Gloria's return to her relatively podunk town is because her boyfriend, Tim, kicks her out of his apartment because, as he claims, of her alcoholism. She views this, initially, as a classic "I need to find myself" moment, as many films tend to do, and places all of the relationship's problems on herself. She knows she is an alcoholic and works to address that during the movie, but she does it, at first, to prevent herself from going on a destructive path, first with Tim, and then with the citizens of Seoul. Tim, claiming that he has a job assignment, comes to town and tries to reunite with Gloria, who obediently comes to his hotel room when he calls. But it's this discussion in the apartment when Gloria realizes that Tim, too, is toxic in his own way; Oscar is more nakedly manipulative, but Tim spends most of their reunion chastising Gloria for being a waitress and, when she stands up for herself, he begins to openly mock her. At this point, Gloria has her full realization that she's in at least *two* deeply poisonous relationships, and decides to work her way out of both of them.

In Seoul, Gloria calls Tim to apologize for leaving him behind—she had earlier promised to go back with Tim to provoke Oscar—and tells him that she doesn't need to explain herself to him, and that, ominously, she is more dangerous than she's ever been, a line that echoes Oscar's earlier warning to Gloria that he was no longer playing "Mr. Nice Guy." Gloria's flipping of the script: her human self coming to Seoul so that the kaiju form would manifest itself back in New Hampshire, is her ultimate freeing of all of her toxic relationships. Oscar is "defeated" and banished, Tim is dumped, and her childhood trauma is alleviated. But Gloria's flaws and foibles remain. The last frame of the film is her reluctance to turn down a drink at a Seoul bar, played for comedy.

I'm going to stop here on this topic, because I don't quite think that *Colossal* would qualify as a feminist film, nor do I think it's completely true in the portrayal of Gloria's often hapless character. But I do feel that *Colossal* is the rarest of films with kaiju in them. It manages not only to have a female lead character, but also one whose inner life and struggles are relatively fleshed out. As viewers, we learn more about Gloria as an individual than we ever do for Asagi Kusanagi in the *Gamera* Heisei trilogy, or Miki Saegusa in her appearances ranging across several films, from *Godzilla vs. Biollante* to *Godzilla vs. Destroyah*.

In fact, Gloria's characterization in *Colossal*, and her relationship to the kaiju within, is the flipside of both Kusanagi and Saegusa: for both of them, their existence is tailored around the kaiju. They interact with the kaiju and it gives them some meaning and depth in doing so. Yet, with

Gloria, the kaiju's existence is almost literally centered around Gloria, as her repressed anger at Oscar coupled with a hefty dose of magic realism creates the kaiju (as does Oscar's intense self-loathing seems to create his avatar robot).

In this regard, *Colossal* manages to successfully tinker with the typical formula of a kaiju film, and, yes, it means far fewer "big dumb fights" (notwithstanding Gloria and Oscar's drunken fistfights), but it also means that the ideas of how humans can be almost as destructive to themselves and to others as kaiju are, comes to the forefront. *Colossal* is somewhat less than a standard kaiju film, and somewhat less than the typical "finding your roots" Hallmark Movie melodrama, but, in between those two poles, lies a unique film that manages to mold—sometimes successfully, sometimes not—kaiju films into a genre that can somehow seek new purpose that steps beyond those "big dumb fights."

And, speaking of "big dumb fights," there's no doubt a place for films such as *Godzilla vs. Kong*, which is essentially the exact opposite structure of *Colossal*: worldwide instead of localized, kaijus with more personalities than the humans, and nothing but fights with human drama functioning as rude interruptions. Perhaps I'm being unfair in this comparison. Perhaps *Godzilla vs. Kong* and *Colossal* are two opposing poles of kaiju film. Perhaps *Colossal* shouldn't even be considered a kaiju film. Yet, it's interesting how *Godzilla vs. Kong* embraces the "big dumb fights" aspect of kaiju films, ladening the plot with ponderous human actions that break up the video-game-like battles that dominate the big screen (or the littler screen, given that *Godzilla vs. Kong* was initially released in the U.S. simultaneously on HBOMax).

In *Godzilla vs. Kong*, humans and human plots are an unpleasant, plodding, and, at times, utterly ridiculous sidelight that exists solely to ferry the viewer from one locale to the next, from one battle to the next. And *Colossal*, just five years earlier, three years before even *Godzilla: King of the Monsters,* flipped that very dynamic, rejecting the "big dumb fights" ideal and instead pushing forward the human drama to provide a somewhat caustic criticism of not only societal and personal ills, but some geopolitical issues as well. I'm loath to say that *Colossal* is a more thoughtful film, but it is one that contains a certain depth to it, as if the kaiju themselves were crowded out of portions of the script to better capture the nuances of the film.

To return to where I started. Certainly, this isn't to say that one film is better than the other, nor is it to say that fans are right or wrong to prefer one film over the other. This is more of a "two paths diverged" moment, with *Godzilla: King of the Monsters* and *Godzilla vs. Kong* showing us one way to make a successful kaiju film, and *Colossal* showing us another,

12. Toward the Past and the Future at the Same Time 159

quite unique, way of utilizing the genre trappings of the kaiju film—many of said trappings to be found in both *King of the Monsters* and *Godzilla vs. Kong*—to provide a new way of structuring the narrative and intent of the kaiju film.

This is ultimately what I mean when I say that stepping outside of the kaiju "boundary," where we label kaiju films as "true" or "correct" if we focus on only a small template of ideology, such as if the film has a Japanese origin, can tell us more about the kaiju genre and what it means. If a film like *Colossal* isn't, in your book, a kaiju film, for whatever reasons, I would still argue that it deserves some conversation, alongside other genre-bending narratives such as *Trollhunter* or *Cloverfield*, because they allow us to understand the borders of the kaiju film. Like Gloria and Oscar, we won't know until we step inside these seemingly rigid boundaries and witness the results; only then can we start to see what impact *we*, as viewers, fans, and critics, have on the genre itself, and how we accept or reject the directions that certain films decide to take.

13

Men as Kaiju: *Big Man Japan* and *Kaiju Mono*

It's quite difficult to make a successful satire, or a successful parody of a genre film. For every *Blazing Saddles*, there's a dozen films that never quite stick the landing, managing to critique a genre while also managing to be a quality genre film all on its own. This is why *Big Man Japan* and *Kaiju Mono* are somewhat startling. They each have flaws, of course, but these films are truly the first quality attempts at interrogating and attempting to understand the somewhat ragged edges of the kaiju genre. They both examine real world sociocultural issues while also occasionally lampooning kaiju films, but they also managed to do so with great respect for the genre, and, along the way, both of these films somehow manage to be decent kaiju films in their own rights.

Both of these very modestly budgeted films can be viewed, simply, as the inverse of one another. In *Big Man Japan*, a loser loses even more when he becomes kaiju-sized, but stays true to himself, even bucking tradition at times. But, in *Kaiju Mono*, the unwilling scientist who becomes kaiju-sized wins everything: fame, women, outright adoration, but loses himself in the process. And they both work to blur the lines between professional wrestling and kaiju battling, which, at times, creates parody, but also highlights the close relationship between the two disparate genres. There's just something intensely masculine about both forms of entertainment.

That's not to say, of course, that women can't be professional wrestlers (they are) or act as kaiju (they have); nor does it mean that women can't be fans of professional wrestling or the kaiju genre (they are). Even so, men tend to dominate both fields, from creators to performers to fandom. Both professional wrestling and kaiju films (as well as a significant amount of science fiction film) tend to allow fans to avoid or otherwise ameliorate what Mark Duffett describes as "gender trouble"—their feminization through the simple act of being a fan. Quite contrary to questioning masculinity, both professional wrestling—and mixed martial arts—and

160

13. Men as Kaiju: Big Man Japan and Kaiju Mono   161

kaiju film, often reinforce masculinity.* And *Kaiju Mono* and *Big Man Japan* enjoy poking at the standard, stereotypical boundaries of masculinity as well as the kaiju film.

Professional wrestling, of course, may have been one of the progenitors of kaiju film, or at least the relationship between the two, especially in the earliest eras where two humans wearing costumes fought as the central focus of the event. It has been a worldwide phenomenon for almost a century now. Don't believe me? Ask a Japanese person about Rikidozan, Giant Baba, or Antonio Inoki. Ask someone from Mexico or Central America about El Santo. And ask an American about Andre the Giant (who is French, but was most "over" in the States during the end of his career). Each of these wrestlers penetrated mainstream pop culture, and along with making millions during their career, managed to routinely appear on television, in film, and other mainstream outlets.

It's like what I always say about *Moby Dick*: if you've never read it, you still know a *lot* more about it than you think. White Whale. Captain Ahab. Themes of Revenge and Destruction. Queequeg. That's how you know something has penetrated pop culture consciousness—when people who never pay attention to the form of the delivery (professional wrestling, in this case), but know well the details of the individual.

Naturally, the idea of professional wrestling sharing DNA with the kaiju film isn't a bridge too far. Consider the cultural impact in Japan of Rikidozan,[†] who made a career of being a Japanese superhero, daring to overcome American gaijin:

> Japan had been beaten by the Americans in the war, ruled by the Americans during the Occupation, and outstripped by the Americans in so many ways, material, technological, and cultural [....] But now this big, strong Japanese guy was putting it to the *gaijin*, with style! With every karate chop, Riki struck a blow for Japanese pride [Schilling 194].

Little wonder, then, that the more heroic form of Godzilla that would appear fighting numerous outside threats would adopt wrestling moves

---

*Duffett notes that the "social stereotype" of many men in fandom leads to the unfortunate result of being "socially inadequate and somehow defective in their masculinities" (206). This stereotype—better described as the popular "geek living in his mom's basement" insult—can provoke righteous sensitivity in fandom. One need only take a look at the dislike of many male kaiju fans toward William Tsutsui, who attended G-Fest and playfully poked fun at some of the participants there in *Godzilla on My Mind*. In the vacuum of the "authentic" community, Tsutsui's notes about "the occasional hot shower with one's figurines," the "domestic problems" caused by collecting, and discussions of "plushy monsters and plasticy creatures for human-toy union" (153) still sting in online communities focused on kaiju collecting.

†It should be noted that Rikidozan kept a secret for his entire career: he was actually Korean. Born in Wonsan during the Japanese occupation of Korea, Rikidozan was forced to take a Japanese name and dreaded people finding out he wasn't Japanese (Schilling 195).

162 The Kaiju Connection

into his repertoire, lending itself to the description of "big-time wrestling in seedy latex suits" (Tsutsui 13). One needs only to point at the heightened irreality of professional wrestling, add a different set and a different costume, and you now have, instead of two people battling, a dinosaur and an armadillo fighting.* This all started, naturally, with *Godzilla Raids Again*, "a knockdown dragout with dirt flying and buildings tumbling," and became known as "*kaiju puroresu*—(monster pro-wrestling)" (Gerow 63).

Some of the more infamous Godzilla moments feature wrestling moves: the very long flying dropkick in *Godzilla vs. Megalon* and his improbable, if not physically impossible, flying body splash in *Godzilla vs. Megaguirus* are some of the more memorable moments; Ryfle and Godziszewski describe the Godzilla in *King Kong vs. Godzilla* as an "outsized Rikidozan" (168). And, of course, most of the 1970s Godzilla featured a series of "tag team" battles with Godzilla teaming up with Jet Jaguar or King Caesar while battling another deadly duo, consisting of Mechagodzilla,[†] Gigan, or Megalon.

Just like wrestling matches, the kaiju battles often feature characters or announcers commenting on the action to help clarify what the viewer is seeing. One example would be in *Godzilla vs. King Ghidorah*, during the first battle between the two. Godzilla gets knocked over, and Ghidorah lifts up into the air and stomps on Godzilla several times. "Godzilla is losing!" one character exclaims. "King Ghidorah is winning!" says another. The adoption of kaiju puroresu is just another example of the Godzilla franchise, in particular, embracing prevailing Japanese pop culture. After all, professional wrestling became, through the efforts of Rikidozan, "one of the most popular media phenomena in Japan from the mid–1950s to the early 1960s" (Gerow 64).

This is all based on the ideas of "monsters" in the world as well, and we can see the overlap between kaiju films and professional wrestling there, too. In many ways, Godzilla, who started off life as a monster in *Godzilla* and perhaps stayed that way for a bit longer in *Godzilla Raids Again*, began to take on more "human" aspects as early as his third film,

---

*And professional wrestling, especially in Japan, isn't afraid of exploiting this close connection and embracing some of the silliness. The promotion *Dramatic Dream Team* has promoted matches between wrestlers and an inflatable sex doll—first, Akihiro, and then her "brother," Yoshihiko. A quick spin through YouTube Japanese wrestling clips will reveal numerous matches featuring wrestlers in a wild array of outlandish costumes.
[†]The presence of the evil doppelganger has been a trope in professional wrestling as well, especially as elaborate costumes, mannerisms, and masks have become more popular. In World Wrestling Entertainment and All Elite Wrestling, there have been evil alter egos for characters such as Diesel, Razor Ramon, and the Undertaker, among others. Of course, the doppelganger or "evil twin" storyline has been around for quite some time, but this factor with the wrestling-style chaos in the final battles is amazingly similar.

13. *Men as Kaiju:* Big Man Japan *and* Kaiju Mono   163

King Kong vs. Godzilla. After that, the grandest kaiju of them all rarely retained the animalistic portrayal, and was often humanized or given human qualities, either through mannerisms or physicality. The lone exceptions to this rule really seem to be sparse: *Godzilla, Godzilla Raids Again, The Return of Godzilla,* and *Shin Godzilla* were among the very few films *not* to give human qualities or personality to him,* and Gamera quickly strayed away from being animalistic or monstrous not long into his film career as well.

Films where Godzilla is at his most heroic are the ones where he's most "human," say, in *Son of Godzilla* or *Destroy All Monsters.* Or, he is given somewhat human motivations, for example, when he crushes the morally questionable Mitsuo Katagiri in *Godzilla 2000.* Likewise, even in moments where Godzilla retains his monstrousness at the start of movies like *Godzilla 2000,* he is often placed against an even larger (often literally) example of the monstrous, in this case, a literal alien, Orga. The same occurs in *Godzilla vs. Biollante* and *Godzilla versus Megaguirus.* Godzilla is only a monster until he comes across even bigger monsters. He is, in other words, the Other until he gets out–Othered.

Professional wrestling, to say the least, is enamored with monsters, both in terms of physicality, but also in terms of their gimmicks. There was the "undead" Undertaker, who, early in his career, could tank almost any damage and pop right back up again (except for when Hulk Hogan threw salt in his eyes, which Undertaker had an unexpected vulnerability to). Or Papa Shango, the voodoo-based wrestler who cursed his opponents, forcing them to spit black goo from their mouths. There's also The Fiend, a wrestler with a Slipknot-style mask who is invulnerable to most forms of pain. Outside of the supernatural realms, there's also physical monsters, ranging from the massive Yokozuna, who was often billed at around 500 pounds,† or the powerlifter/strongman Braun Strowman, whose nickname is, literally, The Monster Among Men. And, of course, one of the most famous wrestlers of all, Andre the Giant, who seems to grow larger in every retelling of his exploits, as if he were a modern-day folkloric legend. As in the kaiju film, you're only the biggest monster on the block until a bigger monster comes along.

It goes without saying, of course, that the professional wrestling industry *and* the kaiju film fan base tends to skew overwhelmingly male.

---

*If you're thinking of *Giant Monsters All-Out Attack* I would just point out that Godzilla personifies the forgotten Japanese war dead in that film, so is a somewhat human extension of a kaiju.

†Wrestling, because it is such a show of a sport, tends to "bend" numbers a little, but there were numerous reports that Yokozuna's weight started to go upwards toward 600 pounds by the end of his life.

164 The Kaiju Connection

Inroads have been made for female fans of both genres, but, just a quick glance at the crowd at an WWE or AEW event or the gatherings at kaiju fanfests such as G-Fest shows that those inroads remain relatively minor. This is not to say that the number of females in science fiction and the kaiju film genre hasn't grown; it has, but when you start at such a low number, the growth tends to remain meager—special individual examples aside—for quite some time.

In many ways, both the kaiju film and professional wrestling tend to verify the conventional male narratives for Western society. Confrontation and conflict as the preferred form of settling disagreements and disputes,* and the display of masculinity as an—and I'm trying not to specifically use the word "toxic" here—almost monstrous form of existence. But masculinity has a series of markers in both professional wrestling and in kaiju film that tends to naturally draw male viewers. There is something intoxicating about widespread destruction, both of cities and of bodies, that keeps actual fatalities at a distance but glamorizes or glorifies pain and the ability to ignore or overcome it.

"Hardcore" matches are a constant attraction in professional wrestling, and some of the most (in)famous legends of professional wrestling made their names in "deathmatches" and the like, with barbed wire in place of ring ropes, thumbtacks, clubs, steel chairs, and lots and lots of blood: Mick Foley, Terry Funk, Abdullah the Butcher, and numerous others are well-known in professional wrestling circles not for their physiques or their wrestling acumen, but for their ability to transcend pain and take copious amounts of physical damage.

In kaiju film, the overcoming of pain is often a sequence that bears itself out through numerous Godzilla films. Turn toward Godzilla, beaten and bloodied in *Godzilla vs. Gigan* and again in *Godzilla vs. Megalon*, or his wounded eye in *Godzilla vs. Hedorah*, or when he is impaled by tentacles in *Godzilla vs. Biollante*. In these films, Godzilla is clearly the hero, the monster who has been out-monstered, either through aliens (Gigan and Megalon) or through environmental or genetic mutations (Hedorah and Biollante). In *Godzilla vs. Destroyah*, Godzilla is ultimately defeated by his own body breaking down as well as immense amounts of damage from Destroyah, but we're left with the heartening sight of his nuclear meltdown reviving his son to carry on the legacy.

Shin Ultraman features a battle between Mefilas and Ultraman in which Mefilas simply decides it's not worth his effort to continue the battle and comes to an agreement with Ultraman to stop fighting. "Talking things out peacefully is always the best solution," Kimio Tamura intones. Later, Ultraman, in his human form of Kaminaga, stands down several government officials and a massive entourage of armed police officers by speaking with them about the consequences of their actions.

13. Men as *Kaiju*: *Big Man Japan* and *Kaiju Mono*   165

Fast-forward to the Millennium era and in the films where Godzilla plays the villain, or at least plays the part of an antagonist, the tables are flipped. Upon sustaining too much damage, Godzilla is defeated or otherwise runs away. He is reduced, literally, to a heart in *Giant Monsters All-Out Attack*, and in *Godzilla Against Mechagodzilla*, he gets hit with the Absolute Zero cannon, blowing a massive hole in his chest. Going even further into the Legendary films, Godzilla is knocked down and knocked out several times by the MUTOs in *Godzilla* and nearly killed twice by King Ghidorah in *Godzilla: King of the Monsters*.

Yet, when the shoe is on the other foot, and the more "human" (and, thus, less monstrous) of a pairing is injured, our sympathies, and our cheers, go to King Kong* in *Godzilla vs. Kong*, who is broken, beaten, and killed (kind of) by Godzilla before being revived to save the day. There's a certain performativity to the idea of being manly enough to battle through pain; think about *Gamera 3: Revenge of Iris* when Gamera, outmatched and on the verge of being killed, *blows off his own hand* and wins the day, only to turn to valiantly battle a group of Gyaos who are about to descend. We want the "bad guy" to suffer pain, or to try to escape it through acts of cowardice, before being thoroughly and definitively beaten, and we want the "good guy" to show their value and their worth through self-sacrifice and overcoming obstacles.

Of course, for the kaiju film, some of that may just be the genre-hopping that the kaiju film allows for. Many fans, including myself, stumbled on Godzilla or Gamera while watching late-night (or really really early morning) syndicated programs dedicated to science fiction and fantasy. One night, *The Thing from Another World*, then *Creature with the Atom Brain* another night, and then *Godzilla vs. Megalon*. The "jump" from Sci-Fi fandom to kaiju fandom was a very small one in the 1970s through the 1990s, and the gender divide remained strong for quite some time; after all, science fiction, where kaiju film has most of its roots—tended to be dominated by men from almost any angle, from creators to directors to the fans themselves.

Indeed, many people have noted the continued lack of a female presence in the kaiju films themselves, overall, with Miki Saegusa in a trio of Godzilla films and Asagi Kusanagi in three Gamera films, both sets of films, occurring, interestingly, during the Heisei era. And one could argue that the modern Legendary Godzilla films have featured somewhat more gender diverse casting, although Juliette Binoche herself seemed

---

*Just looking at *King Kong* in 1933, there's a lot to be said about the masculine relationship to pain as depicted in the more "humanistic" form: Kong, when he gets cut on the finger by Denham, looks confused and legitimately hurt; yet, in *Skull Island* and *Godzilla vs. Kong*, Kong is more willing to "tank" the pain and even uses it as an outlet for his rage.

166 **The Kaiju Connection**

somewhat disgruntled by her character's quick exit in *Godzilla*.* Yet, there still seems to be a primarily male-driven perspective on the kaiju genre.

In many ways, then, kaiju film and professional wrestling have a natural connection, and *Kaiju Mono* and *Big Man Japan* exploit that connection in a variety of ways. Both are as subtle as a sledgehammer, but the criticisms of masculinity and superhero worship colliding with the "real world" are very there, and very relevant. What better way to put the male body on display front and center than to have a performer step out of the kaiju costume and appear only in trunks to join the battle?

Kaiju Mono is more frantic than *Big Man Japan*, and, in the opening few minutes, we get numerous potential references ranging from *Noroi* to *Matango* to *Daimajin* to *Ultraman*,† among others. In fact, the references and homages that cut through the film are so dense that it's difficult to keep up with them all. The central focus of the film is the stoic and at times goofy acting of Japanese wrestler Kota Ibushi, who dives into his role with a smirk and a general look of confusion, as if he woke up one day and happened to be acting in a kaiju film and found out he was actually the star.

This only adds to the general hilarity of the movie, as Ibushi seems to swing between flexing his muscles, giving a sly grin, and expressing befuddlement at his newfound fame, but it goes without saying that hiring wrestlers to fight kaiju in *Kaiju Mono* is just a complete dropping of one-half of the battle between rubber suits, and, ironically, this seems to push the question of reality into another direction entirely. Films like *King King vs. Godzilla* end with two rubber suited actors duking it out, and, somehow, that seems more "real" at times than the fights between Kota Ibushi and the rubber suited fiend in *Kaiju Mondo*.

It beggars belief that a reluctant scientist, Nitta, would turn into a gigantic-sized professional wrestler that looks nothing like him after an injection of a super serum derived from mutated mushrooms; a giant ape with a proclivity for blonde women and alcohol fighting an atomic

---

*Of course, there's Kong, too, whose perpetual fascination with women—a characteristic of even the knockoff versions such as Mighty Joe Young and Yeti—belies a somewhat gender-specific viewpoint. This, of course, would be an example of the "male gaze" for Kong as he consistently objectifies and attempts to literally physically possess the woman. If there's not a kaiju-based Bechdel test out there, someone needs to invent one.

†I should mention that *Ultraman* and the numerous series that followed, from *Ultraman* (1966–1967) to *Ultraman Decker* (2022–2023), is as close to professional wrestling as a kaiju-based property can be: Ultraman, in almost every form, breaks out a series of slams, flips, kicks, and chops on the kaiju before inevitably breaking out his Specium Ray (sometimes known as an Ultra Beam) to finish the battle—a classic "finishing move." Ultraman's human form and his combat style are easily transferred to such video games as *Ultraman Fighting Evolution 0* and *Ultraman: Toward the Future*.

13. *Men as Kaiju:* Big Man Japan *and* Kaiju Mono   167

dinosaur seems somehow more palatable. Nitta, however, is spurred forward by a cheap paean to his masculinity, or lack thereof. He is lured into allowing the injection, or at least temporarily dropping his complaints, after seeing the buff men in a wrestling magazine and being convinced that he could be more attractive to women if he were, literally, someone else.

The primary spur for the film is the ongoing battle against Mono, a kaiju complete with apparent rips in her costume, and is a design quite clearly at home with some of the more inexpensive and less inspired designs from *Ultraman* or *Ultra Q*. The presence of Mono is prompted by the discovery of an egg (shades of *Godzilla vs. SpaceGodzilla* or *Son of Godzilla*), and causes the creation of the Anti-Kaiju Mono task force, reminiscent of the G-Force or the Japanese Xenomorph Self-Defense Force. From there, the viewer is bombarded by a hodgepodge of one-off jokes and situations; for example, spies steal the secret formula (an homage to *Godzilla vs. Biollante*, among others), and are tracked down, only to discover that the theft wasn't of the secret formula that turns nerdy scientists into muscle-bound wrestlers, but the secret formula that allows for the expansion of Nitta's underwear as he grows. Americans, apparently, are quite ecstatic about the possibility of being able to stretch their waistlines without having to buy new underwear.

To add to the bizarre suspension of belief that *Kaiju Mono* demands of the viewer, we learn that Kota Ibushi is too nice to win his repeated battles, and the serum needs to have an "evil" gene, which summons forth a different wrestler: Minoru Suzuki, whose wild haircut and facial tics gives him a more maniacal aspect.* Suzuki, known as Evil Nitta, handily beats Mono, but the serum wears off, reverting Suzuki back to his kinder alter ego, Ibushi. Sandayu Dokumamushi,† playing himself, appears at the climax of the film, in all of his dashing glory, to tell Kota Ibushi that the kaiju he has been battling is essentially a seventy-year-old woman.

Kaiju Mono's adoption of professional wrestlers as gigantic kaiju essentially draws the straight line from one genre to the next. Kaiju, much as in professional wrestling rarely sit down to discuss their problems or come to an amicable agreement; one must be dominated and/or defeated in order to provide the climax and denouement for the film, and it's hard to think

---

*Suzuki is affectionately known by wrestling fans in different parts of the internet as "Murder Grandpa," an intersection of his age (54 in 2022) and his heelish enjoyment of violence—not to mention his background in mixed martial arts fighting and his reputation for working "stiff" (for non-wrestling fans, that means he actually hits, but pulls his punches) in wrestling. Put simply, he's a real-life badass.

†*Kaiju Mono* doesn't just pay homage to kaiju films during the extensive parody, but instead brings forth a series of well-known actors from the kaiju world, including Yasuhiko Saijo, from *Ultra Q* and *Gorath*, among other films.

168 **The Kaiju Connection**

of many, if any, kaiju films where there was some sort of amicable parting between rivals.* Masculinity and conflict are the true nature of many kaiju films, and it's pretty much the entire ecosystem of professional wrestling.

There have been more than a few volumes and articles written about the relatively low-hanging fruit of exploring the intersection of masculinity, violence, and performance in professional wrestling, so, suffice to say, there's really not a lot of new ground to break here. Where *Kaiju Mono* succeeds is how it explodes and then subverts the usual expectations of both professional wrestling and kaiju film, essentially flipping the script on both at the same time by embracing and creating a sort of "talk it out" ending that would be anathema to almost any kaiju film—even more progressive and experimental films such as *Colossal* eventually default to a battle, no matter how one-sided—as well as the story arcs that dominate professional wrestling. Two wrestlers generally have some form of disagreement, both of their motivations are established, and the battle is joined, multiple matches leading to what's sometimes called a "rubber" match, where the final victory, and victor, is determined, before new feuds in an endless array of feuds begin.

The violence is the attraction,† and when you have two workers, or two kaiju, battling one another to critical acclaim, then it makes sense to keep the story arc going. There's a reason why Mothra, King Ghidorah, and King Kong appear and reappear in Godzilla's world. They're different enough that their battles are guaranteed to be entertaining in some way. Godzilla is often perplexed by Mothra, and, more specifically, her larva, and usually loses to them rather than the gigantic flying version. And King Ghidorah is the perfect foil for Godzilla: alien, massive, and vicious, outstripping Godzilla in weight class, size, and skill in almost every way. Kong, of course, may give way in terms of viciousness and sheer power, but the intelligence and ability to improvise make him a formidable opponent, too. These all resemble the classic and long-standing feuds in professional wrestling in many ways: a clash of styles that's so different they become almost complementary.

Kaiju Mono, itself more of a parody than a satire, takes a different tack to understanding reality and how we fans interact with "fake" versus

---

Godzilla vs. Kong (2021) features two titular characters who are deeply humanistic in their actions and their expressions. In fact, at one point, Godzilla sneers at Kong when he thinks he has defeated him; so, at the end of the film, Kong and Godzilla part ways, more allies than rivals.

†At first, the Godzilla franchise avoided bloody depictions of violence, mostly because Ishiro Honda and Eiji Tsubaraya "felt that such bloodshed was inappropriate on the big screen," even as numerous franchises such as *Ultraman* and the Gamera franchise featured copious amounts of "slicing, dicing, beheading, and otherwise mutilating monster foes" (Ryfle and Godzisewkski 198).

13. *Men as Kaiju:* Big Man Japan *and* Kaiju Mono   **169**

"real" in our perspective toward kaiju films and professional wrestling. *Big Man Japan* is a wholly more somber and absurd work, a little less blunt and far less nuanced than *Kaiju Mono* in its jokes and its seriousness, and manages to hover more toward a satire of the genre, working to expose those fine lines in fandom and in kaiju film itself. In fact, the absurdity that runs through *Big Man Japan* creates a more authentically absurd atmosphere, including in one sequence where we learn that Big Man Japan, after winning a battle, needs to sleep in order to shrink back down to regular size. Inside a house where numerous revelers, including his agent, hold a party for his latest victory, he fills an entire room, asleep, in a sequence that could have been pulled straight from an Ionesco play.

Big Man Japan has garnered some minor critical attention, which is somewhat more than *Kaiju Mono*, and *Big Man Japan* has prompted effective explorations of Americanism and the homages—or not—the film pays to the kaiju genre. Kenta McGrath notes that the film has an "ambivalent relationship with the kaiju film" and praises its "flexibility and durability" as a part of the kaiju genre (124, 137). Ultimately, *Big Man Japan*'s critiques of the international role of Japan, as well as the near-incessant questioning of how Japan is understood and depicted internally, dominate much of the narrative. However, *Big Man Japan* resembles *Kaiju Mono* on a much more literal level, in how it portrays the masculine alongside the kaiju film as well.

All throughout *Big Man Japan*, the viewer is constantly exposed to this bizarre and reality-bending juxtaposition of "the real world" and the fantastic. For every CGI-propelled battle sequence, there's bookending frank discussions of the realities of loneliness, dementia, divorce, child estrangement, remembering the "golden times," and even the capitalistic takeover of historical traditions. This sequence: realistic documentary followed by CGI battle followed by realistic documentary, flip-flops throughout the film until Big Man Japan is confronted by a demon who appears out of nowhere and beats him senseless. In response, he flees, and his downfall begins to spiral; although ratings have gone up for that battle because he is providing unique and unintended comedy to viewers through his cowardice, he labors under the assumption that he's somehow become less than his genetic forefathers, who wholeheartedly embraced their heritage as Big Man Japan.

And then the final sequence, both absurd and brilliant at the same time: the demon reappears, and instead of a CGI "final showdown" that pins the plot for so many kaiju film, the sequence inverts, and the viewer is moved from CGI to a "real" practical-effects driven final battle. Big Man Japan receives assistance from a family of Ultraman/Kamen Rider clones, who defeat the demon as Big Man Japan cowers in the corner behind a group of buildings. Writ large through the sequence are the poor practical effects—the camera stays distant for long segments so it's easy to see the edges of the plaster and cardboard "city" and the painted backdrop, and the ill-fitting uniforms. Instead of a soundtrack that we normally associate with kaiju fights, explosions, screaming, and the crackle and rip of fire moving across a city, we get only the theme song of the Ultraman clones, played on an almost endless loop. The only sounds we hear of the "battle" outside of the song itself reveal the clunkiness of the set. Footsteps are hollow, uniforms squish, and vehicles rattle, belying their emptiness and falsity.

Essentially, the "real"-appearing CGI, propelled by computers almost more than people, is flipped to focus on the "fake"-appearing practical effects, in all of their glory, stripped of the studio magic that helps nudge along believability. What *Big Man Japan* does so well—and where *Kaiju Mono* slips—is to force the viewer to question their own relationship to reality itself, and what's "real" and what's not. In an era of increasingly CGI-laden films (and the Legendary Godzilla franchise is just one of them), where CGI generates not only the backgrounds and the environment, but superpowers, individuals through motion capture, and so on, the "fake" reality of traditional 1950s through 1980s special effects has all but disappeared.

Younger audiences can look at, say, *Destroy All Monsters* and feel that it has "cheap" special effects compared to films like *Avengers* or *Justice League*, and they would be right; missing in the discussion is that ballet of behind-the-scenes actions of directors, actors, puppeteers, and musicians all working in tandem to produce the best sequence they can, and relying on the viewer to accept the results, maybe even help them fill in ideas that may not have been flawlessly executed. Of course, there's plenty of people behind the scenes in the CGI spectacles that dominate the current Hollywood blockbuster superhero industry, but there's a decided loss of artistry and just general problem-solving and fortitude in these films: person runs here, jumps over this, fires a beam from their palms. All computers with human oversight. There's a loss of connection there. People making films for people, but instead, marketing agents and computers making films for people.

In the end, what *Big Man Japan* does is point to the viewer themselves in those final battle scenes, revealing that the "reality" of kaiju film—and professional wrestling—relies primarily on the fans, and what they choose to accept or not accept, what they choose to deem as "cheesy" and thus lovable, or "fake" and condemned. There's a reason why a "fake"-looking film featuring Guilala is roundly ignored or castigated while a "fake"-looking film featuring Gamera or Godzilla is appreciated in spite of its faults.

13. *Men as Kaiju:* Big Man Japan *and* Kaiju Mono 171

We're willing to forgive and forget, to plug in those gaps in the plot, to turn our head a little to the side, to explore the history of the film and tell other fans "yes, but the suit was falling apart and they didn't have time to fix it!"

Much the same occurs, of course, with professional wrestling; bigger productions such as the WWE and AEW can keep the viewer at a distance and up close at the same time; compare this to the local professional wrestling shows run by independent promoters, which often is a series of steel chairs for the fans, rings that sounds like concrete, and wrestlers who generally just aren't as presentable as their "bigger" counterparts. Their outfits are a little dirtier, a little cheaper; their acne is a little more on display, and their skills are just not as solid as their fully professional counterparts. It's easy to believe, in other words, that same juxtaposition in *Big Man Japan*: reality intruding on the fantasy. Yes, in this high school gym, there's someone dressed up like an Australian hunter who is from Peoria and whose day job is an accountant at the local car dealership. And that Australian hunter comes back out after a match where he took several blows to the head and smiles happily as he adjusts the PA system for the remaining matches or signs autographs for some local kids.

How do we take those people seriously? Do we cheer for them? If they are the hero of the tale that we are willing to spin for them, do we keep watching rather than ask for a refund? Does it matter if they are wearing a rubber costume and are behind cameras? If we transfer the ring in a high school auditorium to a miniature city, does it matter in any way? How far does our suspension of disbelief go?

Aaron Gerow notes the overwhelming assumptions of a certain sort of "childishness" that permeates both professional wrestling and kaiju cinema; after all, it's plainly obvious that professional wrestling is scripted (or "booked," if we want to use the wrestling parlance), and it's even more obvious that kaiju film requires a massive suspension of disbelief as well (68). Real and unreal, adult and childlike, are somewhat fake categories, and an adult watching a kaiju film, or professional wrestling, is unfairly stereotyped as gullible or otherwise lacking in maturity. Gerow notes that "pro-wrestling is fundamentally a product of the spectator's processes of reading and imagination" (75), and I would argue this transfers over the kaiju film as well, and probably in a more naked form than in *Kaiju Mono* and *Big Man Japan*.

In other words, the viewers are a part of a tacit agreement with whatever they see on the screen or whatever they are watching in the ring. As professional wrestler Johnny Valentine once said, "I can't make them believe professional wrestling is real, but I can make them believe *I'm* real." Do it with gusto, passion, and an open mind, and the viewer will believe *you* even if they don't believe anything else, and, really, for the kaiju on the screen, who rarely get anywhere near any sort of scientific validity or muster, it's the viewer's choice to imbue them with meaning. The actors inside those suits, the directors, the musicians and composers, are all "in" on this reality, so how do you keep viewers? You convince them that even though *Godzilla* the film isn't real, Godzilla is. One, a whole complex mixture of circumstances, interactions, and storylines; the other, the symbol of whatever the directors and writers nudge the viewer toward.

In the end, *we* provide the reality, and *we* provide the credibility. Everything else is just costumes and firecrackers.

14

When Even Humans Are (Almost) Kaiju: *The Amazing Colossal Man* and *Attack of the 50 Foot Woman*

In 1957 and 1958: *The Amazing Colossal Man* and then *Attack of the 50 Foot Woman*. These films come right on the heels of the Americanized version of 1954's *Godzilla*, with the title *Godzilla, King of the Monsters!*, released in 1956, complete with a uniquely American perspective and character: Steve Martin, played by Raymond Burr. It feels like it was almost a matter of time before American film producers began to run through all of the creatures and animals they made gigantic: dinosaurs, ants, octopi, grasshoppers, and simply shot toward the inevitable conclusion. What if we made *people* big?

If there's any sort of connection between *Godzilla, King of the Monsters!* and our giant-sized humans, however, it mostly centers around the most basic aspects of the concept of supersized creatures running through the world and causing untold destruction. Audiences saw it in 1953 with *Beast from 20,000 Fathoms* and again in a succession of films, including *Them!* a year later, *Tarantula!* in 1955, and *The Giant Claw* in 1957. Eventually, somewhere, a studio executive wondered to themselves why they were spending so much money on costumes, puppets, and makeup, when it would be much cheaper to simply have people playing the role of the kaiju beast. Remove the costumes, save money, and create a more readily identifiable—and presumably—sympathetic protagonist.

So were born the triumvirate of film oddities I want to discuss here: *The Amazing Colossal Man, Attack of the 50 Foot Woman*, and *War of the Colossal Beast*. Though not technically kaiju films based on the definitions we've explored, I feel that these three movies provide us with a way of further determining the borders and edges of what the kaiju genre actually is. Of course, it's easy to say "humans can't be kaiju," but there's some humanity lost in these films—that's the point, especially in *War of the*

Colossal Beast. When do humans no longer retain their human-ness and when do they become beasts comparable to some of the most devastating members of the kaiju genre? How do Glenn Manning and Nancy Archer stack up to the Godzillas and Gameras of the world, if they do at all?

Of course, it isn't that big of a stretch. As we've seen with *Big Man Japan* and *Kaiju Mono,* "human kaiju" aren't necessarily unheard of. And there's a large number of humanoid kaiju that appear throughout the kaiju genre. Kong, of course, but also, and perhaps most importantly, Ultraman (and the various iterations of Ultraman), who not only appears human-like in appearance, but actually *is* human for much of his life. Add to this other humanoid kaiju such as Frankenstein and Gaira and Sanda, and the line seems to blur a bit. It feels, in some ways, a bit of a disservice to simply call Glenn Manning and Nancy Archer just "giants." Their roles seem to be somewhat more important, somewhat more worthy than just "big person," and it's quite possible that one could interpret Glenn Manning, especially in *War of the Colossal Beast,* as someone who isn't too far in terms of attitude and posture, from Gaira.

And, most importantly for this essay, where does this line exist, where humans turn into massive, unidentifiable beasts, and nudge more and more toward at least something else, if not entirely kaiju? When do they become monsters, if we, in fact, spurn the kaiju label here? As we have seen, although the definition shifts with society, there's always an element of social disapprobation to the term, rendering the labeled "monster" an outcast. But there's more to it than that in these films. There's a decided emphasis on physical deformity or oddity as well. Yes, you may immediately respond, growing to fifty or more feet tall is indeed an oddity. But, if we take a look at *Kaiju Mono* and *Big Man Japan,* the size of the humans in those individual films are not necessarily monstrous.

Even *Big Man Japan,* which places emphasis on the unnatural nature of Masaru Daisoto's transformations, stays firmly planted on the non-monstrous side of things. Neither *Kaiju Mono* nor *Big Man Japan* asks us to see the giant heroes as anything other than humans, grown large. No, there's something else at work here with *The Amazing Colossal Man* and *Attack of the 50 Foot Woman,* an additional depth that these films symbolize. While both Manning (at least in *The Amazing Colossal Man*) and Archer retain their innate human-ness on the outside—they are, after all, just people who have grown large—it's important to note that their subjugation to their newfound giant stature causes a further descent into monstrosity, the opposite of *Kaiju Mono* and *Big Man Japan,* where being a giant does not lessen one's humanity.

You won't be surprised to know that there's a significant body of literature surrounding the role of giants in literature and various world

14. When Even Humans Are (Almost) Kaiju

cultures. There's no need to spend a significant amount of time discussing this research, but I did want to provide some additional context in how giants appear in Western literature, and how their legend and folklore informs the role of Glenn Manning and Nancy Archer:

> The monster appears to be outside the human body, at the limit of its coherence; thus he threatens travelers and errant knights with dismemberment or anthropophagy,* with the complete dissolution of selfhood. [...] the giant is humanity writ large, a text literally too big to ignore [Cohen xii].

Cohen also notes that the giant also functions as a positive symbol, "a builder of cities" and "a base of heroism" (xii), but, as we will see, neither Manning nor Archer quite rise to that level.

This is heady territory, of course, and the idea of medieval giants influencing a small number of American B-movies in the 1950s may seem like a stretch. But the giant in our public conception, especially when they are human, is a part of a long and almost completely uninterrupted series of symbols and ideas, including "hubris or arrogance," and "play the necessary foil to God's righteous demonstration of superior power" (Asma 73). Set aside the religious context here. Replace God in this sentence with either "America" or "masculinity" and you can see how Manning and Archer retain their disruptive nature through becoming giants.

And, we also need to return to the ever-thin edges of the term "monster" itself. We can easily see the term bandied about for true monsters—those with supernatural powers, for example, but can humans be "monsters"? The films seem to arrive at different answers in how they provoke our sympathy, but monsters "define us by stalking our border and mirroring our traits" (Mittman and Hensel xiii), so we are to understand not only that Manning and Archer turn into monsters, but, more importantly, that *we* could become monsters just as easily as they could.† Like Godzilla and his nigh-endless parade of NotGodzillas who appear to attack him or Japan, Manning and Archer function to remind us and the cast of the film, of course, about their own capacity to become monstrous at a moment's notice.

---

*I find it interesting to consider how the massive beasts that roam the screens rarely eat people. Manning and Archer certainly could not have functioned in their form as cannibals, especially in the 1950s; it would strip away all sympathy. Eating people is usually reserved as a shorthand for audiences to know who the antagonist is going to be; after all, a true hero wouldn't eat people, would they? See: Baragon in *Frankenstein vs. Baragon,* Gaira in *War of the Gargantuas* and King Ghidorah in *King of the Monsters,* as notable (but not exhaustive) examples.

†Interestingly, in *Shin Ultraman,* after the alien Mefilas makes Asami larger to show the world that he had the technology to make human giants, Asami returns to normal size, only to find that the true madness begins: endless government tests and experiments, coupled with her sudden dominance on social media (with the insinuation that some of the social media posts objectify and sexualize her) strip away her autonomy and her anonymity.

Why would Manning represent a foiling or challenge of America? A former soldier horribly burned and mutilated by a plutonium blast, Manning's sudden growth brings numerous military men and law enforcement officers to the foreground as they attempt to stop him. He is a living reminder of what should be ignored: the perils of nuclear power, and as the protectors, projectors, and progenitors of nuclear power, it falls to the military to make sure that the idea of nuclear weapons or radiation's being "bad" be quickly silenced. It isn't until *War of the Colossal Beast* that we get Major Baird, whose sympathy seems to lie less with Glenn Manning and more with Manning's sister Joyce. Baird, even though he eventually agrees merely to capture Manning (more on that later), routinely insists that he has to protect "people" by killing Manning if and when he gets the chance. Being a giant killer is quite the feather in a military man's cap, one would think.

For Nancy Archer, she is clearly and somewhat unwittingly a force to disrupt masculinity in *Attack of the 50 Foot Woman*. Almost every man in her life, from the police department to her husband to even her butler, seems to take turns castigating her, treating her like a child, or otherwise ignoring her. And, of course, the plot to kill her for her money can't be forgotten. Although Archer continues to call out for her husband Harry after she grows, she accidentally kills him. It's worth it to note, too, that Archer is ultimately, like Manning, killed by law enforcement. Even though I don't think she's quite the feminist icon that she's portrayed to be (more on *that* later, too), I do think her presence as a giant shocks and challenges the masculine hegemony that clearly dominates the town she lives in.

I've spoken earlier about how Kong and his various spin-offs (or knock-offs), and his "beast" nature, are integral to our understanding of how we, as humans, can relate to him as viewers. Along with this, I argued that searching for some form of human-ness within the characterization and actions of the beast, whether they be overly large Yetis, apes, or relics of a forgotten time, allows the viewer to avoid, mentally, the "monster" label, even if they can't fully sympathize with the actions of the character. In this instance, we can apply that idea as well: finding the dividing line where "monster" and "human" and "human enough" may reside.

When we first see Glenn Manning, he and a few of his fellow Army men are huddled in a trench, waiting for a test of the new plutonium bomb. The bomb does not trigger when it's supposed to, so the men are obliged to wait it out, for fear of being exposed to the blast when it does happen. Improbably, an airplane crashes on the testing site as Manning and his group watch, and Manning claims he can see the pilot of the aircraft struggling to get out. After some back and forth, Manning decides to go rescue the pilot, and this is where our primary characterization of Manning

14. When Even Humans Are (Almost) Kaiju   177

comes from, and it's unfortunate. He's very brave and tries to save someone's life (good!), but he's also incredibly stupid (bad!), as he ignores numerous commands and is, of course, exposed to the plutonium blast because of course the bomb explodes as he races to the downed airplane.

Maybe it's my cynicism at this point, but one would think that an American viewer of *The Amazing Colossal Man* in 1957,* who is fully aware of not only the power of atomic weaponry but also the deadliness of radiation, would agree that Manning's heroism comes tinged with quite the slice of a "what was he thinking?" It's almost at the level of Konga standing there and watching while people shoot at him.

And, to make things worse, this is really the last we see of Manning as a hero: a split-second decision where he fails to understand, or to balance, the circumstances he finds himself in. In fact, our next visual of Manning is that of a horribly burned person, a small touch of body horror that presages what we may see in films such as *The Fly*, *The Blob*, and *The H-Man* (all released a year later in 1958) and *The Human Vapor* (1960). So, we're immediately given Manning, who makes an admittedly unselfish decision to save someone, but he does so at a risk many people would not have taken, and then we see Manning as a large mass of burned flesh. Already, he's dehumanized, so his eventual turn into someone who's gone bad is predictable.

Where the movie truly gets bizarre is that Manning's skin not only recovers, but he starts to grow at an alarming rate. We learn, though, that Manning's body is outpacing the growth of his heart, and, if he doesn't drop dead from *that* strain, he'll soon go insane. His size is definitely a punishment, a plutonium-laced disease to be cured, and when we see Manning as larger for the first time, he asks his girlfriend, Carol, "what sin could a man commit in a single lifetime to bring this upon himself?" After noting that the 1950s were a heyday in "reconfiguring the category 'monster,'" Jeffrey Jerome Cohen continues:

> His becoming a giant amounts to a discovery of the truth of what he always already was, beneath the suburban miniaturization of his life. The giant's monstrosity is his insistent, exorbitant exhibition of what he is supposed to repress; the fantasy he embodies is that such "primal" wildness is somehow related to a purely natural state, to the lives of (male, aggressive) animals [Cohen 143].

Thus, after setting the stage for Manning to be emblematic of the typical 1950s male, we see his interior, non-conformist pressures literally grow in

---

*One of the more unexplored aspects of *The Amazing Colossal Man* is how the final portion of the story is framed by breathless news reporting, not unlike the previous year's American release of *Godzilla, King of the Monsters!* One sequence for *The Amazing Colossal Man* even features our intrepid reporter pulling back the drapes of his window, seeing Manning, and reporting live from the scene of the rampage.

178   The Kaiju Connection

front of us, and, as you probably noted, my usage of this passage is geared toward pointing to the use of the word "primal" and "animals" in describing Manning's transformation from brave soldier to rampaging beast.

It's easy to see, then, how the film's whole rubric in the first hour or so is to ensure that we, the viewers, have little sympathy for Manning, and that his sudden growth is some sort of penance; as he grows even larger, he stops the self-loathing, and he instead begins to revel in his newfound weirdness. This is rather transgressive. He embraces the removal of the last shred of his humanity, claiming that he's a "circus freak" and that *he* isn't growing, but *they're* shrinking. Although the movie takes pains to explain that this is Manning's loss of his sanity, there's a certain sense throughout the film that we're watching a man losing not just his sanity, necessarily, but his humanity. This is symbolized in numerous instances, from the first time we see him picking up a massive cooked turkey, ripping it in half, and eating it with his fingers, bones and all. Then when Manning escapes, we're told that he's been eating cattle, whole, and that missing cows are a sure sign that Manning is in the area.

It's a bizarre thing to watch *The Amazing Colossal Man* alongside *King Kong* (1933), because we almost have a complete inversion of the formula. In *King Kong*, a primitive beast receives some humanization through his interactions with people, and we're expected to sympathize with him, especially with Kong's fondness for at least one person he meets. As the iterations of Kong progresses, he turns more and more human until he is almost a large substitute for humanity in *Godzilla vs. Kong*. But in *The Amazing Colossal Man*, we see a person slowly turned into a beast, rejecting not only society and his own sanity, but his own humanity. His long-time (and long suffering) girlfriend, the only person in the film who seemed to understand Manning as a human, is ultimately rejected by Manning, although he will later enact a sort of Reverse Kong. He'll pick up Carol, but he does so in rage and insanity. There's no long-lasting pleas from Carol; we see him pick her up and then we just see him from a distance as he stands over Hoover Dam. She simply asks him, once, to put her down, and he does so, without apparent recognition, which allows the Army to blast him with rocket launchers and bullets. He then falls into the Dam, supposedly to his demise.

Before his untimely end, Manning's "rampage" is mostly him walking through Las Vegas as people gather below; he tears apart large advertisements, picking up a massive crown, breaking off a sign in the shape of a large woman's shoe, and, finally, when the police begin to shoot at him, various palm trees, a car, and a large cowboy display, which he chucks at the crowds, forcing them to scatter. Like Ah Wang, Manning temporarily suspends his rampage to peep at a woman taking a bath in her apartment. She screams in terror and he angrily smashes her window.

14. When Even Humans Are (Almost) Kaiju   179

Cute critiques of masculinity aside, there's little here to work with in terms of establishing Glenn as a "human," but plenty to try to establish him as a "monster." Although his basic shape and form is that of a person, his psychology and his size render him to our eyes as the distinct Other. Even though there's a potential cure waiting, the police, Army, local businessmen and citizens ("are you going to stand by and let him destroy property?") can't seem to wait to embrace the opportunity to kill him, to remove this massive reminder of the loss of humanity from our minds.

So, the question is less of when Glenn Manning stops being human, and more of when he fully becomes a monster, if he ever does. After all, he doesn't seem to kill but one person, and the people of Las Vegas may actually be somewhat thrilled to see some of the gaudier massive advertisements be destroyed. While Manning tumbles into Boulder Dam, then, we're left with a very distinctive notion that he stopped being human the moment he was exposed to plutonium—at first, left horribly burned and near death, then improbably (*unnaturally*) healing, and growing larger, ultimately losing his sanity. There's precious little in *The Amazing Colossal Man* that makes Glenn Manning humanistic; he joins many of the characters who are transformed into monsters, or accidentally becomes monsters: Delambre from *The Fly*, Griffin in *The Invisible Man,* West from *The Incredible Melting Man*. All of these characters start out human, are manipulated and scarred by science, and soon become physically monstrous. The cost of their transformation is their sanity as well as their ability to be a part of society. Not only does society reject them, but, often, their loved ones are frightened or disgusted by them, further punishing their mental health.

It's easy to say that Glenn Manning turns monstrous in *The Amazing Colossal Man*, but he never quite provokes our sympathy, as a human anyway. For someone who is identifiably human at the start of the film, we as viewers have a difficult time accepting him as human because of the paper-thin plot and characterization (although Glenn Langan does his best to portray Manning's madness through a series of frowns and blinks). Manning even loses the ability to speak coherently after his final monologue, stripping away, beyond his physical shell, the last vestiges of humanity, and much of what he says beforehand is tinged with anger. Manning's character, in as many words, pushes us away. We can *see* he is human, but we stop *feeling* his humanity within minutes of the movie's start.

This theme goes even further with *War of the Colossal Beast*. A quick and rather shameless cash-in sequel, *War of the Colossal Beast* presents Glenn Manning (now played by Dean Parkin) as a fully hideous, animalistic creature, one who is "desubjectivized," and is "inhuman, wholly animal. Suspended no more between categories, easily labeled and easily

180 **The Kaiju Connection**

dismissed" (Cohen 142). Manning wanders through the rural country-side of Mexico, stealing food trucks and eating what he can, like a giant of medieval yore hunting down travelers and merchants. When we first see the "new" Glenn Manning, he's strikingly horrible. Reduced to only grunts and growls, his appearance is equally devastating. Half of his face is missing, with one eye socket empty and half of his lips are pulled away, revealing his jagged teeth. And there's no indication, even as his sister Joyce confronts him, that he immediately recognizes her or anyone else.

Before the climactic set piece—Manning's rampage through Los Angeles, culminating in a confrontation near the Griffith Observatory—Manning is captured and held in an aircraft hangar, where the military brings in scientists to try to determine if Manning can be peaceful. So, they hook him up to an EEG and show him images from his past—his college, the ship he came back on after the Korean War, his own face—but they receive no response. Manning is too far gone, and he's no longer capable of remembering anything about himself. The military's new solution, before Manning's inevitable escape, is to put Manning on a ship and drop him off on his own little Monster Island "about 60 miles off the coast," where the military will drop food supplies to him regularly.

War of the Colossal Beast, not surprisingly for this era's low-budget creature feature genre, wears its purpose on its sleeve, and the nature versus nurture debate is really only a passing thought. Of course, Joyce thinks Glenn Manning is still a human, somewhere in there, but Major Baird, tasked with protecting the population from Manning, leaves no doubt: "Look at it this way," he tells Joyce, "Glenn has become a total stranger to you. He's not your brother anymore, but a monster, with the instincts of a wild beast, and there's nothing you and I, or anyone else, can ever do that will change him back to what he once was." Baird is fully on board the "he's a monster" train.

There's a tragedy to be had in there, somewhere, but to consider Manning as a comparison to Kong allows us to understand how *War of the Colossal Beast* manages to reveal that the human Manning is more primal and more aggressive than his similarly proportioned ape counterpart. Manning, in his bestial nature, warped and mutilated by science and militarized violence, does not provoke the same sympathy in the viewer as Kong does, who is human enough to be frightened, to have feelings, and essentially eschew violence as much as he possibly can. Kong essentially functions as a hero, Manning as a sort of self-loathing supervillain, and, as such, his actions during *War of the Colossal Beast* further help us understand what makes the Kong story so special and long-lived.

"There's no place in the civilized world for a creature that big," Major Baird tells Joyce. He's In this way, the film clearly spells out the overall

14. When Even Humans Are (Almost) Kaiju   181

thesis of Manning's slow de-evolution into something less than human. Even so, there's still a rather cloying moment as Manning is surrounded at Griffith Observatory. Joyce, ever plucky, still believes in her brother, hijacks a Jeep and confronts him as he holds a bus of schoolchildren over his head. Her constant pleas for Manning to recognize her finally leads to some success, though not in the way she intended. Manning grunts out the name "Joyce," sets down the school bus, and promptly electrocutes himself* by grabbing the nearby power lines. Manning's moment of lucidity allows him to understand that every claim Baird made is essentially true. He's an animal with no place to survive, and the world is safer without him. Like the Yeti, there's an understanding of a creature without a safe home, and, as such, their discovery or awakening ultimately must lead to rejection or destruction.

It's clear that we're supposed to think that Manning's brief moment of awareness prompted a conclusion different from Joyce's and even from Major Baird's. Manning realizes, for just a few moments, that his existence needed to be eradicated. He was a man trapped in the body and mind of a beast, and no amount of isolation or slideshows would prevent that. He had turned into a creature that couldn't be borne by society.

Unlike Manning, Nancy Archer is presented in somewhat positive light; at the start of *Attack of the 50 Foot Woman*,† we see Archer driving her car recklessly before coming across an alien ship, which seems to happen routinely in the 1950s. She screams as a giant hand reaches out to grab her, and then impressively runs back to the town, a sizable distance, on high heels. But, in the moment between the alien grabbing at her and her reappearance at the bar, we meet Harry, her husband, and his girlfriend, the amazingly named Honey Parker. There, we learn Nancy's details. She's an alcoholic who recently recovered from a mental breakdown. She's also an heiress, and there's nothing more than Harry would want than for Nancy to be committed so he can be together with Honey (although his relationship is public enough that neither of them are fooling anyone in town about the true nature of their romance), and Honey wants the money via Harry, leading her to innocently suggest that, maybe, just maybe, it would be unfortunate for Nancy to die and leave all of her money to Harry.

That's the background of manipulation there, and for all of the

---

*Of course, things are left open for a sequel: Manning doesn't fall over after the electrocution. He simply disappears.

†Just as an aside, Manning is said to have been 70 feet tall and then 60 in *War of the Colossal Beast*; Archer, of course, is 50 feet tall, and the original Godzilla (1954) is 164 feet tall; for the American re-cut of *Godzilla, King of the Monsters!*, Godzilla is described as being 400 feet tall. The alien who attacks Nancy Archer, however, is described as 30 feet tall.

182 **The Kaiju Connection**

numerous thin plot points in *Attack of the 50 Foot Woman*, this opening exposition dump gives us a somewhat sympathetic backstory. Nancy Archer is a bit too dependent on Harry, perhaps, and certainly too dependent on alcohol, but she's not prone to stupid but heroic decisions like Glenn Manning (her dead sprint away from danger being a key indicator of that trait). She is, however, prone to mental illness, and, so, we get a revisit of the "will go mad as they mutate" trope. So, the scene is already set for Nancy to go full-on monster.

Yet, there's something about Nancy's behavior that remains somewhat sympathetic, all the way up until she actually begins to grow. She is cast as a victim, and she, along with some prodding from Harry, questions her own sanity. At one point, she cajoles Harry into taking her through the surrounding desert to try to find the alien spaceship, and, of course, they can't find it, making Harry even more smug than usual, as Nancy has promised she would commit herself if she found no evidence of her alien visitor. And then: eureka! The spaceship itself, sitting calmly in a field. Nancy is so excited by this confirmation of her sanity that she runs up to the object that brought her mortal terror just days prior; it's only when the giant hand makes another appearance that she screams. Harry, who we already know is an absolute cad, runs away, abandoning Nancy entirely.

This time, Nancy's interaction with the alien spacecraft and all of its radiation begins to make her grow. While Honey and Harry plot to inject her with an overdose of her medication, Nancy's growth is finally shown in the form of what's basically a massive papier-mâché hand. We're told that this is a horrifying thing because the camera focuses on Nancy's nurse screaming and clutching her head and screaming, and just for good measure, screaming again. It's all scary! A woman! Grown large!

Where Glenn Manning lost his sanity as a result of his growth, Nancy simply becomes more obsessed with Harry, constantly calling his name as she begins to erupt through the roof of the house. There's no real sense of independence for Nancy, no reckoning where she suddenly decides to disavow Harry. Not even a proclamation of her hatred for him or a desire to kill him. She just calls his name exactly as she does at the start of the film when she's pining for him.

The movie ends with a line that's no doubt supposed to be an homage to *King Kong*'s thesis of "It was beauty killed the beast," but this one lands with a thud: "She finally got Harry all to herself." For those who have viewed *Attack of the 50 Foot Woman* as a proto-feminist work, this line deeply complicates things, because it shows a vital misunderstanding of Nancy Archer's role in her own life; her growth doesn't necessarily drive her *insane*, it drives her *dependent*. There's the idea that Nancy turns

14. When Even Humans Are (Almost) Kaiju   183

into a "dominant erotic figure" (Williams 270), who attacks the patriarchal forces in her town.

The argument continues that she moves from dependence on Harry in a miraculous transformation when she gets larger, as she "changes from whining dependent wife into erotic giant out to wreak vengeance on the community which oppresses her" (Williams 269). But, there's no real attack, nor is there vengeance or a sudden understanding of her independence. As Nancy bursts out of her home, her cry, over and over again, is for Harry. And her rampage through the town is simply her walking toward the bar where Harry and Honey are known to hang out. Unlike *The Amazing Colossal Man*, there's no smashing of numerous landmarks; Nancy makes a beeline to her husband motivated by her "psychological dependence in which possessiveness governs her desire for Harry" (Williams 269).

Her "attack" on the bar where Harry and Honey are yet again canoodling is her attempt to find Harry and reunite with him. Nancy's punch through the roof causes a cave-in that kills Honey. Nancy picks up a befuddled Harry and absconds with him, falling victim to a potshot from the sheriff which hits a nearby electrical tower, causing both Harry and Nancy to die.* So, in the movie, we go from "poor Nancy" to maybe even being goaded into begrudgingly saying "poor Harry, too." Unfortunately, while we sympathize with Nancy at the start of the film, the narrative tends to push her away from the reader's sympathies. She doesn't eschew her "previous whining dependence," nor does she suddenly understand "the real nature of her oppression" (Williams 271). The film decides to point us toward a decidedly anti-feminist outcome.

Alas, while it would be nice to understand Nancy Archer as a feminist icon, outside of the poster design and some very few beats within the film, that simply doesn't happen; her depiction is of a mentally ill woman who is unhealthily obsessed with her manipulative and dastardly husband. Yet, even though she doesn't align with our more postmodern understandings of feminism, Nancy Archer still retains some sympathy. She's a victim, caught in a loveless marriage that she desperately wants to make successful. At one point, she says to Harry that he is a "parasite" before adding "I need you all to myself." It's sad, in a way, but it also pushes away our sympathies.

Attack of the 50 Foot Woman, then, doesn't truly have a "full" monster as the giant(ess). No, in this instance, Nancy Archer retains much of her humanity—she's *not* insane, after all, that's established—but she is a

---

*"She's squeezing him to death," we're told, but there's no confirmation that she killed him, or if the electricity did the trick.

confused and psychologically injured woman. Her butler, Jesse, seems to be the only person in the film who can be bothered to see this. To every other male, she's a source of money and funding, and little more. As the film's cast expands toward the end of the film, we can almost universally dislike everyone, especially Harry and Honey,* but Nancy is free of our scorn or hatred, earning only our confusion. She's earned *some* sympathy, at least.

But all of this aside, the true question to consider is whether or not Nancy Archer progresses to becoming a monster like Glenn Manning does by the end of *The Amazing Colossal Man* and certainly by the end of *War of the Colossal Beast*. It seems like she doesn't, in spite of her size. Her sanity is confirmed; she just happens to be jealous or obsessed, or jealously obsessed, with Harry. Compared to Gloria from *Colossal*, Nancy Archer seems almost designed to reinforce the notions of the stereotypical "clingy" female. Gloria rejects both of the toxic men in her life, purposefully manipulating one and presumably killing the other by outwitting him. Nancy certainly earns our sympathy, but it's almost by default. Harry and Honey are the truly "bad" people in this film, and perhaps Honey is an even worse person than Harry for suggesting murder several times as the key to her own ability to get access to Nancy's wealth.

But Nancy isn't a monster in human skin as Glenn Manning appears to be in *The Amazing Colossal Man*, and she certainly isn't as monstrous as Manning in *War of the Colossal Beast*, who has physical deformities alongside his animalistic loss of sanity. Nancy Archer, in spite of her size, remains defiantly human, and the flaws she had when she was small pretty much stayed exactly the same size as she grew. She doesn't suffer from mental illness as she grows, and she doesn't find herself becoming more animalistic or monstrous; in fact, her final very slow and very silent march toward the town seems almost ephemeral, as if she somehow reached some higher plane of understanding about "possessing" Harry, and the sudden powerful means to do so. From Nancy Archer's perspective, perhaps being a giant isn't a curse like Manning feels it is. For her, perhaps becoming a giant is exactly what needs to happen for her to finally "have" Harry.

As with *Colossal*, however, the discussion about the presence of feminism or feminist ideals within the film is another method, another side avenue, to interpreting the film. For our purposes, we're not necessarily focusing on feminist theory here, but it's hard for me to ignore the re-humanization of Nancy Archer in our overarching "is she a monster

---

*Very little has been written about Honey's role in the film. Though derided as a "floozy" for the entirety of the film, she has quite a bit of admittedly malicious intelligence. It can be argued that she's probably the smartest person in the room at any time during the film. She knows exactly how to get what she wants.

14. When Even Humans Are (Almost) Kaiju

or human?" focus. There's points to be made here that our sympathy with even an unhealthily obsessed Archer doesn't change even as she grows, and her destruction of the town is simply focused on her toxic relationship with Harry, and, to a lesser extent, Honey. Ultimately, Archer never reaches "monster" status, so it's a reasonable—yet bizarre—argument that a film that pays such direct homage to *The Amazing Colossal Man* has little in common with it from this particular perspective. One has a giant monster in human skin; the other has a giant misguided human.

This is a lot of words for three films that were low budget cash-ins, with *The Amazing Colossal Man* essentially spawning its own sequel as well as its own homage in *Attack of the 50 Foot Woman*.* Yet, if we consider our definitions from the very first chapter of this book, I would argue that there's some merit to the argument that Glenn Manning, at least, has some resemblances to the same questions that haunt non-kaiju "big monster" films, and we can see that when *The Amazing Colossal Man* and *War of the Colossal Beast* is stacked against the other "giant person goes on a rampage" in *Attack of the 50 Foot Woman*.

Ah, but there's another film to consider, one that actually has Japanese origins and inherently qualifies as a kaiju film: *Frankenstein vs. Baragon*, released in the United States as *Frankenstein Conquers the World*. In this instance, we see a sort of reversal of Glenn Manning's character arc: a relatively dashing and brave man slowly metamorphosing into an insane, giant monster now turns into a monster becoming more human, even though his physical monstrousness remains.

The Frankenstein in this instance is originally introduced to us as a heart brought over to Japan by the Nazis, and left with the Japanese Navy. The bombing of Hiroshima irradiates the heart, and, a decade or so later, Japanese officials find a feral boy living on the streets. This is our Frankenstein: starting life in a more animalistic pattern, feeding himself on wild animals and any other creature he can capture in order to get the sustenance he needs. Sound familiar? Don't forget that Glenn Manning, toward the end of *Attack of the Colossal Man* is relegated to feasting on any animal he can find after he escapes from the Army base where he's being held.

And so, Frankenstein is cared for by a group of scientists who notice that he's mostly immune to radiation. Although Frankenstein never fully progresses to human, he shows consistent signs that would place him almost alongside Kong in basic understanding and relatability. He tries to set traps (and fails), and runs in fear from a gathered military force. At the center of all of this is his fondness for Seuko, Dr. Bowen's lab assistant.

Attack of the 50 Foot Woman received its own parody, *The 30 Foot Bride of Candy Rock* (1959), a Lou Costello comedy vehicle that's best known for two things: being the last movie he filmed before he died, and for being the first movie he starred in without Bud Abbot.

This isn't to the level of a somewhat unhealthy attraction, however: unlike the various women Kong fell in love with, Seuko and Frankenstein are fairly platonic.

Unlike Kong, there's no one-sided "romance" with Dwan or Ann Darrow; Frankenstein clearly adores Seuko, but he does so in a more innocent, childlike manner. Glenn Manning initially has an attachment to his girlfriend in *The Amazing Colossal Man*, but as he grows and goes more insane (and eventually loses his sanity completely), he is unable to recognize his sister outside of one fleeting moment in *War of the Colossal Beast*.

No one, of course, is going to say that the Frankenstein character in *Frankenstein vs. Baragon* is a good-looking character; after all, he's pretty much entirely generated from a heart. So, set aside physical demeanor and form as an indicator of evil; it's the *actions* that determine our sympathies, and Glenn Manning, even if he were horribly scarred as in *War of the Colossal Beast* would most likely still retain our sympathy if he exhibited any form of sympathetic humanity: rescuing orphans from a burning building, saving a young woman from a dinosaur, sacrificing himself on behalf of someone else, and so on.

Manning's physical scars, then, are a sort of visual shorthand that works for the viewer to further reinforce his interior monstrosity. Manning is poisoned and broken, both inside and out, the hollowed eye socket an emblem—and reminder—of his departure from humanity. Meanwhile, Frankenstein is, in spite of his inability to communicate any better than Manning, somehow more along the evolutionary scale: He cares for people and interacts with humans, even helping those who sought to injure him. His moral code is intact, and, besides, even though Frankenstein doesn't quite "look" human, he seems to fall more along the Neanderthal imagery than Manning, whose human facade is cracked and disrupted.

It's ironic to think that a man and woman we see at the start of a film as fully fleshed, but perhaps flawed, individuals, would be moderately less sympathetic than a character who developed and grew from a disembodied heart, but here we are. To make the discussion even more complicated, Frankenstein himself can be considered a kaiju, if we accept our definitions and categories offered at the start of this book: he isn't a Japanese creation, but he appears, like King Kong, in a Japanese kaiju film and functions like a kaiju as well, in every way we can imagine. His size, his "monstrousness," his battles, and even his later heirs apparent, Sanda and Gaira, all point to his innate kaiju nature. Frankenstein can, and has been, adapted numerous times in numerous cultures after *Frankenstein vs. Baragon*, but *this* version of Frankenstein is wholly kaiju.

This means, of course, that Glenn Manning, in particular, isn't a kaiju, but he's also something more than just a human turned into a monster. His

14. When Even Humans Are (Almost) Kaiju

sheer size places him outside of the spectrum of what the films he appears in would consider "humanity"; in fact, each film gives the viewers solid alternatives, so that we see the mirror, fractured beyond all repair: Glenn and his fiancée Cathy and the doctor who tries to save him, Dr. Lindstrom, and Glenn and his sister Joyce and Major Baird. *The Amazing Colossal Man* and *War of the Colossal Beast* take pains to make sure that viewers understand that Manning is human in shape only. His soul, his mind, and, later, his face, are all ruined and rendered incomprehensible.

And so, our conclusion is a problematic one, but ultimately one that illustrates through kaiju films and through the films of human giants, how we perceive monstrosity, and, more so, how we attach our own values to monstrosity. Through Glenn Manning and Nancy Archer, we can more easily understand how other giant creatures, from Gappa to Kong, and how other kaiju, including Gamera and Godzilla, can at once be "human" and "monster," often at the same time.

Conclusion

So, there you have it, a long treatise on the kaiju film and films that hover around the edges of the genre. Like our ancestors from centuries ago, we have collectively incorporated and adopted giants and giant monsters into our culture and, more importantly, into our pop culture. Within these new realms and domains where giant monsters walk the Earth, we experience the rigidity of our moral structures, the fleeting borders of our definitions of humanity. Within the kaiju film genre, and all of the films inspired by the kaiju film, rest our own assumptions about what makes a monster a monster, and, more importantly, what makes a human a human. And, as the kaiju film has progressed over these past few decades, we have seen a more active and much deeper questioning of the purpose of the kaiju film, and what role it should play in our culture. Should humans be kaiju? Can they? And can kaiju achieve a depth beyond "big dumb fun"? And should they?

And, as you've seen, there's a lot left to be said, not just by me, but by many others. Like *The Kaiju Film*, I positioned this book to be another starting point for a series of academic and fan discussions about kaiju and kaiju-adjacent films. In my opinion, and that's what you ask for when you buy a critical text from an author, there's a firm relationship across the kaiju genre in the way that humans are depicted, or how kaiju function in many ways as mirrors of our own identities. This can take the form of a sort of an avatar or icon, like Kong himself, or it can simply be a connection we build with a particular character when juxtaposed alongside another one, like Sanda. And, of course, how we perceive kaiju as witnesses to the film, and whom we identify with, can radically change a kaiju into a hero, or a villain, or the deeper shades of gray in between, as we have seen with the Heisei Gamera trilogy.

In the world of the kaiju film, then, we learn about ourselves, our priorities, and, really, our own relationship with the world, as it ranges from the geopolitical sphere to interpersonal relationships.

And all of this happens alongside a puzzling series of circumstances, sprouting from a fascination with dinosaurs, passing through from West to East, where the brutal ending to a brutal war left scars that eventually created a radioactive kaiju that then marched from East to West, and, at times, became warped into a new life form, stripped of Western responsibility for the very brutality that created it in the first place. It's borne from a desire for a production company to make a lot of money by bringing in children as the primary audience. It's borne from a desire to tell a story on a shoestring budget. And so on.

There's a bizarre aspect to the kaiju film, and to kaiju-adjacent films, as well, that merits further exploration, and it's really the absence of sexuality and bloody or gory human-based violence. The human body generally stays sanctified and pure, unsullied by sex. And, in the kaiju film, even as the kaiju themselves carve one another up, blow themselves apart, and behead one another, the humans who witness the events are often, but not always, uninjured, or, alternatively, killed offscreen, where we, as viewers, can more easily avoid the conundrum of cheering for a monster that kills one of our own, no matter how evil the film may make that person out to be.

As I made a prediction at the end of my earlier book *The Kaiju Film*, it's only appropriate that I make one here, too, with the hopes that in four or five years I can put out another book that is an acknowledgment of how wrong I was in this prediction. But here goes: with Legendary using the license for Godzilla, I can see the Monsterverse getting larger, and Toho happily enjoying the money for wider budgets for their own Godzilla films. We'll continue to see some basic tinkering with the genre, but it's entirely possible that the size of Godzilla's imprint on our current releases—not only toys, but anime, comic books, and a new big-budget blockbuster every few years—will drown out newer and perhaps more nuanced takes on the kaiju film, whether they be legitimately kaiju, or something close enough to it that it will reside within the same family.

We already know a few things that are happening in the near future. Toho is working on their next Godzilla film already. *Shin Ultraman* was just released, and pays campy homage to the *Ultraman* series, a far cry from the darker tone of its cousin, *Shin Godzilla*. We know that Gamera is about to return, this time in anime form, following Godzilla's adaptation to *Singular Point* and the Godzilla Earth trilogy and an *Ultraman* anime series. And, of course, even smaller franchises that were teetering on the brink of irrelevance, such as *Pacific Rim*, got new life from its own anime series, *Pacific Rim: The Black*.

This sort of cross-pollination seems to be drawing more, and younger, eyes to the franchises, and, as such, it's very likely that these experiments will continue, with more adaptations moving already established kaiju

Conclusion 191

properties into the world of anime. Yet, these anime adaptations tend to follow the same tried-and-true formulas that dominate their respective franchises, with little room for experimentation outside of, perhaps, creature design, and slightly longer long-format storytelling.* That's not to say that these works aren't experimental or of quality, but rather that they continue to bump up against the borders of the kaiju genre without necessarily expanding them beyond, well, the borders of anime.

Ah, you say: but look at *Colossal*! There was a smaller feature that attempted a new perspective on kaiju film. After all, *Colossal* was released in 2016, sandwiched between *Godzilla* (2014) and *Godzilla: King of the Monsters* (2019). True; however, *Colossal*, like *Godzilla* (2014), had a lengthy production schedule, and, ironically, both of them were slowed down through legal wrangling with Toho (Patten). And *Colossal* could function as a cautionary tale to studios, as it didn't come anywhere near making back its budget, even though critics seemed to love the film, or at least loved that it took chances. Meanwhile, *King of the Monsters*, considered a bit of a box office disappointment, made more than a hundred times what *Colossal* did in gross revenue. The disappointment of *King of the Monsters* was that it didn't make *more* money, or at least enough to offset its overall budget.

So, then, we receive *Godzilla vs. Kong*, and all of the action and whatnot in that film, and it's a bonanza for Legendary, which followed up the success of the film with a quick announcement for a sequel.

And so it goes. Kaiju fans will never turn down a kaiju-related property, even one that maybe disappoints them or pushes their expectations away, but my prediction will be a little more dire: yes, there will be money to be made. For now. But it feels like the emphasis in *Godzilla vs. Kong* and the "big dumb fun" can only last for so long. A good comparison would be Marvel films: yes, they made (and still make) a good amount of money, but they have ultimately become relatively hollow and no longer exist as a sort of pop culture phenomenon. For a moment in time, Marvel films were an unstoppable juggernaut (reference intended), but the output has recently become more and more uneven, with some films landing, like *Black Panther*, and others landing with a dull thud, such as *Black Widow* (or smaller properties such as *She-Hulk* or *The Eternals*).

I won't go much further there to avoid getting Marvel fans angry with

---

*There's been a lot of discussion about *Singular Point*, in particular, on social media, and anime fans tend to be more forgiving of some of the slower and more tech-y, jargon-y sequences in the show because, to put it mildly, that's anime. Even so, those who praise *Singular Point* while excoriating Godzilla films for their lack of action brush against hypocrisy, for it takes almost two hours before Godzilla appears in any meaningful capacity. That's a lot of text messages about physics before the "star" appears!

Conclusion

me, but the "blockbuster" phenomenon that's currently happening with Legendary could have negative consequences on the genre as a whole: yes, there will be more Godzilla films, and, yes, they will probably make a lot of money. But for how long? And at what expense to the rest of the genre? While we're no doubt at the heyday for big budget films providing us with special effects that those of us who watched Showa-era films could never have imagined, we seem to be at a relatively barren time for other kaiju or kaiju-type films.

Think about all of the properties released during the mid–Showa era, and we covered at least some of these elsewhere in the book: *Space Amoeba, Daimajin, The X From Outer Space, Dogora, Gorath*, and even *Gorgo* and *Gappa* all came into being at the same time Godzilla and Gamera were battling claw to claw in the box office. There's no doubt that many of these films were following a trend, but they also offered something different, a little break from the formulas established in Godzilla films. Being a kaiju fan during this time meant that there were plenty of films—and properties—to choose from, to either enjoy or deride. But they were there.

There's little doubt in my mind that Hollywood is a trend-focused industry that follows profits first. This is why *Pacific Rim*, such a popular film at the time, spawned one miserable sequel *Pacific Rim: Uprising*, and has been relegated to a Netflix anime series, *Pacific Rim: Black*. *Uprising* failed to make money, and so the franchise was set aside. Other films with more ambition than dollars, such as *Reigo: King of the Sea Monsters* and *Raiga: God of the Monsters,* are honest attempts to put relatively new spins on old themes, but their lack of budget and general skill in filmmaking places them far too closely to more dunderheaded films such as *Zillafoot*.

And it's important to think of the kaiju film and the kaiju-related properties that aren't Godzilla that have come out since 2014: *Colossal*, of course, as well as *Pacific Rim: Uprising, Skull Island, Kaiju Mono*, the woeful *Monsters: Dark Continent* … and that's almost all of them. This sets aside, of course, some of the lesser known properties that tend to stick to tried and true formulas, but never really break out on their own, films like the *Deep Sea Monster Reigo* and *Raiga: God of the Monsters*.

Maybe I'm just clutching my pearls here, but it feels like there's little new under the sun, or at least there's not as much growing under the shadow of the massive girth of the Legendary Godzilla. But maybe we don't need new perspectives. Maybe it just needs to be Godzilla and a few of his canonical enemies, and destruction and rampaging galore.

Well. That's that. This has been a volume that I hope continues to engage in academic conversation, even though this is one that isn't as sweeping as *The Kaiju Film*, and it reflects more of my musings and considerations rather than academic-ese. As you've noted by now, there's

Conclusion 193

probably things you agree with, and that's great, and there's things you probably disagree with, and that's almost better, especially if you decide to write an article refuting my points. Go do it!

There's a bumper crop of kaiju properties sort of milling about under a much larger and much more highly-budgeted property. What happens next to the genre is a question, I think, that is too large, too current, for us to see up close. Perhaps with some distance and some time, we'll be able to make things out just a little more clearly, just as the next great beast awakens and pulls themselves upright.

This is the end of the book proper, so it's only appropriate for me to return to the start. I think that there's significant potential over the next few years for a sort of socially conscious, or at least socially aware, subset of kaiju films that retain the kaiju and the destruction, but also manage to probe our society and its various mores a little more deeply. If the massive big budget spectacles from Legendary don't drown them out, there is a place for these movies, from *Trollhunter* to *Monsters* to *Colossal* to *Shin Godzilla*, and all of the potentials beyond. And, perhaps there will be more space for insightful and cutting commentary on not only kaiju film, but the role of the kaiju film in our lives. More films like *Big Man Japan* or *Kaiju Mono* may shine a light on some of the aspects of our relationship with kaiju.

This new Reiwa era is just beginning, and we can see that the kaiju film genre is already undergoing some dramatic changes. There's more and more interest in kaiju, and they're probably as mainstream as they have ever been across the world. Anime series for Godzilla and Gamera, new Godzilla films in both the East and the West, and no doubt a whole series of smaller projects slowly coming to fruition.

Some will succeed; others will fail. Some will fly under the radar; some will come dangerously close to the bright lights of overexposure.

But it's a great time to be a kaiju fan, isn't it?

Filmography

King Kong (1933)
Son of Kong (1933)
Mighty Joe Young (1949)
The Beast from 20,000 Fathoms
     (1953)
Godzilla (1954)
Godzilla Raids Again! (1955)
The Amazing Colossal Man (1957)
Attack of the 50 Foot Woman (1958)
Varan the Unbelievable (1958)
War of the Colossal Beast (1958)
Konga (1961)
Mothra (1961)
Gorath (1962)
Mothra vs. Godzilla (1964)
Frankenstein vs. Baragon (1965)
Gamera, the Giant Monster (1965)
Daimajin (1966)
Daimajin Strikes Again (1966)
Ebirah, Horror of the Deep (1966)
Gamera vs. Barugon (1966)
Return of Daimajin (1966)
War of the Gargantuas (1966)
Gamera vs. Gyaos (1967)
Gappa: The Triphibian Monster
     (1967)
King Kong Escapes (1967)
X from Outer Space (1967)
Agon: The Atomic Dragon (1968)
Destroy All Monsters (1968)
Gamera vs. Guiron (1969)
Space Amoeba (1970)
Gamera vs. Zigra (1971)
Godzilla vs. Hedorah (1971)
Godzilla vs. Mechagodzilla (1974)
Terror of Mechagodzilla (1975)
King Kong (1976)
Mighty Peking Man (1977)
Yeti: Giant of the 20th Century
     (1977)
The Return of Godzilla (1984)

Godzilla vs. Biollante (1989)
Godzilla vs. King Ghidorah (1991)
Godzilla vs. Mechagodzilla II (1993)
Godzilla vs. SpaceGodzilla (1994)
Gamera: Guardian of the Universe
     (1995)
Gamera 2: Attack of Legion (1996)
Godzilla (1998)
Mighty Joe Young (1998)
Gamera 3: Revenge of Iris (1999)
Godzilla 2000 (1999)
Godzilla vs. Megaguirus (2000)
Godzilla, Mothra, and King
     Ghidorah: Giant Monsters All-
     Out Attack (2001)
Godzilla Against Mechagodzilla
     (2002)
Godzilla: Tokyo S.O.S. (2003)
Godzilla: Final Wars (2004)
King Kong (2005)
Gamera the Brave (2006)
The Host (2006)
Big Man Japan (2007)
Cloverfield (2008)
Reigo: King of the Sea Monsters
     (2008)
Raiga: God of the Monsters (2009)
Trollhunter (2010)
Godzilla (2014)
Colossal (2016)
Kaiju Mono (2016)
Shin Godzilla (2016)
Kong: Skull Island (2017)
God Raiga vs. King Ohga: War of the
     Monsters (2019)
Godzilla: King of the Monsters (2019)
Godzilla vs. Kong (2021)
Shin Ultraman (2022)
What to Do with the Dead Kaiju?
     (2022)

Bibliography

Alt, Matt. *Pure Invention: How Japan's Pop Culture Conquered the World.* Crown, 2020.

Ashcraft, Brian. "*Godzilla: King of the Monsters*' Director on the Movie's Biggest Spoiler." *io9.* June 4, 2019. Retrieved from: https://gizmodo.com/godzilla-king-of-the-monsters-director-on-the-movies-b-1835229543.

Asma, Stephen. *On Monsters: An Unnatural History of Our Worst Fears.* Oxford UP, 2009.

Balmain, Colette. *Introduction to Japanese Horror Film.* Edinburgh UP, 2009.

Beck, Horace. *Folklore and the Sea.* Mystic Seaport Museum, 1997.

Berkowitz, Joe. "*Godzilla vs. Kong* Reveals America's Conflicted Feelings About Its Monstrous Sins." *Fast Company.* March 31, 2021. Retrieved from: https://www.fastcompany.com/90620558/godzilla-vs-kong-hbo-max-america-conflicted-feelings-monstrous-sins.

Bernstein, Abby. *The Art of Godzilla: King of the Monsters.* Titan Books, 2019.

Bogue, Mike. *Apocalypse Then: American and Japanese Atomic Cinema, 1951–1967.* McFarland, 2017.

Bradbury, Ray. *Dinosaur Tales.* iBooks, 2003.

Cohen, Jeffrey Jerome. *Of Giants: Sex, Monsters, and the Middle Ages.* U of Minnesota P, 1999.

Cwik, Greg. "Juliette Binoche on Making Quentin Tarantino Cry and Why Kristen Stewart is a 'Great Actress.'" *Indiewire.* April 6, 2015. Retrieved from: https://www.indiewire.com/2015/04/juliette-binoche-on-making-quentin-tarantino-cry-and-why-kristen-stewart-is-a-great-actress-63454/.

Duffet, Mark. *Understanding Fandom: An Introduction to the Study of Media Fan Culture.* Bloomsbury, 2013.

England, Norman. *Behind the Kaiju Curtain: A Journey onto Japan's Biggest Film Sets.* Awai Books, 2021.

Forsberg, Aaron. *America and the Japanese Miracle: The Cold War Context of Japan's Postwar Economic Revival, 1950–1960.* U of North Carolina P, 2000.

Gerow, Aaron. "Wrestling with Godzilla: Intertextuality, Childish Spectatorship, and the National Body." In *Godzilla's Footsteps: Japanese Pop Culture Icons on the Global Stage,* edited by William Tsutsui and Michiki Ito, Palgrave Macmillan, 2006, 63–82.

Gordon, Joan. "Alien Invaders or Alien Invaded." In *Aliens in Popular Culture,* edited by Michael M. Levy and Farah Mendlesohn, Greenwood, 2019, 9–12.

Greene, Barbara. "A Modern Monster: *Shin Godzilla* and Its Place in the Discourse Concerning 3.11 and National Resilience." In *Japanese Horror Culture: Critical Essays on Film, Literature, Anime, and Video Games,* edited by Fernando Gabriel Pagnoni Burns, Subashish Bhattacharjee, and Ananya Saha, Lexington Books, 2021, 21–39

Hart, Adam Charles. *Monstrous Forms: Moving Image Horror Across Media.* Oxford UP, 2020.

"Jun Fukuda: Quotes." IMDB. Retrieved from: https://www.imdb.com/name/nm0297974/bio?ref_=nm_dyk_qu#quotes.

"Kathi Maio on Finding Her Inner Kaiju." *Fantasy & Science Fiction,* vol. 133, no. 3/4, September 2017, pp. 178–182. EBSCOhost, https://search-ebscohost-com.ezrcc.vccs.edu/login.aspx?direct=true&db=a9h&AN=125074846&site=ehost-live&scope=site.

Bibliography

Keller, David H. "The Jelly-Fish." In *American Fantastic Tales, Volume I: Terror and the Uncanny from Poe to the Pulps*, edited by Alice Brown and Peter Straub, Library of America, 2009, 583–587.

Lemay, John. *The Big Book of Japanese Giant Monster Movies: Showa Completion 1954–1989*. Bicep Books, 2020.

Maio, Kathi. "On Finding Her Inner Kaiju." *Fantasy and Science Fiction*, September/October 2017, 178–182.

Marshall, W.J.T. *The Last Dinosaur Book*. U of Chicago P, 1998.

McGrath, Kenta. "The Confused Nation: Hitoshi Matsumoto's *Big Man Japan*." In *Giant Creatures in Our World*, edited by Camille D.G. Mustachio and Jason Barr, McFarland, 2017, 123–137.

Mittman, Asa Simon, and Marcus Hensel. "Introduction." In *Classic Readings on Monster Theory*, edited by Asa Simon Mittman and Marcus Hensel, ARC Humanities Press, 2018.

Miyamoto, Yuki. "Gendered Bodies in Tokusatsu: Monsters and Aliens as the Atomic Bomb Victims." *Journal of Popular Culture* vol. 49, no. 5, 2016, 1086–1106. Web.

Mullis, Justin, et al. "Introduction: What Is Kaiju?" In *Giant Creatures in Our World*, edited by Camille D.G. Mustachio and Jason Barr, McFarland, 2017, 1–16.

Nakamura, Miri. *Monstrous Bodies: The Rise of the Uncanny in Modern Japan*. Harvard UP, 2015.

Noriega, Chon. "Godzilla and the Japanese Nightmare: When 'Them!' Is U.S." *Cinema Journal,* vol. 27, no. 1, 1987, pp. 63–77. JSTOR, https://doi.org/10.2307/1225324. Accessed 12 Feb. 2023.

Parry, Richard Lloyd. *Ghosts of the Tsunami: Death and Life in Japan's Disaster Zone*. MCD, 2017.

Patten, Dominic. "*Godzilla* Rights Holder and Voltage Settle *Colossal* Battle Over Anne Hathaway Pic." *Deadline.* October 30, 2015. Retrieved from: https://deadline.com/2015/10/godzilla-toho-colossal-settlement-anne-hathaway-voltage-pictures-1201599004/.

Pearson, Ben. "*Godzilla Vs. Kong* Director Adam Wingard on That Neon Action Scene, Bringing Out Emotion in the Monsters, and More [Interview]." *SlashFilm*. March 29, 2021. Retrieved from: https://www.slashfilm.com/580163/adam-wingard-interview-godzilla-vs-kong/.

Perine, Aaron. "*Meth Gator* Poster Released After *Cocaine Bear* Success." *Comic Book*. February 24, 2023. Retrieved from: https://comicbook.com/movies/news/cocaine-bear-meth-gator-poster-asylum-movie/.

Poole, W. Scott. *Dark Carnivals: Modern Horror and the Origins of American Empire*. Counterpoint, 2022.

Quizon, Jonathan. "Ken Watanabe Interview—*Godzilla: King of the Monsters*." *Screen Rant*. June 3, 2019. Retrieved from: https://screenrant.com/godzilla-2-king-monsters-ken-watanabe-interview/.

Rawle, Steven. *Transnational Kaiju: Exploitation, Globalisation, and Cult Monster Movies*. Edinburgh UP, 2022.

Raymond, Charles Nicholas. "Why Godzilla Laughs in *GvK*: His Out of Character Moment Explained." *ScreenRant*. May 11, 2021. Retrieved from: https://screenrant.com/godzilla-laugh-gvk-reason-scene-explained/.

Ryfle, Steve, and Ed Godziszewski. *Ishiro Honda: A Life in Film, from Godzilla to Kurosawa*. Wesleyan UP, 2017.

Sanz, José Luis. *Starring T-Rex!: Dinosaur Mythology and Popular Culture*. Indiana UP, 2002.

Sax, Boria. *Dinomania: Why We Love Fear, and Are Utterly Enchanted by Dinosaurs*. Reaktion, 2018.

Schilling, Mark. *The Encyclopedia of Japanese Pop Culture*. Weatherhill, 1997.

Seitz, Matt Zoller. "*Colossal*." *RobertEbert.com*. April 7, 2017. Retrieved from: https://www.rogerebert.com/reviews/colossal-2017.

Stanford, Claire. "A Monstrous Burden: The Original Godzilla Illuminates the Plight of Japanese Survivors of the Atomic Bomb, but What Can It Say about the Present, about the Violence Endured by Asian Americans during Covid-19?" *American Scholar*, vol. 91, no. 4, October 2022, 90–95. EBSCOhost, https://search-ebscohost-com.ezrcc.vccs.edu/login.aspx?direct=true&db=a9h&AN=158644217&site=ehost-live&scope=site.

Stein, Michael. *Alien Invasion: The History of Aliens in Pop Culture.* IDW Press, 2020.

Tsutsui, William. *Godzilla on My Mind: Fifty Years of the King of Monsters.* Palgrave MacMillan, 2004.

Wada, Kiyoshi. "The History and Current State of Drug Abuse in Japan." *Annals of the New York Academy of Sciences,* 2011, 62–72.

Wallace, Daniel. *Godzilla vs. Kong: The Art of the Ultimate Battle Royale.* Insight Editions, 2021.

Weismann, Brad. *Lost in the Dark: A World History of Horror Film.* UP of Mississippi, 2021.

Williams, Tony. "Female Oppression in *Attack of the 50 Foot Woman.*" *Science Fiction Studies,* vol. 12, no. 3, November 1985, 264–273.

Worthington, Clint. "Ultraman's 10 Wildest Monster Enemies." *SyFy Wire.* April 4, 2019, https://www.syfy.com/syfy-wire/ultramans-10-wildest-monster-enemies.

Index

Agon, the Atomic Dragon 5, 6, 12, 41, 56*n*, 56–61
The Amazing Colossal Man 7, 8, 23–24, 62, 128, 173–180, 177*n*, 183–187
Attack of the 50 Foot Woman 7, 8, 23, 25, 62, 173–174, 176, 180–185, 185*n*

The Beast from 20,000 Fathoms 8, 31–32, 42, 64, 111–112, 114
"Besides a Dinosaur, Whatta Ya Wanna Be When You Grow Up?" (short story) 31
Big Man Japan 5, 7, 19, 83, 84, 86, 160–161, 166, 169–172, 174, 193
Bradbury, Ray 31–32, 64

Cloverfield 7–8, 15, 17, 19, 20, 72*n*, 79, 156, 159
Colossal 5, 7, 9, 10, 11, 14, 17, 19–20, 21, 88, 143–159, 168, 191, 192, 193

Daimajin (trilogy) 40, 44–45, 45*n*, 129–130, 156, 166, 192
The Day the Earth Stood Still 42, 63, 108
Dinosaurs 26–33
Dogora 40, 41, 57, 192
Dougherty, Michael 118–119, 143

Edwards, Gareth 115, 143–144, 151–152

"The Fog Horn" (short story) 31
Frankenstein Conquers the World (Frankenstein vs. Baragon) 57, 67–68, 89, 129, 174, 175*n*, 185–186
Fukuda, Jun 146

Gamera 3, 40, 48
Gamera 2: Attack of Legion 72–73, 79, 101–103
Gamera 3: Revenge of Iris 16, 72, 79, 96–97, 103*n*, 103–105, 108, 156, 165
Gamera: Guardian of the Universe 96, 100–101, 103, 104, 105, 108
Gamera the Brave 73*n*, 92*n*, 96, 106–107
Gamera vs. Barugon 57, 92, 96*n*
Gamera vs. Gyaos 81, 96
Gamera vs. Jiger 62*n*

God Raiga vs. King Ohga: War of the Monsters 6, 76, 82, 85–88
Godzilla (1954) 3, 5, 5*n*, 6, 9, 11, 12, 16, 17, 29, 31, 32, 33, 34, 35–37, 38–39, 39*n*, 41, 43–44, 56, 57, 58, 60, 64, 66, 66*n*, 67*n*, 79, 80–81, 84*n*, 87, 88, 89, 115, 117, 124, 132, 156, 162, 172, 173, 181
Godzilla (1998) 5*n*, 12, 18*n*, 66, 97
Godzilla (2014) 12, 40, 43*n*, 82–83, 85, 96, 109, 111–113, 112*n*, 113*n*, 114–117, 120, 132*n*, 143, 144, 151, 156, 164, 166, 191
Godzilla Against Mechagodzilla 42, 51*n*, 65*n*, 80, 88, 165
Godzilla: Final Wars 51*n*, 66, 66*n*, 68*n*, 71, 79, 90, 91, 92, 93, 95, 97
Godzilla, King of the Monsters! (1956) 177*n*, 181
Godzilla: King of the Monsters 95, 109–111, 113–117, 118–120, 175*n*, 191
Godzilla, Mothra, and King Ghidorah: Giant Monsters All-Out Attack 9, 12, 40, 71, 80–81, 88, 89, 92, 96, 97, 104*n*, 107, 163*n*, 165
Godzilla Raids Again 6, 15, 29, 32–33, 34–39, 40, 57, 80, 117–118, 120*n*, 162–163
Godzilla: Tokyo S.O.S. 47, 51*n*, 90, 94, 105*n*, 148
Godzilla 2000 65n, 70, 71, 120*n*, 163
Godzilla vs. Biollante 9, 41–42, 51*n*, 69, 79, 88, 144, 149, 157, 163, 164, 167
Godzilla vs. Destroyah 32, 51*n*, 157, 164
Godzilla vs. Gigan 147, 148, 162, 164
Godzilla vs. Hedorah 34, 35, 38, 74–75, 82, 97, 147, 148, 164
Godzilla vs. King Ghidorah 32, 51*n*, 71, 94, 149, 162
Godzilla vs. Kong 2, 5, 7, 8, 40, 51*n*, 84, 95, 98, 109, 112, 114, 119, 119*n*, 120, 121, 131*n*, 138, 139*n*, 139–142, 143–150, 158, 165, 168*n*, 178, 191
Godzilla vs. Megaguirus 42, 51*n*
Godzilla vs. Megalon 35–36, 146, 147, 148, 162, 164, 165
Godzilla vs. Mothra 94
Godzilla vs. SpaceGodzilla 32, 42, 51*n*, 69, 70, 82, 167

201

Index

Gorath 41, 44–45, 44n, 51n, 55, 57, 60, 73, 167n, 192

The Incredible Shrinking Man 22, 62, 68

Kaiju Mono 5, 7, 7n, 8–9, 19, 83, 84, 86, 160–161, 166–172, 167n, 174, 192, 193
King Kong (1933) 3, 4, 5, 6, 8, 12, 19, 21, 30n, 31, 31n, 38, 48, 50, 121–122, 124, 127, 135, 137, 138, 139, 142, 165n, 178, 182
King Kong (1976) 12, 127–128
King Kong (2005) 12, 129
King Kong Escapes 8, 90n, 124–125, *125n*, 126n
King Kong vs. Godzilla 30, 36, 56, 57, 67, 123, 142, 147, 148, 162–163
Kong: Skull Island 8, 22, 30n, 51n, 78n, 111, 114, 121, 138–139, 144, 146, 165n, 192
Konga 5, 22, 121, 133–136, 138, 142
Kusanagi, Asagi 100–101, 103, 104–105, 157, 164

Matango 19, 23, 166
Mighty Joe Young 22, 136–139, 142
Mighty Peking Man 5, 22, 79n, 121, 127, 129–133, 136, 137, 139, 142
Mothra 40, 46–48, 56, 100
Mothra vs. Godzilla 34, 41, 57, 94, 96, 124n
Mystery Science Theater 3000 2n, 76, 99

Pacific Rim 9, 19, 82, 100n, 160, 192
Pacific Rim: The Black 190, 192
Pacific Rim: Uprising 192
Pulgasari 20, 20n

Raiga: God of the Monsters 3, 6, 76, 81–85, 87–88, 192
Rampage 14, 85, 88
Rare Exports 16, 20
Rebirth of Mothra (trilogy) 47n, 106–107

Reigo: King of the Sea Monsters 3, 6, 12, 76–79, 79n, 81, 84, 85, 86, 87, 88, 102n, 192
The Return of Godzilla 5n, 11, 27, 40, 41, 50, 51n, 52, 64, 83, 87, 110, 120, 144, 153, 163
Rodan 40, 91

Saegusa, Miki 69, 70, 157, 165
Shin Godzilla 2, 5, 5n, 8, 10, 11, 40–41, 48, 52n, 55n, 52–55, 64, 80, 81n, 83, 86–87, 88, 156, 162, 190, 193
Shin Ultraman 4, 18, 41n, 64n, 80, 81n, 110n, 164n, 175n, 190
Son of Kong 8, 22, 30n, 121, 122–123, 138, 139, 142
Space Amoeba 18, 40, 48–50, 50n, 73, 90, 192

Terror of Mechagodzilla 41, 95, 146
The Thing from Another World 1, 42, 165
Trollhunter 14–16, 20–21, 25, 82, 159, 193
Tsutsui, William 94n, 161n, 162

Ultraman (television series) 4, 12, 57, 89, 90, 90n, 166, 166n, 167, 168n

Varan the Unbelievable 45–46, 56, 58, 60, 62, 156
Vigalondo, Nacho 150–152

War of the Colossal Beast 173–187, 181n
War of the Gargantuas 38, 62, 64, 66, 66n, 68, 79, 126, 129, 175n
What to Do with Dead Kaiju? 9, 11, 86–87
Wingard, Adam 139–140, 145–146

The X from Outer Space 1, 5, 18, 62, 64, 73–75, 86, 90, 192

Yeti: Giant of the 20th Century 5, 9, 22, 24, 79n, 121, 126–129, 133, 136, 138, 142